# MIRACLES OF OUR OWN MAKING

# Miracles of Our Own Making

## A HISTORY OF
## PAGANISM

### LIZ WILLIAMS

REAKTION BOOKS

*Published by*
REAKTION BOOKS LTD
Unit 32, Waterside
44–48 Wharf Road
London N1 7UX, UK

www.reaktionbooks.co.uk

First published 2020
Copyright © Liz Williams 2020

Printed and bound in Great Britain by
TJ International, Padstow, Cornwall

A catalogue record for this book is available from the British Library

ISBN 978 1 78914 221 1

# Contents

# Introduction

What do we mean by 'paganism'? The term 'pagan' is often bandied about, with varying claims for its etymology, but it is not always obvious what it refers to – and in what kind of context. The word itself comes from the Latin *paganus*, and is generally held to mean 'country dweller'. But in modern times, in the West, it – and more specifically the term 'neopagan' – has come to have a different meaning: the range of alternative spiritualities that involve the worship of multiple gods and, often but not invariably, the use of magic. We are thus going to be looking at what a pagan is as defined by the *Oxford English Dictionary*:

> *A person holding religious beliefs other than those of the main world religions*

And

> *A member of a modern religious movement which seeks to incorporate beliefs or practices from outside the main world religions, especially nature worship*

In this book, however, we are also going to look not only at the history of paganism in the UK, but at the development of magical practice more widely. The dictionary definition of 'magic' states that it is

*the power of apparently influencing events by using mysterious or supernatural forces.*

Many pagans treat their spirituality as a religion, rather than as a method of dealing with the world. Most pagans believe in science. But many also do believe that magic works, although there may not be a direct relationship between cause and effect. It is perceived as being subtler than that, and is often concerned with personal transformation. We will see that, over time, magic has sometimes been intertwined with pagan beliefs, and sometimes it has been separate. But independently or together, paganism and magic have a continuity of history in Britain and beyond, and we are going to examine the linear development of both.

It is a long history. The human desire to control reality is probably as ancient as we ourselves are, and there is evidence that people have been practising magic from very early times. The oldest burial in Britain – the so-called 'Red Lady' of Paviland in South Wales (actually a male), dating from 33000 BC – contains grave goods made of mammoth ivory, whose purpose is unclear but which are likely to be of religious significance. Sumerian accounts list magical practices, and we know that the ancient Egyptians, Greeks and Romans practised spells and divination. In Britain and Europe, 'cunning folk' worked among their communities from at least the Middle Ages, and some of the practices they upheld are with us today. We will be looking at these ancient roots throughout this book.

But anybody who is interested in contemporary British paganism and magical practice – although over the course of this book we will encounter customs and beliefs from around the world – will soon become aware that there are a great many claims about their origins, ranging from the notion of an unbroken underground tradition dating from the time of the ancient Druids, to assertions that our knowledge comes from lost Atlantis, or a matriarchy of Celtic warrior priestesses, or a wide variety of other sources. Disentangling these claims can be an uphill task, for the stories about the roots of this modern spirituality are interwoven with political, religious, cultural and ideological narratives that may tell us more about the time in which they were written (including the present day) than the ancient pagan world.

So where does contemporary paganism originate? Does it really have ancient origins? Or is it a completely modern invention – the religious equivalent of historical re-enactment? As far as we can tell, there is some truth in both claims. Modern paganism does have a very old ancestry, but its roots are long, spindly tap roots that may go back quite far but which are not easy to trace and – in the UK, at least – do not really allow us to claim an unbroken line of descent from the magical theory of 3,000–4,000 years ago. Traces of Egyptian magic persist into English medieval magic, but they are only traces, not solid practices that have existed in an unmodified form for thousands of years. The current worship of Celtic gods – many of whom weren't gods in the first place – is largely revivalist, not ancient: much of it goes back to the nineteenth century at the earliest.

Magical practice is clearly ancient. And by the dictionary definition, paganism itself is genuinely very old. However, despite the claims of twentieth- and twenty-first-century practitioners, it is highly unlikely that there are many – or perhaps any – unbroken traditions of pagan worship, certainly in the UK. Although there are people living today who may indeed have had cunning folk among their ancestors, you should be very wary of anyone of British ancestry who claims to come from an unbroken hereditary tradition. Magical practice of varying kinds has a continuity, but the evidence for strong unbroken systems of pagan belief in this country is simply not there.

Modern Wicca, for example, gained momentum in the 1950s, drawing material from esoteric traditions such as Theosophy and Rosicrucianism, and from Freemasonry. Western neopaganism as a whole draws on folklore, on literature and on the work of groups as diverse as the late nineteenth-century occult society of the Golden Dawn and the Woodcraft Folk. Its origins lie in medieval grimoires and the poetry of William Butler Yeats; in the spiritualism of Madame Blavatsky and the Eastern interests of a former tea planter named Gerald Gardner. We will meet many of these people as we progress through this book. We will look at other traditions and their origins, too, trying to unravel the Ariadne's thread of information and misinformation. Since this is a historical and not a theological work, we shall not be examining in detail the elephant in the room: the question of the veracity of divine or supernatural origins for these beliefs. But that question must nonetheless be kept in mind by the reader.

When we are talking about paganism or magical practice, we need to be cautious about who is making a claim: whether it is in a history book, for example, or in a work of popular fiction, or on the Internet. The last in particular is a minefield, with a multitude of websites and forums generating some extraordinary assertions and drawing on earlier misinformation in order to promote ideological agendas. In this, paganism is in line with pretty much every other religious and political belief system, but this is not much help to the newcomer, who can find the sheer volume of contradictory information bewildering.

Our remit here covers a huge span of time, but we will strive to be as in-depth as possible, and we will also try to address – and debunk – some of the prevailing myths about British paganism and magic, and about their origins. To do so, we will be trying to examine what is fact and what is fiction, as well as where these claims come from and why they were made.

This is obviously a developing process. The history of magic and of paganism has not been a priority of academic researchers until relatively recently, and even now there are large gaps in the study of magical practice in Britain, and corresponding gaps in our knowledge. Claims made outside academia are wider but do not always weather the standards of academic workings and cannot be verified, despite, in some cases, substantial stridency in favour of their truth. And there are quite a few modern theories reliant on earlier works which simply have not stood the test of time.

We need to note, for example, inaccuracies in the work of late nineteenth- and early twentieth-century authors who did not have access to the sort of historical evidence that we have today. Historical accuracy is a process, not an event, and an understanding of the workings of history is of great help to anyone looking at the way in which paganism (and indeed anything) has developed.

Many authors have already done a great deal to correct such inaccuracies and deconstruct prevailing myths. Ronald

Hutton and Owen Davies, for example, have brought enormous academic rigour to the study of contemporary paganism, and I would recommend their work to anyone wanting further in-depth analysis of its various facets. There are pagans involved in university history departments, in archaeology, in museum work and conservation, and all of these people take a dim view of some of the wilder claims. For instance, we are just about losing the long-held 'fact' that nine million witches were slain at the stake during the 'Burning Times'. This comes from an eighteenth-century misapprehension of how to treat statistics – which Hutton unpacks in his *Witches, Druids and King Arthur* (2003) – and has been repeated ever since; so often that it was treated as gospel during the 1970s and '80s and has only relatively recently been discarded. But for every rejected 'fact' there are a dozen more: we have a veritable hydra.

Hutton has been kind to a number of his less thorough contemporaries by deploying the term 'romantic truth'. Epistemologists might not be totally happy with this, but within the context of religion it makes a certain amount of sense – particularly for a movement that has as a large part of its impetus artistic and literary influences as well as spiritual ones, and a religion which, unlike Christianity, Judaism and Islam, is not text-based, reliant upon a single main book. We can use 'romantic truth' as inspirational. We can use it creatively in our practices (for instance, the spiral path around Glastonbury Tor can be walked as a ritual act and treated as a labyrinth, even though it was not constructed as a maze: it is the remnants of a medieval field system). But what we cannot do is claim that it is objectively true.

We especially cannot make a claim for truth if we cannot provide any evidence for it. It is common for people who are new to paganism to encounter some outrageous claims: some organizations seem to be competing for the title of 'oldest known'. Some individuals go to remarkable lengths, too: I knew a young man who actually made an 'ancient' *Book of Shadows*, constructed out of parchment and stained with tea, which he used to attract people to his teenage coven. There were apparently several hundred pages of this thing, and for a seventeen-year-old boy it was a substantial artistic achievement, although one must question his honesty. People who 'just know' that they are the reincarnation of an Egyptian priestess and who insist upon the unverifiable truth of this are delusional, unlike people who treat the possibility that they are such a reincarnation as a form of ritual performance or as an aspect of an inspirational personal narrative. Feelings are not facts, and however deeply you might feel something, you cannot claim that you 'know' it unless you have reasonable evidence for it: evidence that is at least consensual (agreed upon by people who know the field) and backed up by archaeological or text-based research. Religion is not science, and as such it is not subject to the methods of scientific enquiry, but we should not throw the baby out with the bathwater: you cannot make claims about your past life as a pagan high priestess in medieval Wales if there is absolutely no evidence that they *had* pagan high priestesses then (which they did not). So there is a middle ground to be trodden here between 'romantic truth', historical fact and outright myth-making.

However, why should it matter to us whether our practices are old or not? Just because a practice is not provably ancient, that does not necessarily mean it is not viable. Paganism is one of the spiritual paths that privileges antiquity. It maintains that the older something is, or the longer we can show people to have been practising it, the better it is. This supposition itself needs to be challenged. Why does 'old' equate with 'good' or 'more authentic'? What does it say about us that we need to anchor our modern beliefs in the ancient world – a world that bears little resemblance to our own, and which had many customs that we would regard as abhorrent today?

Some of the reasons are, I suppose, due to a feeling that we in the West have lost contact with some essential facets of existence. The natural world is one of these. Many people say they are attracted to paganism because of its emphasis on nature – on the trees, fauna and weather of the British Isles. Given that a great many pagans currently live in cities, this is understandable. That feeling of reconnection is something that pagans often comment upon: a grounding of their spiritual practice. Indigenous tribes are perceived as never having lost this connection, and their knowledge is seen as valuable. There is some justification for this. The writer Robert Macfarlane's recent observation that words such as 'acorn', 'bluebell' and 'newt' no longer feature in the *Oxford Junior Dictionary* and have been replaced by terminology from information technology, such as 'broadband' or 'cut and paste', is a depressing one to any country dweller who values the natural world around us, a world that is still vibrant and evolving, no matter how much it may be threatened by housing developments or motorways. Paganism offers a way back into this threatened realm, a world that is still seen as offering a magic of its own.

I sympathize with that aim, but I also believe that we must be cautious. We find claims for antiquity in all pagan paths: in contemporary ceremonial magic, in Druidry and in Wicca, all of which possess reasonably clear lines of historical descent, which I have traced in the chapters to come. In the meantime,

I suggest that we consider the words of the twentieth-century occultist William G. Gray on the subject of the lineage of our magical traditions and organizations:

> It is incorrect to assume that any organization must be authentic merely because it can trace a line of descent several hundred years long; the organization's ancestry proves only that it is authentically old, not that it is authentically good or necessarily of great spiritual value. There may be a strong probability that something is worth preserving in its structure, otherwise it would scarcely have survived, but again all this does is demonstrate its durability and persistence, nothing else. A five-hundred-year-old house that has never been modernized might be a very interesting museum exhibit, but who in his/her right mind in our times would care to live in it permanently? Simply because an esoteric concern is old in name or ideology is no guarantee of its goodness or continuing spiritual significance. As a human institution it cannot be older than its most senior member, since it is an inheritance that passes from one generation to the next, and however much they may claim continuity, the people mediating its meaning in modern times are not the same as those who formed and framed it in earlier epochs.[1]

In the last few decades, modern media has popularized witchcraft and Wicca, through TV shows such as *Buffy the Vampire Slayer*, for instance, or *Charmed*. Older readers will remember Samantha and her twitching nose in the American show *Bewitched*, and I suspect that even this amusing and lightweight programme might have drawn people to witchcraft in the 1960s and '70s. I know at least one fifty-something who was enticed into ceremonial magic as a result of watching the film adaptation of Dennis Wheatley's *The Devil Rides Out* through his parents' banisters as a child. These days, urban fantasy provides a huge engine for literature and television, with popular shows like *True Blood* and *Supernatural* drawing major fan bases. The biggest draw of the 2000s has, of course, been the Harry Potter series, which has propelled magical practice very much into the public view again and convinced a generation of children that if they can only get hold of a magic wand, ultimate power will be theirs.

Entertaining though these programmes, films and books may be, they have had mixed results. One benefit is the realization that people who practise magic or who follow a pagan path are not all hygienically challenged Satanists, but can be, for instance, small, blonde, fashion-conscious women. However, an obvious drawback is that a lot of the more bizarre clichés about magical practice stem from pulp movies of the 1960s and '70s: that pagans always do their rituals naked, that they conduct sacrifices, that they worship the Devil. Witchcraft is made to seem sinister at worst and glamorously sensationalist at best. It can have a glamorous side, but fundamentally much magical practice is about developing self-discipline and the transformation of the self. It is not about what you wear and how impressive you look at the end of the day, but whether, for example, it can help you through a night in an intensive care unit when your loved one is dying, or inspires you to go out and plant a tree on a ravaged industrial estate, or can help you deal with an alienated, angry child. Magical practice is about dealing with the real world, not with a comforting fantasy realm. There are too many people who approach paganism and magic with the misapprehension that these practices are either exactly like the world of Harry Potter or, more commonly, that they will award one with attention and power, usually over the opposite sex. Pagans arguably spend more time trying to dissuade neophytes from attempting magic than they do trying to lure people into it: paganism is not a prosyletizing, evangelical religion and some older Wiccans, for example, would prefer that it all went back underground to its secretive 1950s roots. To some extent, this is an understandable point of view. I suspect many critics would secretly love pagans to behave as the protagonists of a Dennis Wheatley novel do, but alas, we are usually far more boring.

Another drawback is that a lot of people have leaped onto the resulting bandwagon. We have seen a great many books on basic witchcraft, many of which have been written without any thorough research going into their preparation. They generate misconceptions. The newcomer might be aware, for example, that there is often a distinction drawn between 'black' and 'white' magic, and indeed magical practice is often defined in these binary, monochrome terms, but they are misleading. Most witches hold that there is no such distinction and that everything depends on the intention that lies behind the spell (just as there is no such thing as 'black' or 'white' legal practice; you can be justified or unjustified in taking someone to court, but the law remains the same). Originally, recent research shows, certain cunning folk were called 'white witches' as a form of abuse by Puritans – to indicate that they were still witches even though they might pretend otherwise. So the very distinction between 'white' and 'black' magic is a Christian construct.

Another misperception is that magical practice through-out history has been entirely positive and dedicated purely to healing. A quick trip to the Museum of Witchcraft and Magic in Boscastle will show that this is not the case. To continue the legal analogy, British cunning folk were more akin to the law-yers of today, who will act for anyone if they are hired to do so. The cunning person would do healing spells and hexes alike. Nowadays, however, the majority of magical practitioners are very averse to performing negative magic, as there is a belief that it will rebound on the person who does it – rather like karma.

However, enough of the drawbacks for now. Let us return to the benefits of media portrayals of witches and occultists: despite the issues above, they do cause people to investigate magical practice. And in a sense, they are our folklore. Whereas, once upon a time, we would have been sitting around the fire telling stories of fairies and werewolves and demons, now we are watch-ing them on Netflix instead. Is there a significant difference? After all, the stories themselves are not so different, although our reactions to them might be. But if the curious newcomer, fascinated by *Supernatural* or *A Discovery of Witches*, is to inves-tigate paganism and magic further, they will find a very different picture from that depicted on the screen. The current lie of the esoteric land in the early twenty-first century is as follows:

**Witchcraft/hedge witchcraft**: more akin to older forms of magic – herb lore, healing, working very closely with nature.

**Wicca**: the more structured and organized form of witch-craft, sometimes called the 'religion' of witchcraft as it deals more closely with devotional practice to the God and Goddess than to actual spellcraft. The term is said to come from Anglo-Saxon, but its founder Gerald Gardner referred to the people involved in it (not the practice itself) as 'Wica' instead. It seems likely that the term 'Wicca' comes from a rival practitioner, Charles Cardell, and was then reclaimed at a later date by Gardner's friend Doreen Valiente. Gardner himself seems to have referred to the path as 'the witch cult'.

**Druidry:** the old religion of the British Isles. Like witchcraft, Druidry is by no means an unbroken set of practices, and moreover, we do not know precisely what the ancient Druids did. Since it was an oral tradition, they did not write anything down, and so, as we shall see, most of what we think we know of their practices stems from Roman writings, which may or may not be accurate. Like Wicca, modern Druidry comes mainly from the 1950s, with some roots in the eighteenth century; it was developed by Ross Nichols, a friend of Gardner. Although its roots lie in an ancient tradition, it is not itself ancient. Today it is similar to Wicca, although less emphasis is placed on spell work and more on meditation and environmentalism. It is often described as a philosophy rather than a religion, and is similar in some respects to Buddhism.

**Goddess worship:** again, this may overlap with Wicca. Many women are drawn to the worship of the Goddess in all Her aspects, rather than the dual aspect of the Goddess and the God. There has been a resurgence of interest in the Goddess over the last few decades and several Goddess temples now exist. Goddess worship can be a healing and empowering path for women, in particular.

**Heathenry:** the Norse tradition, following the worship of the ancient Norse and Germanic deities.

**Shamanism:** a path that is very closely attuned to the natural world and working with spirits, especially animal spirits. Many people who follow this path are drawn to the Native American traditions, and a central aspect of shamanic work is that of healing.

**Chaos magick:** an eclectic form of working which maintains that the 'hardwiring' of all magic is the same, even though the forms it takes might vary – rather like a computer operating system, which remains the same no matter what programs are run by it. So a chaos magician might work with the Hindu pantheon one week, and the next with a Celtic goddess.

**Ceremonial magic:** sometimes called 'High' magic, and often spelled with a 'k' at the end. This stems from medieval and Renaissance magic, which is complex and often involves lengthy rituals. Most contemporary ceremonial magic originates from a group called the Golden Dawn, which was started in the late nineteenth century.

When we look at the history of paganism and magic, especially in the far past, we will rely on a variety of factors. We need to take into consideration the difference between primary sources, defined as immediate, first-hand accounts of a topic, from people who had a direct connection with it, and secondary sources, which are one step removed, although they may quote or otherwise use primary sources. These may cover the same topic but add a layer of interpretation and analysis. Both these types of source material include elements such as written accounts from contemporary commentators (that is, people who were around at the time, such as Julius Caesar) as well as from commentators who were not alive at the time on which they are commenting (such as Gildas, a northern monk who in the sixth century wrote a history of the Britons). We will also be using written accounts from commentators who were not only removed in time but were geographically distant from the people about whom they are writing: ancient Greeks who comment on the Druids, for instance, but had never met one, or eighteenth-century antiquarians speculating about the ancient past. In addition to this, we will be looking at archaeological evidence, myths and legends.

All of these sources can be unreliable in different ways. Written accounts can be biased. Caesar was writing up his own campaigns, for instance, and he was concerned to present a good picture of the brave Roman military in facing barbaric and savage enemies abroad. His writing would have been perused by the elite classes back in Rome, who wanted to be reassured that their commander was doing a good job. Remember, we are talking about an age with no television, no photography, no news media – only written reports and eye-witness statements, if you were lucky enough to meet an eye-witness in an era when travel was also subject to severe restrictions. We know from recent reports about fake news and alleged political influence on social media of how unreliable even photographic evidence and newspaper reports can be – how much more so in an age where travel was slow, people didn't necessarily go that far from home unless they were merchants or in the army, and in which a lot of people could neither read nor write. In addition, just because someone was there does not mean they were telling the truth.

There are also more obvious difficulties with writers who were not there, who never visited Gaul or ancient Britain. Maybe they drew on inaccurate sources, or maybe they just made material up. Writers write for different reasons and sometimes they just want to be entertaining. Accounts of the ancient world – Irish stories about Druids who shapeshift, who speak with the gods, who work magic – are not necessarily lies or intended to deceive the reader. They might have been written just for fun.

Even with visual evidence, such as carvings, we need to be careful not to interpret it too literally. In the case of the Egyptian gods, for instance, the ancient Egyptians may not have seen their deities as possessing animal heads: those depictions may have been metaphors (Sekhmet may not actually have the head of a lioness, but is shown with one because she embodies the qualities of a lioness). We should be wary of regarding ancient peoples as any less or more theologically sophisticated than ourselves.

And we must remember that the idea of history as an accurate presentation of factual events is relatively recent. Tacitus wrote as much to create an emotional climate or prove a moral point as he did to tell people what had really happened. Think of Tacitus as writing for the Roman edition of a tabloid. Do we still believe him when he says that the Druids held human sacrifices? For an audience who thought that all barbarians were basically the same? Writers may have written to denigrate the history of a Saxon king, for instance, deliberately omitting mention of important people for political reasons.

Moreover, the time at which something is written is hugely important. Many references from Latin and Greek sources, and others, are – obviously – in translation, and translations can contain inaccuracies.

Historian Kari Sperring says of these early historical periods in particular that there is

> a problem with pretty much every early source ever, because they all omit, mistake or misreport and we lack the control group to test them against fully . . . sources are a quagmire. Things like the Anglo-Saxon herbal are gold, and I wish we had far more like that. But especially for the areas that were never Romanised, we tend to have to work from wobbly stepping stone to wobbly stepping stone and hope not to sink, while also watching for crocodiles, mosquitoes and idiots on the internet.[2]

It is always worth your while to ask two questions: 'how do we know?' and 'who said this first?' What is the documentary evidence? A few minutes with Google can be enlightening. And if you end up on a Wikipedia page, check the footnotes and the sources.

> Fact-checking is a surprisingly addictive and rewarding habit to get into. I think some people recoil from it

because it's seen as a contrary impulse to the religious one, but there needn't be any contradiction involved. Many neopagans find that knowing the limitations of our historical sources actually opens the door to the possibility of personal insight. In conclusion I can only echo Professor Ronald Hutton, who said 'I wish that Pagans did usually impose their own narratives on ancient places, and indeed on the past, either by actual research or by genuinely visionary experience.'[3]

I would wholeheartedly support this view. When we are looking at contemporary paganism and magic, we are also looking at the role of historical method: we are back to a consideration of who is making a claim, when, where and why.

When considering the history of paganism and magic in the British Isles, it is also crucial to remember that the influences that make these strands of belief what they are are not confined to Britain alone. Wicca – which Hutton terms 'the only religion that England has ever given the world' – may be home-grown, but its origins are diverse and many are not indigenous. What we now term the 'Western Mystery Tradition' is truly intercontinental. This has long been the case. The people whom we now call the Celts traded and connected with tribes in Gaul and Ireland. The Romans brought their own customs and beliefs. Later, other waves of peoples from the Continent – the Saxons and Vikings – introduced their gods, charms and spells to these shores. Christianity itself, which has informed much British magical practice for hundreds of years, is a Middle Eastern religion. Through the Renaissance, ideas from classical antiquity, ancient Egypt, the Moors and Arabs and beyond informed British practice. The great alchemical endeavours of medieval Spain influenced the work of English magicians. Arabic astrology filtered into Britain from the Middle East. In later centuries, ideas from much further afield continued to affect the big magical orders and individuals alike: concepts from Buddhism and Eastern thought influenced the development of Theosophy, the work of the Golden Dawn and Wicca. Vodou is present within Caribbean and South American communities and the work of white magicians in the UK today; African magical practice is undertaken within immigrant communities; and many people who have worked in witchcraft shops will tell you that Islamic clients occasionally reach beyond their own communities for assistance in dealing with djinn.

These influences are not a one-way street. British magic travels back to Europe and then to the Americas. There are more Wiccans and Druids outside the UK than there are within it. The Golden Dawn and the Order of Bards, Ovates and Druids sent out shoots into the United States and New Zealand that are still present today. In my own premises in Glastonbury, this last spring equinox, we had visits from Mexican Wiccans, Rastafarians interested in the history of Theosophy, American and Australian magicians, and Italians buying books on the Tarot, all in a single day. I have a Siberian shaman contact, influenced by the ideas of Madame Blavatsky, who has been using the income she has received from Russian and Western esoteric tourists to travel to India and engage with Indian spirituality. Magical practice is a melting pot. It is cosmopolitan, curious, experimental and diverse. It is perennially interested in ideas from elsewhere, and it is not static.

If we were to look at Western magic as a whole, this book would obviously be much bigger than it is. So we must be restrained, confining our attentions to the British Isles as much as we can. However, the reader needs to bear in mind these influences from elsewhere and to remember that every aspect of magic in the UK, and every pagan path, has roots that begin abroad.

It is now time to embark upon that history itself. We shall begin with the earliest known origins of paganism and magic in the UK and then progress through the centuries (although, obviously, these beliefs and practices are not confined to neat hundred-year periods, and occasionally we will need to refer to both past and future, beyond the boundaries of the chapter in question). We shall be visiting Celtic, Roman and Saxon Britain, looking at the beliefs and practices of the waves of people who came to these shores, and will continue into the times of the Vikings and Normans. This will be followed by a journey through the centuries, looking at such phenomena as the witch trials, the work of cunning folk and court astrologers, the rise in the use of grimoires and other magical texts and the rise, too, of the great nineteenth-century magical societies.

The history of these peoples, beliefs and practices continues to underpin and instruct the course of contemporary paganism and magic in Britain. When we come to the beliefs of our own century, we will hope to have a more informed understanding of their origins.

# ONE

# Ancient Origins

**M**ost British people have a mental picture of what a Druid looks like. It usually consists of an old gentleman dressed in a long white nightgown, holding a golden sickle and a bunch of mistletoe. Such is the stereotypical image of the Druid, dating from the early nineteenth century in illustrations by people such as Samuel Meyrick, up to Getafix in the Asterix cartoons, who is so kindly and wise that he alone is probably responsible for generations of schoolchildren wanting to find out what Druidry is all about. But what *do* we know about the ancient Druids?

We shall be looking at this question in this chapter, but there is a proviso: we have little concrete information about these ancient pagans. In addition, this is not the only time we shall be looking at Druids in this book, for the ancient Druids are not the only Druids with whom we are concerned. Contemporary Druidry will also fall under our gaze, and, unsurprisingly, this relatively new pagan path does hark back (via a convoluted history) to the original bearers of the name, the priests of the early British tribes before and during the Roman occupation. So we'll consider those early Druids here, and then again later on when we come to an exploration of eighteenth-century magical practice, and then later yet when we look at the pagan scene in the twentieth and twenty-first centuries.

In seeking to understand those first Druids, we are severely hampered by one basic fact: the tribes who now fall under the umbrella term 'Celtic' (a name that is itself beset by problems), and who occupied the British Isles and much of Europe, did not write anything down. They were a culture known for remarkable enamel- and metalwork, and were feared by the Romans, who sought, over hundreds of years, to occupy their lands, but because they did not commit anything to paper, they remain mute: we can only discern what we know of them from the artefacts they left behind, and artefacts are, as we have already noted, prone to being misinterpreted.

So we do not know when Druidry really began. Popular thought still vaguely associates them with Stonehenge, but although there is a substantial amount of archaeological evidence regarding these very early cultures, we do not know a great deal about the builders of Stonehenge themselves or the earlier 'cursus' structures: the great ridges and hollows of the earthworks that are such a feature of Salisbury Plain. We can make conjectures from the burials that we have uncovered; we can surmise – but we still do not *know*.

Nor was 'Britain' a united country. It was made up of different tribes over a very long period of time who had different lifestyles and, presumably, different beliefs. Some people lived in hill forts, some in undefended open settlements or defended homesteads. What we think of as 'Celtic' probably coalesces around the start of the Iron Age (700 BC), but these ways of categorizing periods of time were constructed by much later people. Who knows what age we ourselves will be held to be living in by historians among our descendants? The computer age? The graphene age? We simply cannot say.

What we can deduce from Roman accounts and from the archaeological evidence is that there was some form of religious practice across the British Isles from very early on, in terms of human occupation. So let us start with what we do know.

))O((

What we understand of the Druids comes mainly from written accounts by the Romans and Greeks. The Romans, as an occupying force, encountered the Celts across Europe. They noted that their languages differed between tribes, their gods were different, and they were separated from one another not only by time – for they occupy a span of several thousand years – but by culture and geography. Can we say that the La Tène culture in Switzerland of the late Iron Age is the same as the culture known to Boudicca and her troops in eastern England in AD 60? Would a 'Celtic' tribe in the mountains of Wales have much in common with people on the northwest coast of Spain? Given the silence that these people have inadvertently bequeathed to their descendants, it is very difficult to say.

I once met an old man in a pub in Somerset, in a village called Ashcott, which is four miles as the crow flies from my village of Westhay. He had been a peat hod carrier, one of the last generation of men who had dug the peat and carried it by hand rather than using mechanical diggers. Was he, I asked, local? He looked rather shocked and replied 'No! Oh, no, I'm not *local*. I was born in Westhay.' The idea of what 'local' might mean depends on a range of factors, principally communication and transport. If you think back to ancient Britain – thickly and impenetrably forested, with dangerous rivers and seas – it is easy to see how 'local' could mean somewhere very local indeed, and the idea of the rustic who regards someone from the next valley as a 'foreigner' possibly would not have been far off the mark. Again, we are using the values and concepts of the twenty-first century to interpret the past – maybe the tribes did not think like this at all – but they certainly went to war with one another with alarming regularity, and their identity was tribal. They would have seen themselves as members of the Dobunii or the Cornovii, perhaps something even more family-based and insular than that, rather than 'Celtic'.

So what did classical civilization have to say about these people? From the writings of Roman commentators such as Tacitus, we learn that they were fierce and savage, a people who took slaves and practised human sacrifice. They were tattooed, their hair thickened into punk-like points and dreadlocks by lime, and they went into battle naked and screaming. And that was just the women.

Publius Cornelius Tacitus (*c.* AD 55–120) was a Roman senator and writer who possibly spent his early years in the northeast of Gaul, not far from Asterix's imaginary village. The precise date of the surviving books of the *Annals*, his histories of the Roman Empire from Tiberius (42 BC–AD 37) to Nero (AD 37–68), is not clear, but his writing seems to have been well under way by AD 116. This is what he has to say about the Druids and General Suetonius:

On the shore [of Anglesey] stood the opposing army [of Britons] with its dense array of armed warriors, while between the ranks dashed women, in black attire like the Furies, with hair dishevelled, waving firebrands. All around, the druids, lifting up their hands to heaven, and pouring forth dreadful imprecations, scared our soldiers by the unfamiliar sight, so that, as if their limbs were paralysed, they stood motionless, and exposed to wounds. Then urged by their general's appeals and mutual encouragements not to quail before a troop of frenzied women, they bore the standards onwards, smote down all resistance, and wrapped the foe in the flames of his own brands. A force was next set over the conquered, and their groves, devoted to inhuman superstitions, were destroyed. They deemed it indeed a duty to cover their altars with the blood of captives and to consult their deities through human entrails.[1]

Stirring stuff. But how accurate is it? We do not know whether Tacitus relied on eye-witness reports, although he was writing close enough to the Anglesey episode to have done so. The problem is that concepts of rigorous historical accuracy and methodology had not been established – or were even recognized – in Roman times, and arguably it would have been to the advantage of the Romans to present the tribal peoples of Britain in a fearsome light. In other words, this is propaganda. We do know that Tacitus did not have a lot of sympathy for either Jews or Christians and exhibited a distinct (and for him, understandable) Roman bias, so there is no reason why he should have been any more favourable towards the ancient Celts. Moreover, the very role of history was different: not so much to present historical facts that were as accurate as possible, but to make moral and emotional capital out of distant and hard-to-prove events.

Ronald Hutton, in his work *The Druids* (2007), points out that Tacitus' description covers a lot of ground with admirable economy. The people on Anglesey are presented as ferocious, superstitious and influenced by their women – all qualities designed to make the reader back home in Rome tut-tut in disapproval. Moreover, Suetonius does not quake but deals with the foe firmly, and as a result liberates the island from a set of barbarous religious practices. He was doing them a favour by killing them.

Tacitus was not the only Roman to write about the Druids, however. Julius Caesar also made notes about them in 54 BC, having gone into battle with the southern British tribes and the Gauls.

Throughout all Gaul there are two orders of those men who are of any rank and dignity: for most of the population is almost in the condition of slaves, and dares to undertake nothing of itself, and it has no legal redress. The majority, when they are pressed either by debt, or by the vast size of their taxes, or the oppression of the more powerful, give themselves up in vassalage to the nobles, who possess over them the same rights without exception as masters over their slaves. But of these two orders, one is that of the druids, the other that of the Knights [horse-mounted warriors].

The druids are engaged in things sacred, conduct the public and the private sacrifices, and interpret all matters of religion. To these a large number of the young men resort for the purpose of instruction, and they [the druids] are in great honor among them. For they determine respecting almost all controversies, public and private; and if any crime has been perpetrated, if murder has been committed, if there be any dispute about an inheritance, if any about boundaries, these same persons decide it; they decree rewards and punishments; if any one, either in a private or public capacity, has not submitted to their decision, they excommunicate him from the sacrifices. This among them is the most heavy punishment. Those who have been thus excommunicated are considered to be criminal and immoral: all shun them, and avoid their company and conversation, for fear that they will receive some evil from their contact; nor is justice administered to them when seeking it, nor is any dignity bestowed on them.[2]

Caesar presents the average Druid as a kind of early administrator, policeman and lawyer: the lawmakers of their tribes. One Druid ruled the rest – an assembly with, presumably, an elected head. Caesar went on to say:

The druids do not go to war, nor pay tribute together with the rest; they have an exemption from military service and a dispensation in all matters. Induced by such great advantages, many embrace this profession of their own accord, and [many] are sent to it by their parents and relations. They are said there to learn by heart a great number of verses; accordingly some remain in the course of training twenty years . . . They wish to inculcate this as one of their leading tenets, that souls do not become extinct, but pass after death from one body to another, and they think that men by this tenet are in a great degree excited to valor, the fear of death being disregarded. They likewise discuss and impart to the youth many things respecting the stars and their motion, respecting the extent of the world and of our earth, respecting the nature of things, respecting the power and the majesty of the immortal gods.[3]

Caesar speculates that the Druids' refusal to write things down – in spite of their being apparently literate in Greek – stems from their reluctance for their doctrines to be revealed to the wider community, and also for fear that in committing their religious verses to writing they might relax their diligence in learning and memory.

As well as in the Roman and Greek accounts, the Druids, or *draoithe*, also turn up in Irish law texts of the seventh and eighth centuries. In these, their status is described as decreasing with the arrival and adoption of Christianity, as one might expect, until the Druid is little more than a sorcerer. However, the *draoithe* are also depicted as people who can practise divination and curse: traits of magical practitioners that remain constant down the centuries.

Accordingly, the Roman soldier and historian Ammianus Marcellinus around AD 353 describes the Druids as being in possession of esoteric truths:

Throughout these regions men gradually grew civilised and the study of the liberal arts flourished, initiated by the Bards, the Euhages and the Druids. Now, the Bards sang to the sweet strains of the lyre the valorous deeds of famous men composed in heroic verse, but the Euhages, investigating the sublime, attempted to explain the secret laws of nature. The Druids, being loftier than the rest in intellect, and bound together in fraternal organisations, as the authority of Pythagoras determined, were elevated by their investigation of obscure and profound subjects, and scorning all things human, pronounced the soul immortal.[4]

This is all interesting stuff, but as Hutton comments, where did these people get their information *from*? Either you knew a Druid and questioned him, which only Cicero seems to have done when the alleged Druid Divitiacus visited Rome around 63 BC, or you relied on other people's reports, and many of these commentators were geographically far removed from the places in which Druids lived.

Caesar appears neither to approve nor disapprove of the Druidic custom of sacrifice, but the Romans were not the least bloodthirsty people on the face of the planet, and slave-taking and human sacrifice of some kind were relatively commonplace throughout the ancient world. Lying about the practices of the Gauls would not have served Caesar's purposes. When he turned up in Britain around 54 BC he was regarded as a liberator by the tribes, although this relationship significantly deteriorated until the tribal revolt of 52 BC. Caesar had an agenda of casting his campaigns in the best possible light, but his accounts also make it clear that the military campaign was a part of a diplomatic and political programme focused on the tribal leaders.

Hutton, among others, suggests that Caesar's comments had a twofold purpose: presenting the Druids as nasty, thus entitling the Romans to suppress them, but also as wise and sophisticated, thus rendering them worthy of inclusion in the Roman Empire. However, Miranda Aldhouse-Green, in her work *Caesar's Druids: An Ancient Priesthood* (2010), defends Caesar's reliability, suggesting that if he had made up significant events of the campaign, senators who also had access to eye-witness reports would have challenged his writing, and do not appear to have done so.

We are seeing a snapshot of the Druids at the time of the Roman invasion, rather than their history. No people, whether tribal or otherwise, remain static over long periods, and it may have been that the Druids, too, moved with the times, adopting the customs and perhaps the gods of their neighbours.

Let us have a look at some of the prevailing ideas about the ancient Druids.

### *The Druids wore white robes and gathered mistletoe*

We have little idea as to what the actual Druidic wardrobe looked like. Pliny the Elder speaks of the Druids wearing *candida vesta*, which means 'white garments' – not necessarily robes.[5] (Anyone who has ever tried climbing a tree in a robe will have plenty to say about their impracticality.) It is likely that the 'white garment' was a knee-length tunic. Irish accounts speak of the Druids as wearing feather cloaks – a Druid named Mogh Ruith is described as having a 'speckled bird head-dress'.[6] Quite often, Irish Druids have the nickname 'Mael', which means 'bald', and it is possible that they were tonsured or completely shaved. Later Irish clerics of the early Middle Ages had partially shaven heads and this was frowned upon as non-conformist by other Christians, perhaps because it was a relic of Druidic custom.

Revivalist Druids and attendant artists, such as the nineteenth-century author Samuel Meyrick, pictured the ancient priests in billowing white robes, often with an Egyptian head-covering called a *nemyss*, and this kind of image – wise, dignified and not covered in sacrificial gore – seems to have been met with approval, because it stuck in popular thinking. In a case of life imitating art, many contemporary Druids adopt a similar sort of costume.

There are, however, a few references to mistletoe, for instance in Pliny's *Natural History*. The Druids have been associated with this plant ever since. We do not know what significance it may have possessed for them, however.

### The Druids built Stonehenge

Clearly, someone built Stonehenge. It did not manifest on Salisbury Plain all by itself. The site itself is very ancient, with evidence of pine 'totem poles' in holes dating from 8500 to 7000 BC. The cursus structures and long barrows are later, around 3500 BC, and the stones (bluestones and sarsens) were put in place around 2500 BC. The hill fort called Vespasian's Camp, on the outskirts of what is now Salisbury, is Iron Age, built around 700 BC. But we do not know precisely who built Stonehenge, although new archaeological evidence is coming to light all the time.

We do, however, have a fascinating window into the Iron Age world of 325 BC, given by a Greek merchant called Pytheas. His accounts of Prettanike, or Bretanniai, give our current island nation its name of 'Britain'. Pytheas, in many ways a typical tourist, chatted to lots of people, who told him, for instance, that the mother of the god Apollo was born in Britain and that everyone worshipped him there. Pytheas, cited by Greek authors such as Pliny, mentions a 'circular temple' to Apollo with a big city nearby.[7] Kings ruled the city and were known as the 'Boreades' after the chilly north wind.

Pytheas was not specific about the location of this marvellous place, which has informed years of archaeological speculation. The stone circle of Callanish on Lewis in the Outer Hebrides has been suggested, but the obvious candidate is Stonehenge, with the area known as Vespasian's Camp as the 'city', or other relatively local camps such as Hembury. However, perhaps we should not attach too much to Pytheas' claims for Apollo: the temple may have been dedicated to a local solar god, and the Greek merchant simply translated it into terms with which he would have been more familiar.

It was the seventeenth-century writer and archaeologist John Aubrey who suggested that the Druids were responsible for Stonehenge. The English antiquarian William Stukeley popularized this view in his book *Stonehenge: A Temple Restor'd to the British Druids*, written in 1740. There is also an old legend that Merlin simply flew the entire circle over from Ireland, which I think we can rule out. The priest caste whom Caesar first encountered may not have built Stonehenge, but the precursors of the Druids possibly did.

### *The Druids conducted human sacrifice*

Few people now associate human sacrifice with Druids. But this has not always been the case and the imagery still shows up from time to time. It is through Caesar that we first meet the infamous figure of the wicker man, the icon of the twentieth-century folk horror movie of the same name:

> All the Gauls are extremely devoted to superstitious rituals; and on that account they who are troubled with unusually severe diseases, and they who are engaged in battles and dangers, either sacrifice men as victims, or vow that they will sacrifice them, and employ the druids as the performers of those sacrifices; because they think that unless the life of a man be offered for the life of a man, the mind of the immortal gods can not be rendered propitious, and they have sacrifices of that kind ordained for national purposes. Others have figures of vast size, the limbs of which formed of osiers they fill with living men, which being set on fire, the men perish enveloped in the flames. They consider that the sacrifice of peoples guilty of theft, or in robbery, or any other offense, is more acceptable to the immortal gods; but when a supply of such people is wanting, they have the right to even sacrifice the innocent.[8]

The wicker man and other sacrificial practices are also mentioned by Strabo:

> They would strike a man who had been consecrated for sacrifice in the back with a sword, and make prophecies based on his death-spasms; and they would not sacrifice without the presence of the Druids. Other kinds of human sacrifices have been reported as well: some men

they would shoot dead with arrows and impale in the temples; or they would construct a huge figure of straw and wood, and having thrown cattle and all manner of wild animals and humans into it, they would make a burnt offering of the whole thing.[9]

According to Strabo, the Romans, being civilized, put a stop to this sort of thing.

The idea of a wicker man is reminiscent of references in both Irish legend and the second branch of the Welsh epic the *Mabinogi* to men being lured into a specially built house, which is then set on fire. This might not necessarily be sacrificial, however: it could equally be a tactic of war.

There is also a reference by Lucan in the *Pharsalia* of AD 61–5 with regard to three Celtic deities.[10] Taranis is said to have been propitiated by burning people, Teutates by drowning them and Esus by hanging. Esus is mythologically similar to the Nordic deity Odin, who is also associated with hanging from a tree. (This might explain why Taranis, Teutates and Esus are not very popular gods today.)

And there is Tacitus' account of the Roman attack on the Druid stronghold of Anglesey. While the Romans' attack was almost certainly politically motivated, Tacitus suggests that there were at least rumours about sacrificial practices. He refers to altars as 'soaked with human blood'. Boudicca is also said to have impaled victims during her rebellion in AD 60, but again, she was at war.

The best archaeological data supporting Celtic human sacrifice is the body of the man placed in Lindow bog in the first or second century AD. The body was so well preserved that scientists were able to analyse the man's stomach contents to discover his last meal (a partially scorched grain cake). Lindow Man was possibly a ritual sacrifice; he was strangled, hit on the head and had his throat cut, in quick order, then surrendered to the bog. This pattern fits the 'threefold' death referred to in medieval Irish tales – although commentators have questioned whether there is a connection, and have also queried the nature of Lindow Man's death. There are other bog burials (the Tollund Man bog body in Denmark is very similar) in various places in Europe, as there are grain storage pits and shafts that, once they were no longer used for storage, had human bodies thrown in them, for instance at the Danebury hill fort.

A late Iron Age shaft in Holzhausen in Bavaria with a post at the bottom was possibly used for impaling human victims. When it was analysed, the pole showed traces of human flesh and blood. At Garton Slack in East Yorkshire, a young man and a woman of about thirty were found huddled together in a shaft with a wooden stake between them that pinned their arms together. The woman was likely pregnant, since a foetal skeleton was found beneath her pelvis. It is hard to know whether this was a sacrifice, a punishment or something else. There have also been several instances of foundation burials, often of children, which may or may not have been sacrifices.

So it would seem that the Romans, at least, made claims for human sacrifices on the part of the Druids, and there is some evidence that these claims are true.

*The Celts believed in the empowerment of women*

Inspired by feminist retellings of Celtic myths, and fantasy novels set in the ancient Celtic world (or worlds very similar to Earth in which everyone has Celtic names), some pagans like to envisage Celtic Britain and Europe as peaceful, goddess-worshipping places in which women played a significant and equal role. This is perhaps a bit unfair on fantasy novels: Marion Zimmer Bradley's *The Mists of Avalon* (1983), a book that launched a thousand goddess-worshippers, is not by any stretch of the imagination historically accurate – and has not claimed to be – but nevertheless does try to address the very unequal role of women under the Roman occupation of Britain. (A friend who is a medieval Welsh historian once discovered the book in a Glastonbury bookshop under the 'history' section: rather than succumbing to apoplexy, she moved it.)

Despite the long-perpetuated 'docile female' trope, tribal women appear to have fought alongside the men, and, in the absence of suitable male relatives, they could become tribal leaders. The most famous examples are Boudicca and Cartimandua.

In the case of Boudicca, Prasutagus, king of the Iceni, 'famed for his long prosperity', made the Roman emperor Nero his heir, along with his wife Boudicca and his two daughters. He did so in order to secure his tribal lands against Roman pillaging: if a client king died, the Romans would seize his lands, so Prasutagus tried to get round this by splitting the inheritance legally between his family and his Roman masters. Unfortunately this turned out to be a mistake. When Prasutagus died, Tacitus tells us,

> The reverse was the result, so much so that his kingdom was plundered by centurions, his house by slaves, as if they were the spoils of war. First, his wife Boudicca was whipped and his daughters raped. All the chief men of

the Iceni, as if Rome had received the whole country as a gift, were stripped of their ancestral possessions, and the king's relatives were made slaves.[11]

The Iceni rebelled, bringing other tribes such as the Trinobantes into a revolt. Boudicca took her violated daughters in her chariot on a tour of the local tribes. They were not short of supporters, since the eastern tribes had suffered considerably at the hands of Roman settlers, particularly ex-Roman army veterans. These settlers had driven them from their homes and farms and enslaved them, backed up by serving soldiers who hoped for the same privileges when they, too, retired.

The colony was, moreover, undefended – a lapse in security on the part of the Romans, who had possibly become complacent. Things started to go downhill fast. The statue of Victory at Camulodunum fell over – never a good sign – with its back to the enemy as though it fled before them. Women started coming out with prophecies of destruction and 'ravings in a strange language'.[12] The image of an overthrown town appeared in the waters of the Thames and the sea looked like blood.

Not unnaturally, this disconcerted the Romans. Suetonius was far away, so the colonials asked for aid from the procurator, Catus Decianus, who was not much help. All he did was to send two hundred men with regular arms as back-up for the existing small military force. Not only had the colony not managed to erect defences, they had not evacuated elderly men or women. So when they found themselves surrounded by a barbarian host, they had little recourse.

The victorious enemy met Quintus Petillius Cerialis, commander of the ninth legion, who was coming to the rescue. They routed his troops and destroyed all his infantry. Cerialis escaped with his cavalry into the camp, where its fortifications saved him. Alarmed by this disaster and by the fury of the province he had goaded into war by his rapacity, the procurator Catus fled to Gaul.

Despite Boudicca's reported words below, it does not seem that leadership by women was usual. Tribeswomen might have been fierce, but they did not usually become military commanders. Boudicca, however, had been provoked beyond endurance.

It was customary, she knew, with Britons to fight under female captaincy; but now she was avenging, not, as a queen of glorious ancestry, her ravished realm and power, but, as a woman of the people, her liberty lost, her body tortured by the lash, the tarnished honour of her daughters. Roman cupidity had progressed so far that not their very persons, not age itself, nor maidenhood, were left unpolluted. Yet Heaven was on the side of their just revenge: one legion, which ventured battle, had perished; the rest were skulking in their camps, or looking around them for a way of escape. They would never face even the din and roar of those many thousands, far less their onslaught and their swords! – If they considered in their own hearts the forces under arms and the motives of the war, on that field they must conquer or fall. Such was the settled purpose of a woman – the men might live and be slaves![13]

It is accounts like this that made an early feminist heroine out of Boudicca. But despite marching on Londinium (London) and putting it to the torch along with Verulamium

(St Albans), Boudicca did not succeed. Suetonius faced her army down at what is now Watling Street in London and won. Boudicca herself died shortly afterwards, although the cause of her death is not known. This was a big revolt: over 70,000 people died and Nero considered pulling the legions out of Britain as a result, though he later relented. We are not told how much Boudicca relied on her religious advisers during all of this, although there is a story of her releasing a hare from her skirts and seeing which way it ran as a means of divination.

Cartimandua led the Brigantes, in what is now Yorkshire, from around AD 43 to 69. She remained in power by making deals with the Romans and was described by Tacitus as 'loyal to Rome' and 'defended by our Roman arms'. Her loyalty was proved when she delivered the rebel leader Caractacus, chief of the Catevellauni, who had led a revolt against the Romans, to the occupiers. This went down well with her Roman masters but not with the surrounding tribes, who not unnaturally objected. She also further annoyed them by divorcing her husband, Venutius, in favour of his armour-bearer. This counts as one of the most disastrous divorces of the ancient world: Venutius was popular among the people and declared war against his ex. The Romans stepped in to defend her, but Venutius bided his time until Nero's death caused upheaval in the provinces, and took Brigantia back. Cartimandua fled to the fort of Deva and disappeared from history, and Venutius was eventually ousted in turn by the Romans.

Boudicca and Cartimandua have something in common: initial support from the Romans. Cartimandua had this for longer than Boudicca, but if things had not gone so badly, the latter would probably have gone down in history less as a warrior queen and more as an acquiescent Romano-British matron. Like a lot of women in history, they got to where they were as a result of family connections (both were part of a ruling elite) and powerful masters, rather than because the Celtic tribes were into equality.

These women, however, were political leaders, not Druidesses. There are only three known references to Druidesses, all Roman, and all in the fourth century. In each, the Druidess has a particular function: to predict the rise of a great man.

$$))) \bigcirc (((($$

Everyone writing in the ancient world about the Druids seems to be in agreement that they *knew* a lot. They were law-givers, political advisers, astronomers, medical professionals. Diogenes Laertius comments on them in his third-century work *Vitae*, quoting two other authors: Sotion of Alexandria in the 23rd book of his *Succession of Philosophers* and a person mistakenly believed to have been Aristotle in a treatise on magic. Laertius comments that some people say that the study of philosophy itself originated with the Druids.

They were said to have believed in reincarnation, believing that souls passed into another body instead of being extinguished. Hence the tribes were not concerned about death in battle. Laertius also comments that the Druids taught younger generations about the stars and their movements, and instructed them about the gods.

So who were these 'immortal gods'? It is important to note that the gods and goddesses whom Celtic pagan revivalists

worship these days do not bear much resemblance to the frag-
mentary, incomplete picture we have of the ancient Celtic deities.
We have mentioned that gods like Teutates are not worshipped
now (although they do worship him in *Asterix*). And there are
almost certainly a lot of deities who have simply dropped out
of sight: small gods of rivers and springs and groves.

Laertius says that the Druids worshipped 'Mercury', regarding him as the inventor of the arts and the patron of journeys
and merchants. They also, he says, worshipped Apollo, Mars,
Minerva and Jupiter. The tribal form of Mars was a war god;
the version of Apollo was a healer. The tribes made sacrifices of
animals to these gods after victories in battle, and also gave the
gods the spoils of war. Keeping those spoils for oneself could
result in torture as a punishment.

But these gods all have Roman names. What did the tribespeople call them? This is not clear. These were probably gods
who bore a close enough resemblance to Roman deities for the
Romans to use the familiar names. Laertius also added that the
Gauls believed themselves to have been descended from the god
Dis, and, because of this underworld connection, calculated time
by the number of nights rather than days.

Cicero, a contemporary of Caesar, also comments on the
Druids, particularly on a man known to both himself and Caesar
called Divitiacus, whom we have mentioned above. He was a
member of the Aedui tribe in Gaul, and Cicero tells us that
as well as being knowledgeable about the natural world, he
practised divination by augury.

Diodorus Siculus, in 36 BC, comments too, describing how
the tribes were divided into the *drouidas* themselves, who were
philosophers and theologians; *bardoi*, who sang and made poetry,

and the third group of *o'vateis*, who were expert in the natural world and who practised divination.

Pomponius Mela, the Romans' first geographer, remarks:

They [the Gauls] have an eloquence of their own, and their Druids as masters of wisdom. These profess to know the magnitude and form of the earth and the world, the motions of the heaven and the stars, and the will of the gods. They teach the most noble of the nation many things privately, and for a long time, even for twenty years, in a cave, or in inaccessible woods. One of their precepts has become public, namely, that they should act bravely in war, that souls are immortal, and that there is another life after death. Therefore along with the dead, they burn and bury things which belonged to them while living. Their debtor and creditor accounts were transferred below. Some even went so far as to ascend the funeral pyres of their friends of their own accord, as though about to live with them.[14]

Mela goes on to add that the Gauls buried objects that were particularly important to them in their tombs, which does indeed seem to be the case. One has to ask why, if you are going to be reincarnated, you would need such possessions. Perhaps not all of the tribes believed in reincarnation, and it has also been suggested that the tribes believed their souls were reincarnated in a sort of parallel world: an afterlife, in other words.

Dio Chrysostom in AD 100 says that the Druids were expert in many forms of knowledge. And Hippolytus asserts that the Druids learned much from the Greek philosopher Pythagoras

– and indeed, whichever way the knowledge exchange went, there do seem to be some similarities between the two sets of beliefs, notably the belief in reincarnation.

If you were the adviser of your tribe, you would be expected to come up with the goods: whether your magic actually worked might be debatable, but your star lore, medical knowledge and ideas about military strategy would all be testable, and if they consistently failed, you would be out of a job. For these reasons, I think we can conclude that the Druids, if not all-knowing, did have a considerable amount of experiential and practical knowledge.

Yet the Druids were not the only people practising magic and believing in religion in the British Isles at this time: not just colonized, but colonizer, too, brought their own gods and beliefs with them. We should remember that in religious terms the Romans were primarily syncretic: that is to say, rather than trying to eradicate the deities and practices of the people whom they colonized, they tended to merge them with their own. For example, when the Romans established Bath as a commercial and military centre (with a nice spa attached), instead of stamping out the worship of the local goddess Sulis, who had an oracular shrine in the area, they pointed out to the local tribespeople that Sulis was similar to their own goddess Minerva, the Roman equivalent of the Grecian Athena, who was dedicated to wisdom and learning. It seems that the tribes were satisfied with this, because the cult of Sulis Minerva was established, and there is a head of the goddess still on display at the baths in Bath today.

The Romans seem to have followed this syncretic approach throughout the British Isles and elsewhere. But they did not completely abandon their own gods. There was a temple dedicated to Mars near Bristol, and across the River Severn you can still visit the remains of a complex to a tribal god called Nodens, who became equated with some of the Roman gods (he is a bit like Mercury, Neptune and Mars rolled into one). Romans brought votive offerings to the shrine with inscriptions dedicated to Mars (asking him to curse people for them, not infrequently) and so the shrine had a dual purpose: Celtic gods for the Celts, Roman gods for the Romans. In modern terminology, it was 'multivalent': one place with different purposes.

The Romans did not restrict themselves to Italian gods, either. Bear in mind that legionaries were recruited from all over the Roman Empire. So in addition to gods like Hermes and Mars, we find, dotted across Britain, temples and shrines to other peoples' gods as well. There is evidence for the existence of an Iseum – a temple to the great Egyptian goddess Isis – in London: for example, a flagon with an inscription to the temple. There is also an altar on which the inscription confirms that the temple – which had 'fallen down through old age' – had been restored. This third-century altar, found re-used in the riverside wall, was dedicated by Marcus Martiannius Pulcher, a provincial Roman governor. Other finds include a bone hairpin and some weights depicting the goddess. The Egyptian deity had company of her own kind, too: there is also some evidence for the presence of the Egyptian jackal-headed god of the dead, Anubis. Excavations of a cremation site in Great Dover Street in London revealed a lamp with an image of Anubis on it – although perhaps this was simply imported for ornamental reasons.

Further, Roman soldiers were keen on having a god of their own, a military god, and they found him in the form of

Mithras, who was originally from the region of Persia. Temples to Mithras are located throughout the British Isles. These include Carrawburgh, Northumberland, where there is a third-century Mithraeum, Rudchester near Hadrian's Wall, and Caernarfon in Wales (where the Mithraeum features in the Merlin series of novels written by Mary Stewart). These temples were all situated underground.

One Mithraeum has recently been reopened in Bloomberg's new European headquarters in London. They lie over one of London's lost rivers, the Walbrook, which marked the limits of the Roman settlement nearly 2,000 years ago. As the town increased in size and importance, the banks of the Walbrook were reclaimed and Roman London became not only a major port of trade but a successful economic centre, with a population of around 30,000 people. Parts of these walls survive in an area that corresponds roughly to the Square Mile of the City of London – still London's centre of commerce today.

The temple itself was rediscovered in 1954, after the Second World War had ended but while the effects of the Blitz were still being dealt with. Although there was substantial interest in it, the site was not done justice by its reconstructed location, which was close to the original site. When, in the last stages of the investigation, the stone head of a beautiful young man was found, thousands queued to see it, but Britain was still recovering from the war and there were comparatively few resources available to treat the temple properly. The then prime minister, Winston Churchill, prevented the Legal & General insurance company from destroying the walls, which were kept in a builders' yard until 1962. The god's head and other artefacts were sent to the Museum of London. However, wooden benches discovered at the site, which could have told future archaeologists more about the temple, were simply discarded.

'It was a mystery cult and its rites remain very well guarded mysteries. There is nothing written about what went on in the temples, no book of Mithras,' says Sophie Jackson, the lead archaeologist for Museum of London Archaeology, who has spent many years working on the site. 'The one thing we do know is that no bulls were sacrificed there. It was a very confined space and I don't think anyone would have got out alive.'[15]

One-tenth of the Roman finds now exhibited in the Museum of London come from the Bloomberg site. The very name of the Roman city, Londinium, was discovered here, in early texts on wooden tablets, preserved by the boggy, waterlogged ground. Further finds include the first financial document from Britain, which is also etched on a wooden tablet, a tiny amber amulet in the shape of a gladiator's helmet and a hoard of pewter vessels, possibly used in rituals within the temple.

When we talk in religious terms about the Roman occupation of Britain, therefore, we can characterize it as diverse, cosmopolitan and syncretic. It was a relatively tolerant place, at least through the lens that we turn upon it centuries later, once the potentially dangerous caste of the Druids had been subdued. A place with many gods and goddesses from many countries, worshipped by a population that was partly native, but which also came from all over the Roman world. It must have been a fascinating place, with people who almost certainly resented their colonizers, but one can imagine it also as being a country that was opening up to new and interesting religious ideas and practices, with people exchanging information and concepts. Look how popular New Age beliefs and paganism are these days, with people merging lots of different spiritual practices and worshipping lots of different gods. Are we the new Romans? Perhaps. But the Roman colonization of Britain was not destined to last.

# TWO

# Saxons and Vikings

In AD 410 the Romans began to pull out of Britain. The legions were an occupying force, needed elsewhere to combat the threat to Rome from tribes in the north of Italy. Britain was not worth holding on to, and the Roman emperor of the day, Honorius, let the colony go, leaving the Romano-British to fend for themselves against invaders of their own. Ammianus Marcellinus, writing in 378, suggests there was an alliance between the Picts, Scots and Saxons; this may not have been the case, but it is evident that Britain was under some kind of ingress along the 'Saxon Shore', a line of forts ranging from Norfolk to Sussex. An appeal by the Roman citizens of Britain to Honorius received the reply that they should look to their own defences.

This refusal must have been alarming for the Romans who lived in Britain, but it was not entirely unreasonable. Britain had already demonstrated a treasonous tendency to host pretenders to the Roman throne. Honorius, beset by the Goths, did not have much incentive to regard his British outpost with any great favour.

The results of the Roman withdrawal appear in Bede, Gildas and the Anglo-Saxon Chronicle, much later. They tell us that a war leader named Vortigern (it might be a title, *Vawr-tighern* or 'overlord'; his actual name was possibly Vitalinus) is said to have struck a deal with a couple of Frankish or Jutish mercenaries named Hengist and Horsa to reside in the east of England, providing a barrier between their own invading kin and the British. The mercenaries, the story goes, then mutinied over their rate of pay, and seized the lands they were hired to protect. Hengist and Horsa may be myths but the narrative regarding the underlying political situation has the ring of truth. The Romans had already been bringing northern Europeans into Britain from the third century onwards, along the Saxon shore, to act as mercenaries.

Gildas states that around AD 446 Britain was under constant attack and the Romano-British citizens wrote to the then commander Aetius: 'The barbarians drive us to the sea and the sea drives us back to the barbarians; death comes by one means or the other; we are either slain or drowned.'[1] Aetius did respond, but not very helpfully, by sending a couple of bishops on what was essentially a fact-finding mission.

Our main concern here is that the whole of Britain at the time of the Roman withdrawal was an unstable mess. The Irish were attacking from the west, the Picts were still being held at bay by Hadrian's Wall but posed a threat, Germanic tribes were beginning to assault, or at the very least move into, the eastern and southern shores of Britain and the Romano-British were revolting against Rome itself while some folk still wanted Roman military protection.

When we talk of the 'Saxons', we are really referring to three groups of people: the Angles, the Saxons and the Jutes, all closely linked Germanic tribes from across the North Sea. There is considerable debate as to how far they invaded (as opposed to just settled), how violent they were (there is archaeological evidence for massacres as well as commentary by historians like Gildas), and whether the Saxons turned up and peaceably intermarried into Romano-British society, impressing local women with their blond braids and fancy enamelwork.

In part, we have a similar problem with the Saxons to the one we had with the Celts: very little was written down, although we do have more textual evidence for the Saxons than we do for the Celts, which we will look at shortly. People were not generally literate as we know it, and we have noted that when it comes to interpreting culture, archaeological evidence is limited. We do not fully understand the symbology used in Saxon images, for instance. And accounts written by outsiders, such as the Romans, were likely to have been heavily biased, so, when it comes to the Saxons and the Vikings, a lot of our research is based on later writers, who were Christian. This is not to say that later Christian writers automatically denigrated pagans, but when they wrote down old stories, those stories may already have been greatly altered. Folk tales do not stay static but are adapted by different people, and people who wrote things down often did so for complex reasons and in complex ways.

the people writing down the sources weren't in a vacuum – they introduced stuff they found cool or relevant, from all over the place, or borrowed stories, or added in local colour. They adapted things to make their patron or family look good and their rivals bad. So with later sources, you have to look for writer bias, borrowing and assumptions. Plus, not all sources are equal even when they have contemporary layers. For a start, there's the question of what is deliberately omitted – the Anglo-Saxon Chronicle is pretty much contemporary for the ninth century, but leaves out Aethelred of Mercia and Aethelflaed, to serve West Saxon propaganda that only the King of Wessex was really a king. Then, sources can be aware of and dependent on each other – so what looks like three separate and independent accounts is actually only one, because either one manuscript is the original and the other two copied it, or, more commonly, all three are descended in complicated and different ways from a common original.[2]

It is worth a digression here, to take a look at why – if Celtic paganism was as attractive as its modern adherents claim – Britain became Christian relatively quickly. One possibility lies in an episode involving King Edwin, who invited Bishop Paulinus to speak to him and his court. Bede relates that during Paulinus' visit, someone at the court told the king the following parable:

The present life of man upon earth, O King, seems to me in comparison with that time which is unknown to us like the swift flight of a sparrow through the mead-hall where you sit at supper in winter, with your Ealdormen and thanes, while the fire blazes in the midst and the hall is warmed, but the wintry storms of rain or snow are raging abroad. The sparrow, flying in at one door and immediately out at another, whilst he is within, is safe from the wintry tempest, but after a short space of fair weather, he immediately vanishes out of your sight, passing from winter to winter again. So this life of man appears for a little while, but of what is to follow or what went before we know nothing at all.[3]

The implication is that in Christianity we *do* know what happens outside the mead hall: that is, the soul goes on to an eternal afterlife. This more appealing concept might account for the swiftness of conversions. Edwin converted, as did his pagan priest Coifi, who is said afterwards to have ridden to the temple of Woden at Goodmanham and put a spear through it before burning it to the ground. This may all be apocryphal, a metaphor for the conversion of Saxon kings, but what is apparent is that widespread conversion did take place and was also coming from the north, as Irish missionaries – with the belief that it was their holy duty to spread the word of God – ventured across the sea and down into eastern and southern Britain. The Saxons do not appear to have martyred anyone, unlike in Europe.

Part of this Christianization is perhaps the legacy of Roman syncretism. In Ireland, the goddess Bride seems to have become St Bridget. It also appears that the Christian Church followed the Roman example. When Pope Gregory i sent St Augustine to Britain, he suggested that pagan practices should be incorporated into Christian ones – taking over feast days and so forth. Some historians also believe that the resident Celts effectively became 'Saxonized', adopting the newcomers' customs.

However, those newcomers brought their native beliefs. Around Cambridge, Saxon burial sites contain the bones of people who had originally been buried elsewhere: the migrants brought their ancestors with them. There are indications that the Saxons believed in magic, and that some form of witchcraft was practised. Multiple words relating to magic turn up in the language – *lybcraeft*: magic, *lybblac*: witchcraft, *begalan*: to enchant and *morth weorc*: to kill someone by poison, witchcraft or, in a belt-and-braces approach, both. There was *scinn-lac*:

magical action and *scinn craeft*: magical skill. There were *wicce-craeft* and *wiccedom*, also meaning witchery, terms we shall encounter again much later, in the twentieth century, and *bealo-craeft*: sorcery and evil art. And there are lots of words relating to ghosts and phantoms.

In addition to these clues, edicts were passed against magic, and you do not bother passing a law against something unless it actually exists and presents a problem. For example:

> we have ordained respecting witch-crafts, and lybacs, and morthdaeds: if any one should be thereby killed, and he could not deny it, that he be liable in his life. But if he will deny it, and at threefold ordeal shall be guilty; that he be 120 days in prison: and after that let kindred take him out, and give to the king 120 shillings, and pay the wer to his kindred, and enter into borh for him, that he evermore desist from the like.[4]

The above passage was part of King Athelstan's legal code in the 900s, and rulers continued to take precautions.

> We earnestly forbid every heathenism. It is heathen practice if one worship idols, namely if one worship heathen gods and the sun or the moon, fire or flood, wells or stones or any kind of forest trees, or if one practices witchcraft or encompasses death by any means, either by sacrifice or divination.[5]

These were the words of King Cnut (he of the ill-fated attempt to hold back the sea) in 1020. So it would seem that throughout the reign of the Saxon kings, people were either practising magic or believed to be doing it, otherwise no one would have bothered to mention it. With the rise of Christianity in Britain, we are beginning to see the characterization of magic as something forbidden, dark and suspicious: something opposed to the work of the Church and which undermines its power.

Caesar declared that the Saxon tribes did not worship gods as such, only the sun, the moon and fire. Tacitus reported that the Germanic tribes did not like cooping their gods up in temples, but he does mention some of them via the syncretic process of *interpretatio romana*: conflating Roman deities with tribal ones. Writing about the religion of the Germanic Suebi tribe, Tacitus states that they worship Mercury: 'They regard it as a religious duty to offer to him, on fixed days, human as well as other sacrificial victims. Hercules and Mars they appease by animal offerings of the permitted kind.'[6] According to Tacitus, Odin/Woden is Mercury, Thor is analogous to Hercules and Tyr (distinct from Thor) is Mars, although he also mentions that the Suebi worshipped Isis and it is not clear which Germanic deity he means by that. Woden is also mentioned in a text called the Nine Herbs Charm:

A serpent came crawling [but] it destroyed no one
when Woden took nine twigs of glory,
[and] then struck the adder so that it flew into nine [pieces].
There archived apple and poison
that it never would re-enter the house.[7]

Woden and Mercury are not really that similar (Woden is a god of healing, wisdom and many other qualities, whereas

Mercury is a deity of communication, commerce and eloquence), although both of them carry a staff and wear a broad-brimmed hat, and to an extent they are both cunning tricksters. The mid-seventh-century writer Jonas of Bobbio references Odin, 'whom others called Mercury', but for all we know he might have been talking about Tacitus as one of those 'others'.

Caesar and Tacitus, as we saw in our previous chapter, were writing quite a long time before the Saxons started taking a real interest in Britain, and as we have also noted, religious practices do not stay static: they are in a constant state of development and change. It seems possible that gods like Woden were comparatively recent concepts even in their countries of origin (that is to say, they were newish gods for the Saxons back home), but they were still imported to Britain. The Saxon rulers of Essex, for instance, traced their ancestry back to Woden, rather as Japanese emperors claimed until recently to have been descended from the sun goddess. Divine blood was evidently regarded as desirable. The Merseburg Charms are a principal source of information about gods and goddesses here. Discovered by Georg Waitz in 1841 as part of a ninth- or tenth-century religious manuscript, the 'charm' actually consists of two spells, one of which is about women freeing prisoners and the other about the gods themselves:

> Phol [Baldur] and Wodan were riding to the woods,
> and the foot of Balder's foal was sprained
> So Sinthgunt, Sunna's sister, conjured it.
> and Frija, Volla's sister, conjured it.

and Wodan conjured it, as well he could:
Like bone-sprain, so blood-sprain,
so joint-sprain:
Bone to bone, blood to blood,
joints to joints, so may they be mended.[8]

Spells like this one appear in the later 'black books', the Germanic and Scandinavian grimoires, and more Christianized versions of spells from Orkney and Shetland. Thunor, Woden and Seaxneat are mentioned in the Old Saxon Baptismal Vow (ninth century) as the three main gods whom you are supposed to renounce before being baptized as a Christian. The first two – in their Norse guises as Odin and Thor – are still with us, worshipped and commemorated in the days of the week (Wednesday and Thursday), but Seaxneat/Saxnot has fallen by the wayside, at least as far as most modern British Heathens are concerned. However, he originally appears to have been the dominant god and was later modified into a son of Woden. Possibly – because people are still mixing and matching their deities – he was conflated with the god Tiw. But there are lots more who are not widely worshipped, or even widely known, today: Rig, Ran, Tuisto, Mannus and Irpa, to name but a few. As with the Celtic deities, we might begin to ask why some lasted the distance and others did not.

We might also ask whether the gradual development of one overall deity, such as Tiw or Odin, could have something to do with Christianity. Did the Saxons think that since the Christians had an overpowering sky god, they would have one, too? As seems possible with Odin, these deities may originally have been more like powerful ancestral spirits than what we tend to think of as gods. The historian Bill Griffiths states: 'The Germanic "gods"... were likely to be relatively local, limited in potential, and connected with a particular need or role, not distinguished by status in some fixed pantheon that assisted and reflected a self-perpetuating and wide-ruling state system.'[9] However, some of the Saxon and Viking gods do bear a resemblance to deities further south: Odin is a little like Zeus, Thor resembles Mars, Freya is a goddess of love like Venus. This does not mean that the Germanic tribes necessarily adopted their gods from the classical world – all humans have concepts of love and war – but it is a possibility.

The writer Saxo Grammaticus, in the thirteenth century, states: 'There are some who say that the gods whom we worship only shared the title with those whom Greece or Rome honoured, and in effect borrowed from them the rituals and name, as though claiming to be equal in status.'[10] And a sixth-century commentator said, somewhat cynically, 'The rich Goth imitates the Roman, the poor Roman imitates the Goth.'[11]

References in Christian Anglo-Saxon texts to ancient gods are not common and tend to refer to them as demons. And much of what we now think of as a Saxon pantheon of gods is owed to Jacob Grimm, writing in 1835 at the rise of German nationalism, and subsequently to Richard Wagner. This is obviously much later in the day. Whom we commonly think the Saxons worshipped may bear little resemblance to the deities they actually did honour.

To illustrate the difficulty of pinpointing who believed what, I am going to take as an example the 'goddess' Eostre. I am using her as an example of what happens when modern flights of fancy get interpreted as historical fact. Eostre is an extreme example, but she serves as a demonstration of the twists and turns that belief in 'ancient' gods can take, and serves as a warning not to become too attached to modern conceptions of old deities.

In many modern pagan books that feature the gods of Dark Ages Britain, Eostre is presented as a Germanic goddess. Her name, in the form of 'Ostara', was attached to the spring equinox by the American writer Aidan Kelly in the 1970s and is now a festival celebrated in some form by the majority of modern pagans. 'Easter' is held to come from her name. Most European languages use a derivative of the Latin 'Pascha' for the holiday, which commemorates Christ's death and resurrection, a word that in turn is thought to derive from Aramaic. It is a nice explanation as to why we are different and call it 'Easter'. She is a Germanic goddess, after all.

The only problem with all this is that it is completely wrong. The words 'Easter' and 'Eostre' are not linguistically connected, and the spring equinox (the date on which night and day are of equal length) is an astronomical festival, whereas Easter (the weekend after the first new moon) is a lunar one and has a totally different focus. This is important because the belief that Easter is named after an ancient Saxon goddess and really refers to the arrival of spring is part of a wider belief that Christians 'stole' pagan festivals. There is some mapping, but overall, this is a straw-man argument.

So who was Eostre? For the research on this, we are indebted to a historical researcher and writer, Adrian Bott, who has made it part of his life's work to debunk some of the myths surrounding Eostre. Rather than accepting the received wisdom about her connection to Easter, Bott began a rigorous examination of the origins of her name, linking it back to an obscure reference in the writings of the Venerable Bede (*The Reckoning of Time*, AD 725), which was then picked up by Grimm. Bott questioned the idea that Eostre was an ancient Germanic goddess of the dawn or of springtime, or that she had anything to do with hares, eggs or indeed chocolate.

> Only one piece of documentary evidence for Eostre exists: a passing mention in Bede's *The Reckoning of Time*. Bede explains that the lunar month of Eosturmonath 'was once called after a goddess . . . named Eostre, in whose honour feasts were celebrated.'
>
> However, even this may only have been supposition on Bede's part. In the same section he says the winter festival of Modranecht was so named 'because (we suspect) of the ceremonies they enacted all that night,' hardly the statement of a historian with first-hand information.
>
> Eosturmonath may simply mean 'the month of opening', appropriate for a time of opening buds and arguably a better fit for the rest of the Anglo-Saxon months. They tended to be named after agricultural or meteorological events, hence 'mud-month' and 'blood-month'.[12]

Gradually, however, these findings have begun to disseminate into the wider pagan community in the UK, enhancing our understanding of where this popular part of our celebrations actually originates. Bott's work on the origins of Eostre is to be commended: no one is saying that pagans should not name the festival as they please, or enjoy the concept of a beautiful goddess of springtime. But it behoves us to be aware of where our prevailing myths come from.

As well as more or less inventing a goddess, the Venerable Bede does tell us some things that are more reliable:

> It is told that the king, while he rejoiced at their conversion and their faith, yet compelled none to embrace Christianity, but only showed more affection to the believers, as to his fellow citizens in the kingdom of Heaven. For he had learned from those who had instructed him and guided him to salvation, that the service of Christ ought to be voluntary, not by compulsion.[13]

Pope Gregory was pleased with the outcomes of missions to England and in AD 597 made Augustine 'Archbishop of the English'. Augustine asked Gregory for guidance on ways of dealing with the pagans, and Gregory told Augustine to gather whatever seemed best from the various churches and teach them in the way that seemed appropriate to him, 'For things are not to be loved for the sake of places, but places for the sake of good things.'

Gregory, in the early 600s, wrote a letter to Mellitus (the first Bishop of London in the Saxon period) proposing that pagan temples should be converted for Christian worship. He suggested that since the pagans were in the habit of sacrificing cattle, perhaps they could be persuaded to sacrifice cattle to God instead.

> So when almighty God has led you to the most reverend man our brother Bishop Augustine, tell him what

I have long gone over in my mind concerning the matter
of the English: that is, that the shrines of idols among
that people should be destroyed as little as possible, but
that the idols themselves that are inside them should be
destroyed. Let blessed water be made and sprinkled in
these shrines, let altars be constructed and relics placed
there: since if the shrines are well built it is necessary that
they should be converted from the worship of demons
to the service of the true God, so that as long as that
people do not see their very shrines being destroyed they
may put out error from their hearts and in knowledge
and adoration of the true God they may gather at their
accustomed places more readily.[14]

It is not clear how many pagan sites were actually converted
to Christian worship, however. Some possible examples that we
know of were the temple of Claudius and two other Romano-
Celtic temples in Roman Colchester. But there are few, if any,
examples of Anglo-Saxon churches on top of the foundations
of pre-Christian structures.[15] Building D2 at the archaeological
site of Yeavering in Northumberland is held to be an Anglo-
Saxon temple complex, but this was destroyed some years after
its conversion to Christianity and no church was subsequently
erected on the spot. Goodmanham in Yorkshire used to be
the site of a temple to a pagan deity, variously described as
Delgovine or Wotan, and is mentioned in Bede, who states that
it was destroyed by the pagan high priest Coifi on his conversion to Christianity in the time of King Edwin, AD 627. This
appears to be on the site of the current All Hallows Church.
In Canterbury, King Aethelbert (AD *c.* 560–616) is said to have

worshipped at a temple to Odin before his conversion, and apparently did give the temple precincts to St Augustine to build a church.

We have said that we have a little more in the way of texts from the Saxon period than we do for the Celts. Much of this relates to medical matters. For instance, we have Bald's Leechbook, or the *Medicinale Anglicum*, which was written in the 900s and relates to practices of healing (it even describes a bit of early plastic surgery: how to heal a cleft lip). This is not a magical textbook as such – it is a medical one ('leech' means 'physician') – but it has some interesting hints about Anglo-Saxon supernatural beliefs. Sore feet, headaches, impotence and shingles – we are still plagued by these things today, so it is not surprising to find the Anglo-Saxons being concerned with them. We do not generally believe that illnesses might be caused by elves, however, whereas the Saxons did. Diseases of the head, and mental illness, were sometimes attributed to their malign influence. It has to be said that a lot of these remedies are not what we would refer to today as empirically sound: for instance, mixing the ash of burnt periwinkles with honey and smearing it into your eyes, or using white dog excrement for throat complaints.

We also have the *Lacnunga* (a name given to it in the nineteenth century, although it dates from the tenth), which contains a variety of charms in Old English and Latin, including the famous Nine Herbs Charm previously mentioned. This contains, unsurprisingly, nine herbs (mugwort, plantain and nettle being three of these), which are made into a paste against poisoning. In order for it to be effective, you also need to recite the charm itself, invoking the name of Woden. However, the

*Lacnunga* was not just composed of superstition and old wives' tales: one of its recipes for an eye poultice has been found by researchers to combat the superbug MRSA.[16]

Our concern is not whether combining slugs with holy water is a champion cure for snakebite but how all this medical information relates to Saxon religious practice, or gives an insight into it. Magic and medicine had, and still have today, a closely intertwined history, because illness is one of those areas in which people can become desperate and willing to try anything. Modern medicine works wonders with many conditions, but it cannot cure everything, and one has only to take a look at some of the more extreme claims of faith healing to see how easy it is for afflicted folk and their relatives to turn to magic where science fails. In a pre-science era, how much more pressing it might have seemed to seek out a magical solution for your dying child, for instance. So when we are looking at early medical remedies, there are elements that we might profitably bear in mind with regard to magical theory: is there an astrological component to the remedies, for instance? Is the illness for which they are designed held to have a supernatural component, such as elf shot or cursing? Does the power of prayer enter into the remedy at any point?

))) ○ (((

The Angles, Saxons and Jutes were not the only people to come across the seas from Northern Europe in search of wealth and land. From the late eighth to the eleventh century, the Vikings crossed the sea roads of the North Sea and the Baltic to Britain and Ireland – people from Denmark, Sweden and Norway with gods and beliefs of their own. As with the Druids, each age has a perception of the Vikings: romanticized pirates, brave warriors, noble savages in horned helmets. 'Viking' itself is a later word, introduced during the Norse revival of the eighteenth century. To the peoples whom they encountered, they had many names: 'ashmen' to the Germanic tribes, after the wood of their boats; 'dark and fair foreigners' to the Irish; 'lake dwellers' to the Gaels. To the Franks they were called 'northmen', and the people who were in the process of becoming the English knew them as 'heathens', a term that has survived today.

Their earliest raids on these shores were recorded in the 790s (the first being a raid on the island of Lindisfarne in 793), and their influence in this country lasted until the Norman Conquest – in fact, it might be seen as a part of that conquest, since the Normans themselves were of Viking descent. The Vikings settled in Shetland and Orkney, and in York – itself a Scandinavian word. Yorvik was established in AD 866 and became the second largest city in Britain after London. Viking influence remains in some of the place names around our coasts: the islands of Skokholm and Skomer off the south Welsh coast; Dublin itself. Place names that end in '-by', '-thorp' and '-toft' are of Scandinavian origin. 'Derby', for instance, means 'a village where deer are found'. The area they encompassed – parts of what is now Northern England plus the Midlands – was known as the Danelaw.

Why did they come? There are a number of explanations. The age-old need for land is one of them. The Scandinavian countries are cold and heavily forested. In the eleventh century in Iceland, only the eldest son of each family inherited the family estate, leaving younger sons to go and seek their fortunes elsewhere. It is possible that a similar system was in place in other countries in the eighth century, although we do not know a great deal about Viking inheritance customs at this time. Norway had relatively little farmland, so perhaps some folk decided to look further afield.

Technological advances in the form of shipping were likely to have been a factor. Viking ships were developed to sail into the wind, so no longer needed to cling to the coastline and could sail across larger tracts of water. There were political reasons, too. In Iceland local kings were starting to expand their territories and push out rivals. The growing Carolingian empire was beginning to encroach upon Denmark, and many Vikings who came to Britain were Danes. Fortunes, too, were to be found in monastic communities, which amassed money and valuables. It is highly likely these communities were raided for their wealth rather than because the Vikings did not like Christians. Though they were pagan at the beginning, the Vikings were quite quick to take the Christian God on board (we can tell this from the lack of grave goods in Viking burials in the UK: pagans buried their dead with valuable possessions, and Christians did not). It took a little longer for their original countries to become Christianized: Sweden was the last, in the mid-twelfth century. But precious metals and slaves were a desirable commodity, and it is probable that this was a primary motive for the raids.

As with Celtic and Anglo-Saxon observances, we do not know much about Viking religious practices. There are some mentions of them in the Icelandic sagas – but, as with classical scholars commenting on the Druids, we need to remember that these were written a couple of hundred years after the Vikings had converted to Christianity, so the accuracy of this material is once again a possible issue. However, the myths of the Norse gods survived quite well – in the Eddas, for instance, thirteenth-century Icelandic literary works that relate the origins of the world, tales of the gods, and stories about heroes.

The Prose Edda was written by the Icelandic scholar and historian Snorri Sturluson around 1220, surviving in four known manuscripts and three fragments, written down from about 1300 to about 1600. This consists of a prologue and three separate books – the *Gylfaginning*, which concerns the creation and the future destruction of the Norse mythical world; the *Skaldskaparmal*, which is a dialogue between Aegir, the god connected with the sea, and Bragi, the skaldic god of poetry; and finally the *Hattatal*, which concerns verse forms. As the historian Daniel McCoy says,

> While it would be rash to simply dismiss everything in the Prose Edda that the earlier poems haven't already told us, it would be equally presumptuous to accept every statement of Snorri's at face value. Unfortunately, the latter approach was common throughout much of the nineteenth and twentieth centuries, and as a result most popular introductions to Norse mythology uncritically rehash Snorri's contentions and thereby present a skewed portrait of the old gods and tales.[17]

For instance, Snorri suggests in his Prologue that the Aesir – one of the two main tribes of Norse deities – were actually the Trojans and that Aesir derives from the word 'Asia'. This is quite a claim, but it points to the possibility that he got at least some of his ideas from post-Christian medieval sources.

Other writers include Adam of Bremen, writing in his history of the Bishops of Hamburg in the eleventh century, who gives an account of a pagan temple at Uppsala dedicated to Thor, Odin and Freyr (Freyr's was the statue with the improbably large penis). If war breaks out, sacrifices are made to Thor; if there is a plague, the priest petitions Odin; and Freyr, appropriately, is in charge of marriages. Adam goes into sacrifices in great detail, describing how the sacred grove was hung with rotting male corpses. Whether this was the case or not is debatable: Adam seems to have exaggerated the size of the temple, for example.[18] And while he was a relatively careful scholar, Adam's account might have been influenced by Isidore of Seville's comments on the religious practices of the Goths, Vandals and Suevi some centuries earlier.

Muslim observers wrote about these people, too: the tenth-century traveller Ibn Fadlan writes about the Volga Vikings, including an account of a ship burial accompanied by the sacrifice of a slave girl:

> So they carried her to the ship and she removed two bracelets she was wearing, handing them to the woman called the 'Angel of Death,' the one who was to kill her. She also removed two anklets she was wearing, handing them to the two slave-girls who waited upon her: they were the daughters of the woman known as the 'Angel of Death.' Then they lifted her onto the ship but did not bring her into the tent, and came men with their shields and sticks and gave her a cup of *nabid* and she sang and then drank. The interpreter told me that she [bade] her female companions farewell. She was handed another

cup, which she took and sang for a long time [*sic*], while the woman urged her to drink it and to enter the pavilion where her master lay. I saw that she was confused and wanted to enter the pavilion but put her head between it and the ship. The woman grabbed her head and pushed it into the pavilion, entering at the same time, and the men began to bang their shields with the sticks [so] that her screams could not be heard and [excite] the other girls, who would cease to seek to die with their lords.

Six men entered the tent and all had intercourse with the slave-girl. They laid her down beside her master and two of them held her feet, two her hands. The woman called the 'Angel of Death' placed a rope around her neck with the ends going in the opposite directions, and handed it to two (men) to pull it, and she approached holding a broad-bladed dagger and began to thrust it in and out between her ribs, while the two men strangled her with the rope until she died.[19]

It is with the arrival of the Vikings that the slightly impenetrable Saxon gods take on a more recognizable form to the twenty-first-century reader – at least, one who is familiar with the Marvel Comics pantheon. We have the Allfather Odin, who legendarily hangs from an ash tree for nine days and nine nights in order to snatch wisdom in the form of the runes from the abyss. (It is possible that this is a retelling of the story of Christ's crucifixion.) We have Thor, the heavy-hitting but rather dim god of thunder, and the trickster Loki, as well as the brother and sister deities Freyr and Freya. There are two main tribes of gods, the Aesir and the Vanir, who generally get along but who have on occasion fallen out, with the situation being resolved by the traditional means of sending hostages from each to live with the opposite tribe. So Freyr, Freya and Njordir go and live with Odin and the rest of the Aesir, while Hoenir and Mimir go and live in Vanaheim. This does not go to plan: Freyr and Freya get on well enough in Asgard, but Hoenir is unfortunately not the brightest, except when he has Mimir to counsel him, and eventually the Vanir get fed up with this and, in a moment of irritation, behead Mimir and send the head back to Asgard. Odin is not pleased.

It is possible that this 'two tribe' version of the gods relates to some distant ancestral clash between rival religions: perhaps two peoples who merged, with the gods of the dominant culture taking precedence. The Vanir seem older and are closer to nature and fertility. Their home, Vanaheim, ends in '-heim', which in Old Norse suggests an unenclosed space. Asgard, home of Odin, Thor and the Aesir, is a 'gard' – somewhere fortified. Early Scandinavians seem to have been interested in other cultures and taken aspects of them on board: Ibn Fadlan's account of the Volga Rus suggests that they blended Slavic with Scandinavian practices.

Viking cosmology is very reminiscent of Tolkien's Middle-earth, which is hardly surprising since Tolkien was a scholar of the Norse myths. It has elves, giants and dwarfs (though not hobbits), who fall into the category of Vaettir, nature spirits. Some of these are friendly, like house wights: the 'brownies' of later English legend, who may well have come over with our Viking ancestors.

The world revolves around a massive ash tree called Yggdrasil, which encompasses the known universe. Asgard and Vanaheim are somewhere around Yggdrasil, as is the human world of Midgard. There are the Norns, who are three female entities who guide people's fates, and the Fylgjur, who are guardian spirits – they are female, along with other supernatural beings like swan maidens and Valkyries, the famous spirits who carry fallen warriors off to the afterlife.

As well as the Eddas, we have material such as the Hávamál, which is a poem containing advice on good conduct. It also contains a section on how unreliable women are and how you can seduce them, and a collection of charms, as well as other bits and pieces. Like the Prose Edda, it dates from the thirteenth century, and its most famous section is that which explains how Odin attained the runes:

> I know that I hung on a windy tree
> nine long nights,
> wounded with a spear, dedicated to Odin,
> myself to myself,
> on that tree of which no man knows from where its roots
>     run.

> No bread did they give me nor a drink from a horn,
> downwards I peered;
> I took up the runes,
> screaming I took them,
> then I fell back from there.[20]

We will be meeting the Hávamál again when we come to look at the rise of revivalist Heathenism in the twentieth century, as parts of this early code of conduct have been incorporated into the practice of some of the modern groups.

However, by the time the Vikings settled in England, they were content to adopt Christianity, perhaps alongside their own practices, as is suggested by a coin found in York: it bears an inscription to St Peter (Petri), but the final 'I' of Petri is in the form of Thor's hammer. Viking settlers seem to have intermarried with the locals, resulting in households where religion was mixed. Old Norse itself did not have a word for 'religion' (*heiðinn*) until after the introduction of Christianity: it refers instead to *forn sið* (old custom) or *heiðinn sið* (heathen custom). Scholar Karen Bek-Pedersen states that the belief system should probably be thought of as several systems rather than one. This should not surprise us: we have already speculated on the influence of the classical pantheons on Saxon and Norse belief systems, and these cultures did not exist in isolation but interacted with each other. They may well have taken on other people's spirits and gods. Coexisting as they did with the Anglo-Saxons, the Sami of Finland, the Inuit of Greenland, the Irish and the Baltic peoples, as well as having trade routes to the south to exchange amber and other goods, the Vikings were exposed to a vast area of different influences. This was not an age where angst about cultural appropriation existed. If you liked something, you adopted it, whether it was a new style of tunic, a way of wearing your hair or a nice new god.

## The Runes and Seidr

The magical legacy of the Viking age today is the practice of divination by runes, and, to a much lesser extent, that of seidr (pronounced *say-der*), which is a form of shamanic channelling.

Working with the runes is popular not just with modern Heathens, but with pagans generally. These days, it is a form of divination: a system of symbols that stand for different aspects of life, usually carved onto small wooden tiles. There are a number of variations on this old Northern European system of divination, including the Elder Futhark (AD 150–800), Old English Futhorc (400–1100) and Younger Futhark (800–1100). The Elder Futhark is divided into three sets of eight known as the 'aettir' (each set is an 'aett'). The name 'rune' appears to come from a word that means a 'secret' or a 'whisper'.

Runes originally date from around 150 BC. As an alphabet they were replaced by the Roman letters around AD 700, but their use continued as a decorative system. There is little evidence that they were used for divination, but rather for inscriptions, curses, spells, trading records, deeds and graffiti. In the Hávamál, Odin credits them with being able to restore the dead to life.

Some runes seem to be taken from the Roman alphabet, but others appear to derive from the early Italic alphabets. Like the ogham, the divinatory equivalent often used by contemporary Druids, this is a system whose origins are murky and whose purpose has changed, but which is regarded today as being highly useful nevertheless.

Seidr is, these days, a form of divination and of trance mediumship, and several other things besides. In divination, you try to foretell the future, as we have just seen with the runes. In trance mediumship, a person gives up their body, or at least their voice, to a possessing force: a god, goddess or spirit. This sounds like a frightening thing to do and it certainly can be – the idea of being possessed by an entity is a trope of modern horror films. It is very rarely that dramatic, however. Trance mediumship takes two main forms – one in which the person remains conscious and aware, but has in effect a backseat driver who uses their voice, and one in which the person is unconscious and comes round later with no memory of what's happened. Both of these can take place within a single ceremony.

'Seidr' may mean 'cord' or 'string', which in turn may derive from the words for 'thread spun from a distaff' – there are a number of etymological explanations. Archaeologist Neil Price comments:

> There were seiðr rituals for divination and clairvoyance; for seeking out the hidden, both in the secrets of the mind and in physical locations; for healing the sick; for bringing good luck; for controlling the weather; for calling game animals and fish. Importantly, it could also be used for the opposite of these things – to curse an individual or an enterprise; to blight the land and make it barren; to induce illness; to tell false futures and thus to set their recipients on a road to disaster; to injure, maim and kill, in domestic disputes and especially in battle.[21]

Odin and Freya were supposed to be the experts in this, but the Norns – the three female beings who guide everyone's fate – were important, too. It is the Norns who really control seidr, as they control everyone's fate. But humans could practise it; we have accounts of women called *völur* (sing. *völva*), who travel from town to town performing magic for hire. The name possibly derives from earlier Germanic practitioners called *veleda*, a 'seeress' or 'prophetess', or from the word for 'staff/magic wand carrier'. The *völur* did not have quite the same role as priestesses, which is why I am not using that term, although they did sometimes lead ceremonies. A *spákona* or *spoekona* is a specialized *völva*: a seer (it may be cognate with our word for 'spy'). Priestesses in the Norse traditions were different: *blótgyðiur* (sacrificial priestesses) or *hóvgyðiur* (temple priestesses), who were home-based. However, we need to be careful with the terms 'priest' and 'priestess' when we are talking about the Vikings. These terms do not have the same connotations in Viking society as they do now: they do not denote separate jobs. A person might be a priest, but might also be a sailor, a trader, a headman or a farmer. Their wives and sisters might also be priestesses.

Caesar mentions the *völur* in his commentary on the Gallic wars:

When Caesar inquired of his prisoners, wherefore Ariovistus did not come to an engagement, he discovered this to be the reason – that among the Germans it was the custom for their matrons to pronounce from lots and divination whether it were expedient that the battle should be engaged in or not; that they had said, 'that it was not the will of heaven that the Germans should conquer, if they engaged in battle before the new moon.'[22]

There are some fabulous descriptions of one of these seeresses in *The Saga of Erik the Red*, composed at some point before 1265, which takes place in Greenland.[23] The *völva* wears a long cloak and a headpiece of lamb's wool fringed with catskin. She carries a staff decked with bronze and is adorned by a necklace of glass pearls. She wears calfskin shoes and catskin or ermine gloves that are white and fluffy inside (cats were sacred to the goddess Freya, who brought seidr to the Aesir from her Vanir home: perhaps a folk memory of the shamanic practices of an earlier group being brought into another culture). This *völva* is certainly well-treated, being taken to a special seat in the household and given a dish made of the hearts of each kind of animal in the homestead. Then the women gather around her and sing songs dedicated to the powers with which the *völva* wishes to speak – a kind of summoning. It works: the *völva*, according to the saga, is able to glimpse into the future and avert a famine.

Archaeologists have found around forty graves that belong to women and which contain a type of wand or staff. These are wealthy graves, filled with a lot of artefacts from different parts of the world. One Danish grave has goods from Gotland, Finland and Russia. Some of these graves contain cannabis seeds and the Danish one has a pouch containing henbane seeds: if you throw henbane on the fire, the smoke is mildly hallucinogenic, producing a sensation of flying. The origin of the witch's broom or the wizard's staff? Maybe.

More sensationally, some commentators have suggested that some of the staffs found in these graves have a sexual aspect: phallus rather than distaff. *Völur* were apparently considered dangerous, because they were seductive (like their patron goddess, Freya). Henbane is also an aphrodisiac. But we might note that the sagas were influenced by biblical models, in which witches are scary and female sexuality in general is distrusted.

It seems to have been 'unmanly' for a Viking man to practise seidr. Ragnvaldr Rettilbein, Harald Fairhair's son by a Sami woman, was one, but his father had him burned to death in a hall along with a group of other male practitioners. However, we must remember not to take these accounts at face value.

Ragnvaldr's story may have been written by the storytellers of those who overcame his family, and who sought to denigrate his line.

But what about Odin, who also practised seidr and was called *ergi* (unmanly) as a result? Why should it be unmanly? Possibly because seidr was connected with weaving practices, and this was women's work. The Norns spin and thus create the weft and weave of life. This is a form of sympathetic magic, concerning invisible bonds and fetters controlled from a loom. Oddly, Odin's 'unmanliness' seems to have been part of his strength, perhaps because he had in some way co-opted women's magic. In some societies gender fluidity is seen as a source of magical power.

Part VII of Snorri Sturluson's *Ynglinga Saga* states:

Odin could change himself. His body then lay as if sleeping or dead, but he became a bird or a wild beast, a fish or a dragon, and journeyed in the twinkling of an eye to far-off lands, on his own errands or those of other men. Also, with mere words he was able to extinguish fires, to calm the seas, and to turn the winds any way he pleased.[24]

This is classic shamanic practice: travelling in animal form, seeking to control the weather, looking at people's fates, but also cursing them and swapping around their abilities (which is *not* recommended in today's practice, by the way).

Odin may have been a god and formidable practitioner of seidr, but it was human women who appear to have held sway, as demonstrated by the burial of two Oseberg women around AD 800 who were laid to rest in a ship burial alongside horses, dogs and cows. Their grave goods included items that may have been wands, as well as magical amulets, wagons, tapestries and the aforementioned pouches containing cannabis seeds. However, it may be more their political status than their religious functions that earned them this impressive burial.

So what happened to this influential cadre of women? Where did they go? The *völur* and their practices were eradicated by the Christianization of England, as King Edgar's canon law edict from the tenth century suggests:

> If witches or wizards, perjurers or murderers or impure, corrupt, notorious whores are discovered anywhere in the land, then one should drive them out of the land and so cleanse the people, or let them perish entirely where they are . . .[25]

Was this really successful? It is difficult to stamp out popular religious practices. They tend to go underground, metamorphose, change. Did the 'fountain worship' of the Saxons and Norse folk become transformed into the well-dressing that we still find today in places like Derbyshire? The heathen gods may have become relegated to the days of the week, but witches remained, their folk magic still practised under a more Christian guise. The healing herbs of the Saxon charms appear again in the receipt books of the Elizabethan period and the Civil War.

And the Greenland *völva* of Sturluson's saga appears again, many centuries later, as a fairy:

> No taller than a human finger, fairy spae wives are usually dressed in the clothes of a peasant. However, when

properly summoned, the attire changes from common to magnificent: blue cloak with a gem-lined collar and black lambskin hood lined with catskin, calfskin boots, and catskin gloves. Like human spae wives, they can also predict the future, through runes, tea leaves and signs generated by natural phenomena, and are good healers. They are said to be descended from the erectors of the standing stones.[26]

# THREE

# Magic of the Middle Ages and the Witches Who Weren't

By the tenth century, most of Britain was Christian. These were times of tremendous upheaval. The Normans were disruptive enough, but the fourteenth century saw huge social shifts after the Black Death, which killed a sizeable portion of the British population and led to immense social turbulence.

Does this mean that magical practice went away? We may state with some confidence that it did not. In the centuries after the Saxon and Viking incursions and the Norman Conquest, people still sought to heal and harm, obtain more money and power, undertake love spells and do all the things for which people use magic. Rather than falling under the banner of a pagan religion, however, these practices now occurred alongside – and sometimes under the aegis of – a newly established Church. And they do not seem to have been pagan any more. The existence of an old religion, practised in secret and unchanged in the thousand years or so since the Vikings, is not supported by any evidence, and it is not necessary for people to have believed in different gods and goddesses in order to do magic. Magical practice can be separated from religion; a spell can be cast without reference to a particular deity.

This period also raises the interesting question of why some strands of magic are popular among revivalist pagans and others are not. If the Normans imported their own magic into their new colony, I could find no record of it. This is partly a 'soft' political issue; the Normans, like the Romans, were the oppressors, not the oppressed, and as such they are not as appealing as the perception of the mystic Druids or warrior Vikings. It is highly likely that they had magical practitioners and the later history of Normandy bears this out: it was a centre of masculine witchcraft by the sixteenth century. Here, feared witches were not old women, but shepherds, most likely to be older men or teenagers, and their practice involved, among other things, the use of toad venom and stolen Eucharists. Whether this bears any resemblance to what was going on magically in the French province – or, indeed, Britain – at the time of the Norman Conquest is difficult to say. But it does raise some intriguing queries, and it also brings into question the feminist assertion (which I believe to have a lot of merit, but which is not the whole story) that the witch trials of the later Middle Ages and the seventeenth century were solely a war against women.

During the eleventh and twelfth centuries, people still practised magic (herbalism, for instance), yet despite the earlier Saxon edicts against it, very few people were brought before the ecclesiastical courts in Britain. The Church seems to have focused on heresy rather than folk magic, and a diverse range of people were technically involved in various kinds of magical practice: monks, midwives, physicians, surgeons, priests, diviners and folk healers. Written sources help us to understand what was going on, and while much of this is weighted towards the Church, it does not mean that such sources do not contain some valuable information.

For example, monks were expected to have knowledge of herbalism (think of Brother Cadfael) and healing cures. A twelfth-century priest would sometimes be expected to conduct a version of the old Saxon Land Ceremonies Charm, a fertility ritual for barren fields that took a whole day, during which the priest would sprinkle holy water, honey, milk and herbs over the field while reciting passages from the Bible. It first appears in the *Lacnunga*, which we looked at in the last chapter, and it was written by monks, so it calls upon the Lord and the Apostles. However, some believe that its Christian component was a substitution for earlier pagan elements. Given the date of the charm, they could be right. If so, then it does indicate that the Church adopted at least some Saxon practices.

It is not who you were, but what you did, that seems to have mattered to the clerical authorities. The water is further muddied by some of the Church's own earlier teachings, for instance this statement from about 900 in the *Canon Episcopi*:

It is also not to be omitted that some unconstrained women, perverted by Satan, seduced by illusions and phantasms of demons, believe and openly profess that, in the dead of night, they ride upon certain beasts with the pagan goddess Diana, with a countless horde of women, and in the silence of the dead of the night to fly over vast tracts of country, and to obey her commands as their mistress, and to be summoned to her service on other nights. But it were well if they alone perished in their infidelity and did not draw so many others into the pit of their faithlessness. For an innumerable multitude, deceived by this false opinion, believe this to be true and, so believing, wander from the right faith and relapse into pagan errors when they think that there is any divinity or power except the one God.[1]

What is being said here is that witchcraft is not real and that witches do not exist, but that some people are delusional or wrong and think they do. This obviously puts a big block in the way of ecclesiastical courts prosecuting folk for being witches: you cannot prosecute someone for being something that does not exist.

In the world of late antiquity or the early Middle Ages, it is impossible to define someone as a witch (as opposed, for example, to an amateur herbalist, a heretic or a scold), and none of the legislation of the time attempted to do so. Offenders were designated offenders by virtue of their performing various actions or wearing certain objects declared by the legislation to be condemned or forbidden. For all practical purposes, the 'witch' had not yet been invented. There were only practitioners of various kinds of magic, both male and female, who might belong to any rank of ecclesiastical or lay society, and whose actions might, or might not, bring them within the compass of canon or secular law, depending on external factors that were usually local but could, from time to time, be more general.[2]

So we know that the Church was concerned about some magical practices at this time. A lot of these were to do with healing, but in a pre-scientific era, it is difficult to distinguish between magical forms of healing and natural or Christian ones. For example, Catholic historian Eamon Duffy has pointed out that some healing charms looked a lot like prayers and exorcisms, and thus were acceptable to some clerics. The physician Bernard of Gordon in Montpellier rejected incantations but allowed astrological talismans, although some clerics denounced even these. The issue of sortilegium – magical practices including divination, healing cures, belief in fairies and misuse of Church rituals – is therefore a thorny one.

In addition to what people were doing magically, the early medieval period is important because at that time myths and legends began to develop which continue to exercise a powerful influence on modern paganism. We are going to look at three of these now: the Knights Templar, King Arthur and Robin Hood.

## The Templars

The Templars were crusading Christian knights. What are they doing in a book on paganism?

I do not intend to spend a lot of time looking at the Templars, but we do need to consider them in context, because the influences – and perhaps more importantly the alleged influences – that extend from this fascinating group impact on occultism in later centuries and still have a resonance in much of contemporary pagan practice, not to mention popular culture, as demonstrated by novels such as Dan Brown's *The Da Vinci Code* (2003).

The Poor Fellow Soldiers of Christ and of the Temple of Solomon, known more commonly as the Knights Templar or simply the Templars, were a Catholic military order. They were recognized in a papal bull of 1139 but had started earlier, around 1119, and remained active for the next two hundred years. They were a hierarchical organization led by a Grand Master – a position for life (although 'life' might not have meant very long: all but two Grand Masters died in office). And they were strict: knights had to take vows of chastity, and they were not allowed to leave the battlefield until all Christian flags had fallen.

Distinguished by their dress – a white mantle with a red cross over their armour – they were a crack cavalry force, the SAS of their day. Despite this, significant numbers of the Templars were not engaged in military action. Only 10 per cent of some 15,000–20,000 Templars were actually knights. They arguably established the banking system and invented the cheque, and their fortifications and churches are still found across Europe. They were most active during the Crusades, but once these faded, so did support for the order. King Philip IV of France was opposed to them, probably because he was heavily in debt to the order, and he started a sequence of persecutions, including burning at the stake, which saw the order officially disbanded in 1312 by the then pope, Clement V.

Part of Philip's justification for dismantling the Templars related to rumours of Satanism and a secret initiation ceremony. This is classic disinformation against groups that the authorities do not care for: Jews throughout the centuries have experienced comparable slurs and so do some pagan movements today. We saw it in action with Roman comments about the Druids. The Templars were accused of financial fraud, homosexuality, worshipping idols and spitting on the Cross. Confessions were extracted under torture, although many were later retracted.

The Templars' influence on later occultism comes via the Freemasonry movement, which in turn has deeply influenced various esoteric orders such as the nineteenth-century Hermetic Order of the Golden Dawn and Wicca. There are a host of rumours about Templar practice, notably that they worshipped an idol known as Baphomet, whom we will meet later. As we will see, the Freemasonry movement became interested in the Templars in the eighteenth century, and there have been claims that Freemasonry is directly descended from Templars who took shelter in Scotland after the demise of the order, and who fought with Robert the Bruce at Bannockburn. Masonic historians reject this, but the myth has proved pervasive, as has the story that the Templar fleet made it to Scotland with treasure on board. This is where the legend comes from that the Holy Grail was saved from destruction and placed in Rosslyn Chapel in Midlothian.

As with earlier magical practices, what is important here is not so much what the Templars actually did as what they were later perceived to have done, and the myths that have grown up around them.

## King Arthur

Arguably the most famous of Britain's heroes, Arthur's existence is in considerable doubt: if he was a real person, he is most likely to have been a Romano-British commander (or a composite of commanders) who lived around the fifth or sixth centuries AD, about the time of the Roman withdrawal. He is mentioned in very old texts, for instance the probably tenth-century *Annales Cambriae* (Annals of Wales), which cites Arthur's role in the

Battle of Badon in 516; the Welsh work *Y Gododdin*, which may be as early as the seventh century; and the *Historia Brittonum*, allegedly written by Nennius around 829, which gives details but not dates of Arthur's battles. The latter refers to him as a *dux bellorum*, a war duke. Writing in the period, Gildas does mention the Battle of Badon but not Arthur himself, and we may speculate as to why this is: perhaps he did not exist at all, or perhaps Gildas decided to keep him out of the history books for some reason. Later writers sometimes omitted mention of historical figures because they were on opposing political sides, but in this case we really do not know whether Gildas deliberately omitted Arthur or whether Arthur did not exist in the first place. Gildas does, however, mention Ambrosius Aurelianus, whom Geoffrey of Monmouth describes as Arthur's uncle. Ambrosius, whoever he was, apparently fought against the Saxons. But as for Arthur:

> I think we can dispose of him quite briefly. He owes his place in our history books to a 'no smoke without fire' school of thought ... The fact of the matter is that there is no historical evidence about Arthur; we must reject him from our histories and, above all, from the titles of our books.[3]

This is fair comment given the lack of evidence, and it is why we did not include Arthur in our earlier chapters. However, it is not so much the historical Arthur with whom we are concerned here as it is the legend. The myth of Arthur starts early, as we have seen, but it really gains traction in twelfth-century literature: Geoffrey of Monmouth's *History of the Kings of Britain* of 1138 is a primary source for the myth of Arthur, in which the king is a warrior both in actual and supernatural terms. The stories that arise around him are full of magic, from his adviser Merlin the great magician, to the encounters of his knights with supernatural entities such as the Green Knight, to the magical sword Excalibur. Geoffrey drew on earlier sources such as the work of Isidore of Seville, who mentions an early version of the Isle of Avalon, the island of apples that is ruled by nine sisters (Isidore's island is generally considered to be one of the Canaries). The twelfth-century French writer Chrétien de Troyes added more elements, such as Sir Lancelot and the Holy Grail. The Grail legend is a perennial theme throughout British esotericism; we encountered it briefly in our mention of the Templars, and we shall meet it again across the centuries.

Arthur became a popular figure of legend. French writers made much of him, and the early literature culminates in Thomas Malory's *Le Morte d'Arthur*, written in English towards the end of the fifteenth century. Malory drew heavily on earlier works, such as the Vulgate Cycle, which featured Arthur, but *Le Morte* was more comprehensive. Bringing many of the stories and legends together, it was one of the earliest books printed in England, by William Caxton in 1485. Caxton's edition cemented the popular image of Arthur within ideas about pre-Christian Britain.

Interest in Arthur waned after the Middle Ages but was revived in the nineteenth century with the work of Alfred, Lord Tennyson, and he has remained popular ever since: Arthur, Merlin and Guinevere remain iconic images of British legend, from Mark Twain's time-travelling Yankee, to John Boorman's curious movie *Excalibur*, to the comic knights of *Monty Python and the Holy Grail* and a host of other television shows and films.

Beyond popular culture, esoteric work continues to revolve around this series of myths, known as the 'matter of Britain'.

## Robin Hood

Our third prevailing medieval legend is that of Robin Hood. Robin is similar to Arthur in a number of respects: he might have existed or might not, he may have been a composite of a number of people, and he continues to have an effect on the public imagination in terms of twentieth- and twenty-first-century paganism.

Just as pretty much everyone in the West has at least some knowledge of King Arthur, so too do most people know the basics of Robin Hood (likely, in no small part, thanks to Kevin Costner's portrayal in the 1991 film *Robin Hood: Prince of Thieves*). Robin was said to have been an outlaw in Sherwood Forest, battling the evil Sheriff of Nottingham and waiting with his band of Merry Men and his girlfriend Marian until good King Richard returns from the Crusades to take up the reins of power once more. He steals from the rich and gives to the poor. As such, Robin is not only an Arcadian figure – a personage of the pure greenwood as opposed to the wicked city – but appeals to contemporary left-wing political ideals relating to wealth distribution. He is an anarchic presence under a repressive regime, but he never renounces his essential nobility. The robbing from the rich and giving to the poor business is not explicitly mentioned in Robin's story until 1592,[4] although it is clear from the start that Robin has sympathy for the poor. In *A Gest of Robyn Hode* (c. 1450) it is stated that

he was a good outlawe,
And dyde pore men moch god.[5]

Robin first appears in *Piers Plowman* in the 1370s. He occurs
in the context of a lazy priest who knows songs about Robin,
but does not know the Lord's Prayer. Robin being a contemporary of the twelfth-century king Richard the Lionheart is a later
addition, and so is Robin's identity as the earl of Huntingdon:
the early ballads portray him as a yeoman. His story became
popular not only through literature but through 'Robin Hood
games', which were part of May Day celebrations from the
1400s onwards. In these, people dressed up as Robin and others
of his merry band, including Maid Marian, who often has to
be rescued from nasty knights. In some of these, Marian does
not appear to have been terribly maidenly![6]

I need to stress that Robin is not a pagan figure. He is
a Saxon – perhaps noble, perhaps not – fighting in amus-
ingly cunning ways against the Norman oppressor. Despite
the May Day celebrations, he did not have much to do with
contemporary paganism until the British television series
*Robin of Sherwood* (1984–6). Owing to a somewhat eldritch
sensibility, a theme tune by Clannad, the inclusion by creator Richard Carpenter of twentieth-century pagan elements
and, to be honest, the dark good looks of initial lead Michael
Praed, the programme attracted a swathe of romantically
inclined British youth of the 1980s to real-life paganism. In
the series, Robin – the 'Hooded Man' – has distinctly pagan
affiliations. He is the Chosen One, the spiritual son of a
shamanic version of the wildwood god Herne the Hunter,
and the devotee of a pagan religion that has survived down

the centuries. Like Arthur, he has a magical sword, one of the 'Seven Swords of Wayland'. The Templars turn up in one episode as well, although they are the bad guys. And when Praed's version of Robin sacrifices his life for his friends, Herne chooses a replacement, for Robin (like Merlin and King Arthur himself) is one of those heroes who can take many forms.

## The Witch Trials

It was towards the end of the period covered in this chapter that one of the most notorious episodes in the history of witch-craft took place, over the course of several hundred years: the witch trials. One might think that this section is likely to be enormous, but that is not the case, for one principal reason: a lot of the people targeted during the witch trials of the later medieval, Elizabethan and Civil War periods are unlikely to have been actual witches. Magical practitioners *per se* were not targeted during the witch trials. There was a difference between what were known as cunning folk and witches, and the former were allowed to continue practising magic at a time when persecutions for witchcraft were at their height.

This might seem curious – the 'witch trials' which were not – but if we unpack the nature of the magical practitioner over the course of these centuries, it begins to make sense. In essence, the belief system goes like this:

> *Witches* are evil. They practise black magic and consort with the Devil.

*Cunning folk* are good. They practise benevolent magic, mainly protecting people from black magic, and helping those who have been cursed by witches. People would know about them mainly by word of mouth.

The question arises: if the Church had previously said that witches were not real, how could they prosecute them?

Partly, this was due to the Church changing its mind. The idea that a pact with the Devil could be made had become increasingly popular. The implication of this is that it is not really an individual who is the source of black magic, but Satan, working through them. New texts coming into the country in translation from the Islamic world, such as the Arabic grimoire *Ghāyat al-Ḥakīm*, known as the *Picatrix*, were giving cause for concern among clerics. Things of which heretics had been accused now became things of which witches were also accused: eating babies, orgies, cannibalism, demon worship. Horrible stuff, mainly unprovable or downright falsehoods, but useful if you wanted to get rid of someone. From 1300 onwards the fear of witchcraft, and the targeting of people suspected of it, continued to rise, reaching its peak from about 1450 to the mid-1600s.

Britain got off relatively lightly compared to the Continent. There were thousands of trials across Europe during this time. There are a variety of reasons as to why Britain's witch trials, though bad, were not as extensive as those conducted throughout Europe. England (rather than Britain) was almost the only European state in which legal trials did not change from accusatory to inquisatory justice; which is indeed one reason why it had relatively few trials and a very high rate of acquittal. Written communication was changing from expensive parchment to cheaper paper. With this, it became easier to disseminate magical information but it also became easier for the authorities to seize it and track down the author. In addition, there were political factors. Accusations of witchcraft were made against Henry VII's enemies, for instance, who were gaining power in Wales at the time. And there were also religious issues: by the end of the thirteenth century, magical practice was becoming increasingly linked with Christian heresies. Despite all these factors, the nature of the English legal system still meant that the execution rate was lower than elsewhere.

The answer to how many 'actual witches' there were is not known, but it is unlikely that there were large numbers of people forming covens, cursing and blighting all and sundry and holding sabbats in the woods. There were not huge numbers of persecutions in England, although Scotland was a somewhat different story. So if the nice cunning person in the next village – who gave you charms against black magic and made you healing herbal concoctions, and helped you with your animals – was not persecuted, who was?

In Britain, 'competent, middle-aged, middle-class women were more often picked on, usually because they had a reputation for a hot temper and a sharp tongue.'[7] Such women may also fall into the category of 'people disliked by their neighbours'. Other targets included the mentally ill, those members of the criminal classes who extorted money by means of magical intimidation ('give me a penny or I'll put a spell on you'), and people who genuinely believed in magic and who undertook cursing. Earlier magical practitioners did not have the same squeamishness about hexing people that modern Wiccans do, and without question, some people did practise a form of what is commonly called black magic. Also affected were heretics and people who engaged in possible drug use (for example, of henbane or belladonna).

Let us take a look at a case study, that of the Pendle Witches in Lancashire in 1612. The trial of twenty people, sixteen of them women, took place at the Lancaster Assizes. Many of the accused had been arrested in and around Pendle, and were made to walk all the way to Lancaster across the Trough of Bowland. Eight of them came from Samlesbury, associated with the handsome hall that still stands there today. Eleven people out of the twenty went to trial, nine women and two men. Of these, ten were found guilty and hanged, and one was released.

The trial is significant because it represents 2 per cent of the total number of people hanged for witchcraft through-out the entire period of the English witch trials: the total of people executed was less than five hundred. That is still five hundred people too many, but it is not an enormous quantity. The Pendle 'witches' were mainly from two families, each headed by a matriarch. One was the family of Elizabeth Southerns, aka Demdike, and her daughter Elizabeth Device, plus her grandchildren James and Alizon Device, and the other was Anne Whittle, aka Chattox, and her daughter Anne Redfern. The situation is complicated by the fact that the Demdike and Chattox families seem to have been in competition. They were rivals who accused one another of all sorts, and who seem to have been a kind of mini-criminal gang apiece, competing for the market of healing, extortion and begging.

Pendle is an exceptionally bleak part of the country. You could possibly scrape out a living from sheep farming, but it would in many ways have been hard to survive at this level of society, and it was possibly this that drove people into a life of what was essentially petty crime. Pendle was apparently 'fabled for its theft, violence and sexual laxity, where the church was honoured without much understanding of its doctrines by the common people'.[8] The abbey at Whalley, a major religious player in the district, had been dissolved by Henry VIII, although people still held to their Roman Catholic beliefs. When Elizabeth came to the throne, many of them continued to celebrate the Catholic Mass in secret.

In 1562 Elizabeth passed a law in the form of an Act Against Conjurations, Enchantments and Witchcrafts. This called for the death penalty, but only in cases where harm had been caused. Lesser offences were punishable by a term of imprisonment. The Act provided that anyone who should 'use, practise, or exercise any Witchcraft, Enchantment, Charm, or Sorcery, whereby any person shall happen to be killed or destroyed', was guilty of a felony without benefit of clergy, and was to be put to death. This set the tone for the next few decades of witch trials and culminated in King James's Witchcraft Act of 1604, which also sought the death penalty in cases where harm resulting from witchcraft could be shown. The authorities in Pendle, perhaps seeking favour from the king in the early 1600s, were keen to expose recusants (anyone who would not attend the English Church), and it was in this climate that a pedlar came forward to announce that he had been injured by witchcraft.

What seems to have happened was this: Alizon Device had met the pedlar, John Law, and asked to buy some metal pins. He was not keen to supply them, either because he suspected she was using them for nefarious occult purposes (her mother was known to have been a witch for fifty years) or because he could not be bothered to undo his whole pack for such a tiny item. Alizon took his refusal badly and a few minutes after their exchange Law had what sounds like a stroke. He may not have thought he had been cursed, but Alizon apparently did, as she visited him a little later, confessed and asked for his forgiveness.

It is important to realize that the deaths of which the Pendle Witches were subsequently accused were not a sudden spate of mysterious slayings: they had mostly taken place years before the incident with Law. But after Law's family mentioned the episode to the local Justice of the Peace, Roger Nowell, he brought the Demdike family in for questioning, and it was at this point that things began to escalate. Alizon claimed she had sold her soul to the Devil, and her brother told the magistrate that she had bewitched a local child. Alizon also seems to have told Nowell about the Chattox family, who were in the Demdikes' bad books as a result of a recent burglary. When Anne Chattox herself was brought in, she said she had indeed sold her own soul to a 'thing like a Christian man' in exchange for power and revenge. She also confessed to four murders.

Both Mrs Demdike and Mrs Chattox were in their eighties and blind. Today these dotty, poverty-stricken old women would not get anywhere near a court house, but would be a matter for social services, if anything. However, given that they had all confessed, Nowell sent everyone to Lancaster for trial. Then he got word of a meeting to be held on Good Friday at Malkin Tower, chez Demdike, organized by Elizabeth Demdike. This may in fact have been an illicit Catholic Mass, not a witches' gathering. As a result, eight more people were accused of witchcraft: the Pendle episode was starting to snowball.

The Pendle Witches were a diverse group of people. Also accused were Jane Bulcock and her son John Bulcock, Katherine

Hewitt, Alice Grey, Jennet Preston and the unfortunately named Alice Nutter, as well as the witches from Samlesbury: Jane Southworth, and Jennet and Ellen Bierley, who were accused by a fourteen-year-old girl, Grace Sowerbutts, of child murder and cannibalism. Their trial collapsed when Grace was discovered to have been manipulated by a Catholic priest. The women from Samlesbury were acquitted, but the whole trial likely had little to do with witchcraft and a lot to do with the Catholic/Protestant divide. Alice Nutter was a wealthy widow and a landowner: it is possible she was a recusant, but it is also possible that Nowell wanted her property for himself. Two of her family had been executed for being Catholic and she may not have wanted to implicate anyone else among her relatives. Whatever the case, Nutter was eventually hanged.

Nutter protested her innocence, as did the Samlesbury witches. We have here a combination of people who sincerely believed themselves to be involved in witchcraft and who, for whatever reason, confessed, and people who appear to have had a very tangential relationship, if any, with magical practice. Although they are known as the Pendle Witches, we should not lump them all into one category. Jennet Device, who was nine, gave evidence against her entire family. Again, we cannot be sure why: was it malice, revenge, manipulation (of the kind found in the sort of 'Satanic panic' cases of reconstructed memory of the late twentieth century), bribery or simple terror of the authorities? We cannot say why a little girl would betray the whole of her clan, but whatever her reasons, her mother, brother and sister were put to death. Years later, Jennet herself – or a woman of the same name – was prosecuted for witchcraft and imprisoned.

The case of the Pendle Witches is one example of the many witch trials that were held in Britain during this period. People were accused of witchcraft throughout the nation, and although not everyone who came to trial was executed, many of those accused did end up on the gallows. The most famous trials in England, apart from Pendle, were those instigated by Matthew Hopkins, who remains notorious as the Witchfinder General. This was a self-conferred title that nevertheless, in the chaos of the English Civil War, saw him responsible for the trials of around three hundred women in the 1640s and a hundred deaths. If you mention his name, it is likely to conjure up the image of some stern, elderly fanatic, but Hopkins was young – he was only 27 when he died.

Hopkins was born around 1620 in Suffolk, the son of a Puritan clergyman. He used an inheritance to buy the Thorn Inn near Manningtree in Essex and set himself up as a gentleman; there has been some suggestion that he trained as a lawyer, but no direct evidence of this exists. Hopkins and his associate John Stearne set up as witch-hunters throughout East Anglia. Hopkins claimed to have done this after overhearing a conversation between some women in Manningtree about their consorting with the Devil, but his career seems actually to have begun with accusations made by Stearne. Twenty-three women were tried at Chelmsford by Justices of the Peace overseen by the Earl of Warwick.

Ronald Hutton attributes some of Hopkins's success to the Civil War itself and the collapse of the assize system: normally, these women would have been tried at the assizes. The war left a power vacuum and Stearne and Hopkins seem to have taken full advantage of it. Both claimed to have been hired by

Parliament, and both made a considerable amount of money from witch-hunting, along with their female accomplices. In fact, Parliament expressed considerable concern about their activities. A report from the area to Parliament mentions 'as if some busie men had made use of some ill Arts to extort such confession'.

Their investigations were based on the *Daemonologie* of King James. We know this from Hopkins's own book, *The Discovery of Witches*.[9] Their methods remain familiar to most people today and are the ones most often associated with the witch trials: ducking a suspect to see if she floats, pricking her (it is usually 'her') with a trick needle to see if she bleeds, and so on. Hopkins was warned against ducking people without their permission and gave up the practice around 1645, having to rely on the 'Devil's mark' instead. This is supposed to be a third nipple, but in Hopkins's interpretation it could simply be a birthmark or a mole instead, and unfortunately a lot of people have those.

Not everyone went along with this. One of Hopkins's principal opponents around 1646 was a vicar, John Gaule of Great Staughton, who preached against witch-hunting. Hopkins and Stearne themselves then came to the attention of the justice system, but they prudently retired before they came to court. Hopkins died in 1647, probably of tuberculosis, although there is a legend that he was subjected to his own swimming test. However, the damage had already been done.

Happily, however, it was not to last. In 1712 Jane Wenham of Hertfordshire stood trial before a judge for 'conversing familiarly with the Devil in the shape of the cat' (talking to the cat, in other words). John Powell, the judge, stated, 'There is no law against flying,' when told of Wenham's ability to do this. She was found guilty by the jury and sentenced to hang, but the more sceptical judge set aside her conviction. She was pardoned by Queen Anne and supported by the local gentry for the rest of her life. This was not the last witch trial in Britain – Janet Horne was executed in Scotland in 1727 – but it is often held to mark the end of this period of persecution.

## Cunning Folk

It is important not to get too caught up in the witch trials, since they are a bit of a red herring with regard to magical practice of the period. We need to take note of the confessions, particularly those that relate to working with the Devil: do these really provide evidence of pagan survival? Or are they more likely to be an indication of mental illness, for example? Confessions have, in previous times, been taken as an indication of the survival of a previous religion, a 'witch cult' that lasted secretly throughout the centuries, but it is considered by historians to be very unlikely that a secret pagan cult could have been operating for hundreds of years without someone breaking ranks and mentioning it. The idea informing the belief in a persisting cult is partly that mentions of the 'Devil' tend to relate to a horned god, but, as we will see later on, which god this might have been is very uncertain.

We also need to be careful with the assumption that the witch trials were purely anti-women: the bulk of the people accused were indeed female, but not all. The Demdike and Chattox families seem to have been involved in something genuinely magically suspicious – or believed that they were. Yet many people practised magic openly throughout the period of the witch trials without coming near a courtroom or falling foul of anyone. What was different about their case?

The difference according to the laws of the time is reasonably clear: it has to do with harm. We have mentioned earlier in this chapter that if you were a witch, you were held to be the sort of person who would curse others; but if you were a cunning person, you were considered the sort of person who would *heal* cursed individuals. You might practise magic, but you were anti-witch. You worked good magic against evil magic, or *maleficium*, which included cursing and, interestingly, weather magic. As such, you were on the side of decency, and the authorities would in the main leave you alone. Negative magic was said to come from the Devil, but it is much more doubtful where 'good' magic was supposed to originate: perhaps the angels; maybe there was a touch of brimstone there, too. It was best for your reputation if you were known to have inherited your powers from a relative, or if you occupied a particular position in a family: the seventh son of a seventh son, for instance. Some people claimed that the fairies had granted them their powers, which was a dangerous tactic and got at least one Scottish witch tried: Isobel Gowdie in 1662. Or you could learn from another practitioner: 'Essex cunning-man William Hills . . . was said to have been a pupil of the famed astrologer and almanac writer William Lilly. Anne Kingsbury, of Somerset, likewise said she had acquired treasure-seeking techniques from Lilly.'[10] Puritan writers believed, however, that all magic was hellish in origin. So, if you were a cunning person, you were treading a thin line between acceptance and potentially very serious consequences.

Cunning people were found in most communities and continued to operate widely until quite late into the twentieth century. A friend of mine who lives near Whitby remembers a cunning woman who lived in the next valley and who died in the 1980s. The grandmother of that friend had been a self-described weather witch who worked in Hull to gain good weather for the fishermen. We arguably still have village wise-women today, although they are more likely to use crystals and work in Reiki than in old-school witchcraft. But a national healthcare system, a police force and a legal system have largely rendered the role obsolete.

So what did cunning folk do? The kinds of spells that have persisted are commonplace. The ancient Egyptians would have recognized them; people in the Philippines or Haiti today would find them familiar. They were spells for love and healing, good harvests and protective magic, making money, finding lost or stolen goods, or foretelling the future. Alan Macfarlane suggests that prior to the Reformation, a lot of these tasks would have been carried out by the clergy,[11] since magical practice within the Catholic Church is quite an old phenomenon, but that after the Reformation cunning folk stepped in to fill the gap. Also, not all of them were full-time: several cunning people ran early versions of pubs. Astrologers were most likely the best paid; this is a status issue, as they would have been literate and from the higher and more educated classes. Getting your information from books was valued, but not everyone was in a position to do this, because not everyone had an education.

James Sharpe suggests that there were four main areas of operation: divination and fortune-telling, healing, removing curses, and finding lost or stolen goods.[12] This last is not to be downplayed. Some commentators have suggested that this and healing occupied most of cunning people's time. This was an age before we had a police force, and you would not have much recourse if your possessions were stolen. Also, the cunning person was probably astute enough to keep their ears to the ground in the local community, assuming that they were not involved in the theft in the first place.

There were a lot of ways of describing cunning folk: wise man or woman, witch (white or black), wizard, sorcerer, conjurer, charmer, magician, wight, nigromancer, necromancer, seer, blesser, dreamer, cantel, soothsayer, fortune-teller, girdle-measurer, enchanter, incantatrix and so on. Bishop Latimer noted in 1522: 'A great many of us when we be in trouble, or sickness, or lose anything, we run hither and thither to witches, or sorcerers, whom we call wise men ... seeking aid and comfort at their hands.'[13] And Robert Burton stated in 1621: 'Sorcerers are too common; cunning men, wizards, and white witches, as they call them, in every village, which, if they be sought unto, will help almost all infirmities of body and mind.'[14]

There seem to have been a lot of them, but it is hard to tell what the exact numbers were, largely because they were not reported or documented. It's not even clear whether the majority were male or female. Men certainly practised, but there are accounts of female fortune-tellers, and the lines are blurred because a lot of people would also have engaged in non-magical folk practices. John Aubrey in his *Miscellanies* mentions:

The last summer, on the day of St John the Baptist, 1694, I accidentally was walking in the pasture behind Montague house, it was 12 o'clock. I saw there about two or three and twenty young women, most of them well habited, on their knees very busy, as if they had been weeding. I could not presently learn what the matter was; at last a young man told me, that they were looking for a coal under the root of a plantain, to put under their head that night, and they should dream of who would be their husbands: It was to be sought for that day and hour.[15]

This is not atypical of 'women's' magic: much of it was to do with finding a husband.

Many cunning folk dressed up to create a mysterious ambience. Keith Thomas suggests that a cunning man's greatest asset was the imagination of his customers. Let us not forget that in an era with no TV, people made their own entertainment. They still do: people go to Tarot readers for fun as well as in emergencies, and they prefer it if the reader looks a bit witchy rather than sitting in an ordinary suburban living room wearing a tracksuit.

The cunning person had an arsenal of different techniques. Finding things, for instance, could be done by means of the sieve and shears: Aubrey tells us that

The Sheers are stuck in a Sieve and two maydens hold up ye Sieve with the top of their fingers by the handle of the Shiers: then say by St Peter and St Paul such a one hath stoln [such a thing], the others say by St Peter and St Paul he hath not stoln it. After many such adjurations the Sieve will turne at ye name of ye Thiefe.[16]

This was a common method: it turns up in the Salem witch trials, being used to determine whether someone was alive or dead. Or you could use the Bible, putting a key inside it and slotting the names of possible suspects into the hollow part of the key. The book would wag (twitch and jerk) when the guilty party's name showed up. Or you could use a crystal ball.

For healing, the spectrum of treatment is perhaps broader: the doctrine of signatures was used (for example, gorse flowers were used to treat jaundice, because they were yellow) and those who could read would use herbals such as that devised by Nicholas Culpeper, whose books often gave the magical correspondences of each plant. Some of these old folk remedies have no basis whatsoever in fact; others could be useful. Empirical observation over hundreds of years might suggest that, for instance, yarrow was helpful in treating wounds (it contains antibiotic chemicals). Bay, rue, sage and rosemary – all cleansers – were popular. But you might be told to wear an amulet as well as being given a herbal treatment.

Keith Thomas claims that there were three main areas of healing:

> The first is that disease is a foreign presence, and this assumption was shared by official healers as well. The second is that religious language possessed a mystical power which could be deployed for practical purposes. The third was that the working of certain charms and potions owed their efficacy to the healer himself. It was this last belief which proved so deadly to the healer when inverted.[17]

Relying on prayers had a twofold effect. They were held to work, and if the authorities started investigating, you could always claim that you were reliant only on the word of God and that he was the one doing all the healing, although this got a bit trickier after the Reformation, as you might find yourself using Catholic prayers. Alternatively, you could use magical language: 'abracadabra' was a popular charm, and this is why stage conjurors still use it today. Reginald Scot, writing in the *Discoverie of Witchcraft* in 1584, cites it as a cure for ague. Other charms may have older origins, for instance this one from Lincolnshire:

> Father, Son and Holy Ghost
> Nail the Devil to a post
> Thrice I strike with holy crook,
> One for God, one for Wod and one for Lok.

A remnant of the old Saxon Woden and Loki? Perhaps.

Curse-breaking was another popular form of magic. Witch bottles from medieval times still turn up in the cellars or walls of old houses: these 'bellarmines' are ceramic or glass bottles filled with pins, coils of wool, tangled threads, nails, needles and, sometimes, human urine (of the person who has been cursed). They are supposed to attract negative spells, which become tangled in all the mess in the bottle and cannot get free – a bit like a dreamcatcher.

Other examples of cunning folk dealing with curses include William Drage, an apothecary from Hitchin in Hertfordshire, who assessed his patients carefully:

> Those that vomit, or void by stool, with greater or less torments, Knives, Scissors, Bryars, Whole Eggs, Dogs Tails, crooked Nails, Pins, Needles, sometimes threaded, and sometimes with Hair, Bundles of Hair, pieces of

Wax, pieces of silk, live Eels, large pieces of Salpeter; conclude they are bewitched; and that such have been vomited, or voided by stool, and that from witchcraft.[18]

If you were vomiting up this sort of thing, you might well conclude that you had been subjected to psychic attack. Drage believed in demonic possession, a common enough conviction at the time, and there are many spells that concern it.

While cunning folk did not experience the same levels of persecution as witches, they did not escape attention altogether. Some people believed that 'white' witches were even more dangerous, as they put your immortal soul at risk: while their practices might appear innocuous, this was part of the Devil's deceit (some fundamentalist Christians still say this about practices such as yoga or Tarot reading). And some of their magical practices skirted what was held to be acceptable, particularly love magic, an ethical issue that persists today. A lot of cases involving love magic came to trial. For example, an indictment from 1680 states: 'Kitchell Harrison of the City of York in the county of city of York . . . on 10 Nov . . . at Burstall, exercised divers incantations and conjurations and consulted evil spirits, with the intention of provoking Joyce Massey to illicit love.'[19]

The worry was that love magic could promote social disorder. These cases were dealt with by the ecclesiastic courts and the punishments were not usually as severe as death, but they were punishments all the same: for example, being made to stand in the street with a board detailing your sins. This started to change after 1735 when the new Witchcraft Act got rid of the idea of witchcraft as a legitimate practice, but opened everyone up to prosecution for fraud instead. And although local populaces do not seem to have regarded cunning folk as a threat, unlike witches, this could go either way: if you hire someone to get your stolen stuff back, and they cannot do it, you might be tempted to have a little revenge and shop them to the authorities for fraud, or worse.

> A Butcher in Essex, having lost some cattle, resolved he would go to a Cunning Man to find out what had become of his animals . . . This deceiving witch, seeing his opportunity of gaining a fee for the purpose in hand, used his Conjurations in a room contrived for his usual impostures. Presently, a confederate came in where the two men were, covered over with a bull's hide and a pair of horns on his head. The poor butcher, now sitting and looking in a looking glass made for that purpose, beheld it in the terrible object. It was made less clear to his eye than if he had looked right upon the sight, but he was charged by the Conjuror not to look behind him, for if he did the Devil would be outraged.[20]

The butcher grew suspicious, however, and exposed the cunning man's fraud.

William Lilly himself was denounced in a pamphlet by one John Vicars, and cunning folk often attracted a degree of Puritan ire. At best fraudulent and at worst in league with the Devil, in Puritans' eyes cunning folk as well as witches occupied a precarious social position, although one that was more likely to result in censure than execution.

## A Word about Fairies

I am including a few comments about the belief in fairies in this chapter, since we are in an age here when some of the most famous portrayals of fairykind took place, in the plays of Shakespeare. Oberon, Titania and Puck are arguably some of the best-known British fairies in the world. But where does the belief in fairies originate? Is it really a belief, or just a charming (or sinister) notion?

The first mention we have of fairies in English literature is by Gervase of Tilbury, writing in the thirteenth century: he speaks of a 'portune', a little old man with a wrinkled face who assists on farms. It is likely, though we have no evidence, that people may always have believed, in some form, in minor spirits, sometimes benign, sometimes malicious. Homer mentions fairies in the *Iliad*, although we must be careful of terms in translation. We have noted the Scandinavian belief in elves in earlier chapters, and in Ireland, the supernatural race known as the Tuatha de Danann are said to have been the first people resident on the island.

Our perception of fairies as tiny, winged beings is relatively recent, within the last four hundred years. In Scotland they were seen as dangerous entities who could lead people astray in marshes, and there are tales of fairies throughout the British Isles who are at best tricky to deal with and at worst actively malevolent. Folklorists have suggested that these beliefs may relate to earlier inhabitants of the British Isles – perhaps a small, dark people who lived in the hills, such as the Picts – but this hypothesis must remain in the realm of conjecture.

The influence of fairies on contemporary paganism is not huge, but it does exist: there are versions of Faery Wicca that work with the fae, as they are also called. And cosplaying fairies is popular as well among people who may have pagan leanings: the southwest of England hosts regular fairy balls, which are for dressing up rather than ritual.

)) ○ ((

This period of British history is notable for its social upheaval and religious change, resulting in a significant shift in the view taken towards magical practice. We begin with that practice as something that was undertaken by priests, among others, and which may have been frowned upon by sections of the Catholic Church but that was more or less tolerated. Over the centuries, the religion of Britain itself changed and intolerance and persecution became the order of the day. By the time the last witches were hanged in England, in Devon in 1682, an estimated four to five hundred people had been put to death. Around 90 per cent of these were women. More were executed in Scotland (1,100 to 2,500: it is difficult to give precise numbers, as records have been lost). And we know that five were executed in Wales. Across Europe, the consequences of the witch trials were more severe, and the New World was not exempt either. Most people are aware of the trials in Salem in New England.

However, we have noted that it is important not to conflate cunning craft with alleged witchcraft, and we have also seen that the reasons for bringing people to trial for witchcraft in Britain were quite varied. What we can say is that it is very unlikely that the kind of magic practised in Britain at this time had a significant pagan element, and also that this period of persecution did not cause the demise of magical practice itself, and people continued to visit cunning people for spells and folk remedies. As we shall see, it was in the Renaissance period too that magic began to grow and become more elaborate.

# FOUR

# High Magic and the Seventeenth Century

European thought developed substantially throughout the period known as the Renaissance. With the rise in literacy and a renewed interest in classical philosophy, art and learning, educated men, in particular, grew interested in the 'spiritual sciences' of magic, and the interrelation of the world with the wider cosmos. The 'practical' magic undertaken by cunning folk was not the only sort of magic practised in Britain from the medieval period onwards. As society, and ways of looking at that society, continued to grow more sophisticated, a different kind of magic, often looking back to Graeco-Roman classical principles, emerged, aimed at ascertaining the place of humanity within the universe and at spiritual development. To differentiate it from the work of the cunning folk, some historians have used the term 'high magic' (as opposed to 'low magic'), but it would be a mistake to adopt these labels too rigidly, or to assume that this is a definition that was used by practitioners of magic at the time. Some cunning folk had access to books in which so-called 'high' magic was delineated, and some 'high' magicians went in for the kind of treasure hunting more commonly supposed to be the domain of the cunning person. As is the case now, people met one another and exchanged ideas, often regardless of their social standing.

We are looking narrowly at the British Isles here, but it is important to remember that ideas regarding the occult were going to and from the Continent at this time. Spain had been producing an enormous body of lore around alchemy. Occult literature (such as the seventeenth-century French text *Comte de Gabalis* – the possibly satirical but influential 'Count of Cabbala') was coming out of France and being disseminated across Europe, including Britain.

'High' magic is generally associated in the British Isles with social elites, ranging from court astrologers to the king himself. The monarchy may not have practised magic themselves, but those of royal blood were held to have a healing touch – their very flesh was said to contain a kind of medicinal power. An illustration of this is from a letter sent to one John Brown, who was collating information about the 'touch' in 1683:

> Mr. Brown,
>
> . . . I was very much afflicted with the Distemper vulgarly known by the Name of the Kings-Evil, from seven years of age, until the time that I received His Majesties most gracious Touch: I was so much afflicted with it, that at some times my Face would be so Tumefied, that I could hardly see out, or speak plain: my Cheeks and Neck were full of Glandules, and I had such a running Ulcer in my upper Lip, that at some times it appear'd like a Hare-Lip, and in a very bad condition I continued from the year 1648, until the year 1662, at which time all my Friends advised me to get the Favour of being Toucht . . . So . . . I waited upon His Majesty as I was directed, and received His Divine Touch; which had

so good effect upon me, that in two or three days I was very much at ease; and by that time I got home, which was within a fortnight, I was perfectly well, to the great Glory of God, the Eternal Honour of His Sacred Majesty, and the Lawful Heirs of the Crown, whom God preserve.

from

Your Humble Servant, Philip Williams. From my House at the Globe in Whites-Alley in Chancery-Lane London, Dec. 10. 1683.[1]

This relates to Keith Thomas's earlier assertion regarding the belief that some forms of healing depend for their efficacy on the powers of the practitioner themselves. In terms of royal healing, the practice is said to have begun in the eleventh century with King Edward the Confessor in England and Philip I in France. The English and French kings who followed were thought to have inherited this 'royal touch', which was also supposed to show that their right to rule was God-given. In huge ceremonies, kings touched hundreds of people afflicted by scrofula (which often goes into remission on its own). Coins were minted that, when touched by the king, also had the power to heal: these were known as 'angels' up until the 1620s, when they were replaced by medallions, which were worn as amulets. Queen Anne, who died in 1714, was the last monarch to continue the practice.

These examples of royal magic, when the touch is direct, are what is known as the 'laying on of hands': the idea that a healing power can be directly transmitted through a human medium. This was not confined to the king or queen; however, their touch seems to have possessed extra potency because of their royal status. It is a practice still found today in the form of folk healers, though it is more common to the New Age or some forms of Christianity than to paganism.

Other forms of 'high' magic include alchemy, astrology and divination. To practise alchemy you needed to be a kind of proto-chemist, possessing lab equipment such as alembics. To study alchemy, you would need to be literate and numerate, as you would to practise astrology. Astrology occupied an ambivalent position as to whether it was low or high: it depended on what you used it for, and although it was regarded as a legitimate form of science, some of it was considered dubious. Divination is probably the clearest crossover between high and low magic.

## Alchemy and Hermetic Magic

Changing lead into gold has an obvious appeal, but alchemy was not just about the transformation of base metals: it had a direct influence upon the basics of what is known as Hermetic magic, the transformation of the self. We will meet the word 'Hermetic' with increasing frequency throughout this book, and will devote some time to it in detail a little later.

Alchemy itself is old. A story that it had been established by the Egyptian god Thoth continued into the Middle Ages, and it was practised throughout the Islamic world. We must remember that the seventeenth century was a time when science and magic were still intertwined. Isaac Newton, for instance, returned to his studies in alchemy at the end of his life, believing that physics was something of a dead end.

(His writings on alchemy are now widely available, and there are a lot of them.) Newton undertook a translation of the *Smaragdine Tablet*, a work purporting to date from the classical period but probably Arabic in origin. He stated that Alexander the Great had found an emerald tablet in a tomb belonging to the god Hermes-Thoth, also known as Hermes Trismegistus (Thrice Great Hermes). This tablet detailed the principles of alchemy and other aspects of natural philosophy, and it is one of the foundation stones of Hermetic magic. From the 1100s alchemy began to become popular among British magicians, starting with Robert of Chester, Abbot of Pamplona. Robert described his work in *The Book of the Composition of Alchemy* (1144), and his teachings were taken up by later practitioners such as Roger Bacon and George Ripley. Chaucer, even, satirizes alchemy in *The Canterbury Tales* (*c.* 1376). In the 'Canon's Yeoman's Tale', the titular character insists on telling everyone how clever his master is. The other pilgrims are less convinced and ask how it is that the Canon is dressed so shabbily if he has the ability to turn lead into gold.

To take a much later example, the English physician Robert Fludd further popularized alchemical practice, travelling to Europe in 1598 and studying a form of medicine based on the work of Paracelsus (1493–1541). The latter believed in the doctrine of signatures, which we have noted already: the idea, for instance, that if a plant resembles a body part, it is able to cure an affliction of that part. Fludd brought his alchemical ideas back to England, joined the Royal College of Physicians in 1609 and worked on the principles of spagyrics, which involves the doctrine of signatures and drawing up a horoscope for the patient prior to treatment. This might all sound a bit New Age now, but where Paracelsian medicine proved really valuable was in its empirical outlook, relying on observation and experience rather than theory. For example, Paracelsus insisted that wounds should be kept clean instead of being treated with concoctions such as cow dung or burned feathers. Fludd's medical practice was apparently quite successful, and if he followed Paracelsus' less peculiar and more empirical notions, no wonder.

But though science won in the end, alchemy did not completely die. It is still practised today across the world, both in its transformative efforts on the soul and on metals and chemicals. It is a vast, complex area of study that may have lost out in terms of practical, experimental application to physics and modern science, but which is still held to be of value in terms of magic. There are people who practise spagyric medicine, and a small number of magical practitioners who run alchemical labs, as well as annual conferences on alchemy.

From the seventeenth century onwards, Hermetic principles become increasingly important to magical practice, particularly to 'high' magic. We have seen that the word encompassing these various principles derives from the entity known as Hermes-Trismegistus, and that Hermetics involves alchemy. It also includes astrology, theurgy (the operation of the gods upon human affairs) and the idea of reincarnation. Describing the attraction of Hermetics, Tobias Churton, Professor of Western Esotericism at the University of Exeter, writes:

> The Hermetic tradition was both moderate and flexible, offering a tolerant philosophical religion, a religion of the (omnipresent) mind, a purified perception of God, the cosmos, and the self, and much positive encouragement

for the spiritual seeker, all of which the student could take anywhere.[2]

Today, the Hermetic Fellowship states that

the new figure of the Hermetic Renaissance Magus entered the cultural consciousness of the era. Ficino's [1433–1499] 'Natural Magic' moved out of the shadows of the grimoires and once more into the light of general philosophical and theological consideration. A student at Ficino's Florentine Platonic Academy, the brilliant and daring enfant terrible Count Giovanni Pico della Mirandola, added the crucial catalytic element of the Jewish Qabalah to the new Pagan-Christian Hermetic amalgam, and transformed Hermetism forever. It is here that Hermeticism was born ... once more entering into a syncretic union, this time with Christianity, Renaissance Neo-Classicism and Humanism, Natural Magic, and Qabalah.

Hermeticism has of course included the beauty of Rosicrucianism since the seventeenth century, and has illuminated the symbolic ritual of Freemasonry since the eighteenth. It was the motivating force behind the foundation of the most influential esoteric schools of the fin de siecle – Theosophy, the Hermetic Order of the Golden Dawn, and the Martinism of Papus – and the great Occult Revival to which they gave birth, and has strongly influenced the twentieth-century Pagan Renaissance.[3]

It is hard to overstate the impact that the ideas contained beneath the label 'Hermeticism' have had on esoteric thought since their inception, or the number of groups that have adopted them as a cornerstone, Rosicrucians, Freemasons, late nineteenth-century ceremonial magicians, Wiccans and twentieth-century occultists among them. Central to Hermetics is the idea of the Kabbalah.

## Kabbalah

Also known as the Qabbala or Cabbala, Kabbalah (literally 'received tradition') is a system of thought that originated in Judaism but was later adopted into ceremonial magic. More widely, it underpins a lot of Western magical thinking. This process of integration began during the Renaissance and continued through the next two centuries, when Kabbalism and occultism became enmeshed in British magical practice. There are innumerable manuscripts in Hebrew and Arabic that have never been translated,[4] and the magical use of these texts differs quite considerably from the Judaic form, so we must be as careful as possible not to confuse these different versions.

Kabbalism is based around a cosmological concept: that the universe we are capable of apprehending emanates from the mind of God, and is divided into ten zones, called sephiroth, in a diagram known familiarly as the Tree of Life. The higher one goes up the tree, the closer one gets to God, and the more difficult it becomes for us to understand our place in the scheme of things. Our human brains simply cannot cope with the vastness of these upper realms. Our own world of Earth is situated right at the bottom of the tree and is known as the realm of Malkuth. The remaining spheres are linked to the other planetary bodies, starting with the Moon and progressing through Mercury, Venus, Mars, Jupiter, Saturn, Neptune and Pluto/Uranus (the correlations of the upper levels of the tree to specific planets may vary. The outer planets of the solar system were not yet discovered when the Kabbalah was being developed, and their attribution came later).

The Kabbalah has been linked to astrology and the Tarot. Many of the cards in the more old-fashioned decks, such as the Rider Waite, feature two pillars because the Tree of Life has a right- and a left-hand side. These are sometimes represented by two columns onto which the tree is mapped, the pillars of Severity and Mercy, perhaps also representing male and female, although some people disapprove of mapping gender onto the tree. The ten zones can, however, represent a human figure, with each sephiroth symbolizing a part of the body – rather like the Eastern concept of the chakras. There is a central pillar, too, of Balance.

The tree is also divided into three triangles – the upper triangle of Kether, Binah and Chokmah; the middle triangle of Geburah, Tiphereth and Chesed; and the bottom triangle of Hod, Netzach and Yesod, with Malkuth right at the base. The top triangle represents the universal spirit, the middle triangle the soul, and the bottom triangle – pointing towards the material world – the personality.

But what is Kabbalah actually for? Basically, it offers a map of the magical universe. The planets all have different qualities: each one rules a different day, and the hours throughout that day. This ties into cosmological ideas – 'as above, so below'. If the Renaissance magician wanted to get more money for his client, for instance, he could work with the powers of the planet Jupiter, which are tied to wealth, and he would do so on a Thursday, the day ruled by Jupiter. He could look up the planetary hours on a table and do his ritual work on the hour ruled by Jupiter on that Thursday, to give the spell maximum chance of success. The Kabbalistic sphere for Jupiter is represented by Chesed, which has various qualities and symbols attached to it that the magician might work with, visualizing and perhaps making a physical representation of the colours, numbers and qualities of the sphere. If he was undertaking a love spell for a client, then the relevant sephiroth would be Netzach, which correlates with Venus. In this case, any magical work would be done on a Friday, the day that is governed by Venus. And so on.

The Kabbalah can be used as a meditation or visualization tool: as a 'mind map' to explore the psyche, a means of travelling upon the astral plane in a structured format, or as a form of prayer, or an adjunct to understanding the Tarot.

## Divination and the Tarot

Moving on with our assessment of more learned forms of magic, the arts of divination are still one of the main elements of modern magical practice, just as they were in ancient times. Most people would like to know what the future holds.

Divination takes a number of common forms – scrying via a crystal ball or a dark mirror, the runes, the ogham and the Chinese system of the *I Ching*. But in Western Europe, one of the oldest and most respected forms of fortune-telling remains the Tarot.

The roots of the Tarot are unclear, although the most widely accepted origin story among historians is that in 1781 Antoine

Court de Gébelin wrote a nine-volume esoteric work called *Le Monde primitif* (The Primitive World). He had, so he said, visited a female friend who had shown him a new card game that was becoming increasingly popular. It featured a set of decorated cards called *Tarocchi* in Italian and *les tarots* in French. Court de Gébelin was fascinated and had, he claimed, a revelation that this was Egyptian in origin. He called the cards the 'Book of Thoth', after the Egyptian ibis-headed god of scribes and learning. Thoth himself, so Court de Gébelin's story goes, had given the images of the Tarot cards to his disciples and they sent them down through the centuries in the form of a game.

Court de Gébelin and a later admirer of his, the comte de Mellet, who linked the Tarot images to the letters of the Hebrew alphabet, were Freemasons, and it has been suggested that Court de Gébelin's story about being introduced to the Tarot by a lady friend was simply a disguise for the cards' Masonic roots. We can see already that accounts about the foundation of these cards are starting to become confused. Many more claims have been made for them – that they come from ancient Atlantis, or are the creation of Cathar-inspired papermaking guilds, or represent Chaldean phases of the moon. There are almost as many origin stories for the Tarot as there are Tarot cards.

What we do know is that the Tarot gradually began to gain recognition in Italy throughout the Renaissance, and may have been devised as a form of flattering accessory to the Visconti-Sforza family of Milan around 1450 by one Bonifacio Bembo, an artist from the north of Italy. In this early stage, the cards are a game – *Tarocchi*. But writers have suggested they were not merely a game, nor simply a list of medieval stereotypes.

There may indeed be links with the Kabbalah. The 22 Tarot 'trumps' may connect with the 22 letters of the Hebrew alphabet, although there is no reference to the Tarot in Kabbalistic literature until the nineteenth century, when the occultist Éliphas Lévi drew parallels between the two. A coincidence? Or a secret 'book' that would be clear only to initiates? We may never know. Whatever its history, the Tarot has gone through many forms and changes across the centuries, and is still doing so today.

The Tarot itself is divided into two main types of cards. The Major Arcana (arcana means 'secrets') are the 22 cards that follow a symbolic journey through life, beginning with zero, the Fool, who blithely steps from a cliff. If you look at the Major Arcana, you will see that the cards are numbered, and you can follow the Fool's progress through the deck as he meets figures and situations that represent archetypal people and events in our lives: the Emperor, the High Priestess, Justice, the Lovers, and so forth. It is in the Major Arcana that the Death card so beloved of occult thrillers is found, halfway through rather than at the end of the journey, for the Fool must pass through Death in order to find eternal life, journeying down into the hinterlands of the underworld before rising back up again on the Day of Judgement and effectively becoming reborn into the World. The Major Arcana represent the journey of each person's spiritual life, in essence.

The Major Arcana are the most important cards, indicating significant trends and influences whenever they turn up in a reading. Some like to compare them to Jungian archetypes and, indeed, there is even a Jungian deck. The two systems go nicely together. Many of the symbols in later decks come from Masonry, through the Golden Dawn.

The Minor Arcana, 56 cards in number, are parallel to the suits of the playing card deck – swords (spades), wands (clubs), cups (hearts) and pentacles (diamonds). These are also linked to the four elements and represent 'everyday' situations: the Two of Cups, for instance, symbolizes the beginning of a relationship, as cups refer to the emotions. Pentacles are concerned with money and work, swords often concern difficult situations, and wands are to do with energy and communication.

It is a big system and can entail a lifetime of study, but it is used very widely by modern pagans and occultists. It would be hard to find one who has not either studied the Tarot or at least had a Tarot reading at some point. It is also used in New Age thought and work. Tarot's influence pops up in all sorts of areas – from blockbuster movies (for example, the James Bond film *Live and Let Die*) to psychoanalysis. And like the Kabbalah, it links many different groups, people and systems of esoteric thought.

## Astrology

Astrology – the consideration of a person's character and their future by looking at the stars – almost needs no introduction here, since, like divination, it is still one of the most popular forms of magical practice throughout the world today. It and the zodiac are ancient and are found in various forms in most countries. Like other forms of Western magic, such as herbalism, astrology is based on the idea of macrocosm and microcosm: that the movements of the stars and planets can affect human fate. It most likely dates from around the second millennium BC, and derives from calendrical systems used to predict astronomical phenomena. We find astrological precepts among the Babylonians, the Maya, the Chinese and most other civilizations. The stars and their regular motions are a source of perennial fascination to those on Earth.

The first astrological text published in Europe was the *Liber planetis et mundi climatibus* (Book of the Planets and Regions of the World), which appeared between AD 1010 and 1027. It is alleged to have been written by Pope Sylvester II, whose wide-ranging academic interests covered mathematics and astronomy and who reintroduced the abacus and the armillary sphere into Europe. He is also said to have introduced the decimal system, adopting it from Arabic mathematics. European thinkers continued to study astrology from this point on, with considerable debate as to how it should most properly be used.

Astrology has for most of its history been regarded as a scholarly tradition and a respectable study for academics. It is only relatively recently, with the rise of science, that its authenticity as an empirical discipline has been questioned. From the Enlightenment onwards it began to decline, and it is currently regarded by many people as something that is fun and interesting, but not necessarily to be taken very seriously. During the period in British history that we are currently considering, however, it was an accepted part of academic enquiry and many top-ranking political figures relied upon it. We shall use John Dee as a case study.

One of the most famous magicians of the Elizabethan period, Dee was astrologer to Queen Elizabeth I. He may also have been a spy, occasioning exciting possibilities of an early James Bond (rumours about Dee's work for the 'government' were extant as early as the seventeenth century). Born in

1527, Dee was a remarkable man, expert not only in the occult sciences, but in navigation and mathematics. A great deal of his time and energy were directed towards the expansion of the emergent British Empire on Elizabeth's behalf, training explorers in navigation. He was a fellow of Trinity College, Cambridge, and while still in his early twenties was invited to speak at the University of Paris on the subject of Euclid's geometry. In 1554 he was offered a readership in Mathematics at Oxford, but declined to accept it.[5]

Dee was also focused on Hermetic magic and spent much of his life developing a language named Enochian, said to be an angelic tongue channelled by his associate Edward Kelley. He regarded every aspect of his work – astrology, mathematics and the angelic tongue – as being a quest for the universal verities, all parts of a single whole that would explain the underlying mechanisms of reality. It brought him to the attention of people in high places: Elizabeth asked him to choose the date of her coronation, by astrological means, in 1558.

Dee wrote extensively on a variety of subjects, and in 1564 published the *Monas hieroglyphica*, a Kabbalistic interpretation of an esoteric glyph of his own design. Around this time, he also wrote a preface to Henry Billingsley's English translation of Euclid's *Elements* (c. 300 BC), which bears testimony to the esteem with which he was held within the mathematical community. In many ways, he was a typical polymath of his time. Like Newton, he was engaged in both magical and scientific enquiry, the two not being subject to the separation that exists in our own age.

Dee's friend Kelley was a strange man who came to live with him from 1582 until he was ejected by Dee's wife, whom he had apparently annoyed. According to some sources, Kelley's ears had been clipped, suggesting that he had a previous conviction. Kelley turned up again a few months later, announced that he had been operating under a false name and moved in once more. In the 1580s the Dees, Kelley and Kelley's wife went on a trip around Europe, visiting crowned heads, communing with angels and getting up to a number of adventures (wife-swapping was said to have been involved at one point). It is hard to know whether Kelley was a criminal, a lunatic, a visionary or all three.

Dee returned to England to find that his precious library at his house in Mortlake had been ransacked by his brother-in-law, Nicholas Fromond, whom he had left in charge. Elizabeth gave Dee a college position in Manchester but he returned to Mortlake after Elizabeth's death, having little political patronage to fall back on. He died in 1608/9, apparently in penury. His obsidian scrying mirror, which is Aztec in origin, is still to be seen in the British Museum, and a copy of his 'Holy Table' – used for divination – can be found at the History of Science Museum in Oxford.

Other well-known practitioners of this time include Richard Napier, born in Exeter in 1559 and another devotee of angelic magic. Napier, a rector, claimed to communicate with angels such as Raphael and Michael, and combined an interest in angelic magic with astrology, alchemy and medicine. Again, this would not have been particularly unusual at this time, but it was somewhat controversial owing to his clerical role; however, Napier did not come to any censure from the authorities. His papers were subsequently bought after his death by Elias Ashmole, founder of the Ashmolean Museum in Oxford and a friend of the antiquarian John Aubrey and the astrologer William Lilly. Most of Napier's papers are still there today.

Lilly, born in 1602, describes how he became interested in astrology:

> It happened one Sunday 1632, as myself and a Justice of Peace's Clerk were, before Service, discoursing of many Things, he chanced to say, that such a Person was a great Scholar, nay, so learned, that he could make an Almanac, which to me then was strange: One Speech begot another, till, at last, he said, he could bring me acquainted with one Evans in Gun Powder-Alley . . . that was an excellent wise Man, and study'd the Black Art.[6]

This was typical of cunning folk as well: you got to hear about a learned person who knew things, and you learned your trade from them. The line between 'high' magicians and cunning folk is often blurred, as we have noted, and things become further confused because the Church on occasion at least tolerated or ignored the presence of magical practitioners seeking treasure in Church properties. Lilly in his *Life and Times* relates that the king's clockmaker, David Ramsay, hearing of a treasure buried in Westminster Abbey, turned up at midnight with some divining rods and a sack for the treasure (he was, however, allegedly beset by demons and fled). And in Europe 'wandering scholastics', usually penurious students or monks, advertised themselves as treasure seekers and healers and sold amulets, combining learned magic and cunning practice.

Not everyone who took an interest in magic persisted with it, however. The English antiquary Abraham de la Pryme (1671–1704) seems to have become interested in magic as a result of supernatural 'disturbances' at the family home, but he received a stern letter from one Edmund Bohun urging him to cease his enquiries. And apparently he did so.

## Grimoires

With literacy in English increasing among the British population during the Renaissance, and the developing sophistication of printing presses, the printed word was becoming popular and magical texts flourished. The word 'grimoire' is familiar to many people today through works of contemporary fiction. But what is a grimoire?

Etymologists generally consider that the origins of this word are the same as the roots of the word 'grammar'. A grimoire is a grammar of magic: a how-to guide. The term only gained currency in the English language in the early 1800s, with the publication of Francis Barrett's famous grimoire *The Magus*.

> Grimoires are books that contain a mix of spells, conjurations, natural secrets and ancient wisdom. Their origins date back to the dawn of writing and their subsequent history is entwined with that of the religions of Judaism, Christianity and Islam, the development of science, the cultural influence of print, and the social impact of European colonialism.[7]

Such texts appear far back in the history of magic: the Egyptians possessed them (on papyri) and so did the Babylonians (on cuneiform tablets). The magic of both of these cultures, distant though it may seem, does have a relevance to Western magic of the Elizabethan and Renaissance periods and later: names that may be derived from the Babylonians appear in grimoires written in English, and there is some evidence that there are remnants of Egyptian spell work in these texts also. Magic was integral to Egyptian religion, although it tended to focus on minor rather than major deities, with the addition of Hellenic deities such as Hekate. However, the distinction between religion and magic in these ancient times is not precise; while they seem to have been separate to some degree, there is also overlap.

Typically, grimoires contain spells, recipes for making talismans, charms and other magical preparations, and instructions for summoning demons. For example:

> Hundreds of spells, incantations, and omen-inscriptions have been recovered, and these not only enlighten us regarding the class of priests who practised magic, but they tell us of the several varieties of demons, ghosts, and evil spirits; they minutely describe the Babylonian witch and wizard, and they picture for us many magical ceremonies, besides informing us of the names of scores of plants and flowers possessing magical properties, of magical substances, jewels, amulets, and the like. Also they speak of sortilege or the divination of the future, of the drawing of magical circles, of the exorcism of evil spirits, and the casting out of demons.[8]

Some of the demons of the English grimoires appear to derive from the gods of the Chaldeans and Canaanites: Beelzebub/

Baal, Moloch, Ishtar (Astarte). The use of the magic circle, in which the magician works and which we will describe later, turns up in Babylonian magic, too, and may have started there.

Also of relevance to later British magical practice are the Greek Magical Papyri (known as the PGM, from Papyri Graecae Magicae). Dating from Graeco-Roman Egypt of the second century BC to the fifth century AD, these texts contain spells and rituals. Copies began to be seen on the antiquities market in the early nineteenth century, but elements of Egyptian magic seem to have made their way into earlier British texts. Ronald Hutton, in a series of recent talks, refers to elements of Egyptian spellcraft that resurface in the Renaissance period, such as the use of hoopoe's tongues – not a bird native to the British Isles. It is Hutton's contention that Egyptian magic is the engine of much later practice, based on the claim that the Egyptians embraced magic, unlike the Greeks, who often seem to have regarded at least some forms of magic ('low' or Goetic magic as practised by lower-class practitioners) as dubious and dangerous.

Some of these papyri appear to be scholarly, while others are likely to be the personal texts of travelling magicians. They contain material similar to the Greek *defixiones*, or curse tablets. Many of them have references to magical figurines of various kinds. The legacy of these may be the 'poppets' of English witchcraft and the dolls found in traditions such as Vodou.

When you are looking at the history of the grimoire, you are really taking into consideration the mindset of the magician throughout the ages: enquiring, curious, cautious yet experimental, jealously guarding magical secrets and engaged in a continuous process of one-upmanship against other magicians.

As ever, the Church took an ambivalent attitude to these works. Anything that was held to be natural magic (relating to herbs and healing) was tolerated, whereas the 'darker arts' described in many grimoires, such as necromancy and demonology, were proscribed. But the Church was unable to stop ideas and concepts filtering into Britain – the Crusades, for instance, introduced a lot of Arabic magic to the West, such as the text known as the *Picatrix*, which describes celestial magic and the making of talismans. In the sixteenth century books such as the *Key of Solomon* began to circulate (as with many forms of magic, if something is seen to have ancient roots, it benefits from a certain gravitas; the *Key of Solomon* was almost certainly not written by King Solomon). The first book of the *Lemegeton* – or *Lesser Key of Solomon* – is known as the *Goetia* (pronounced Go-ee-sha) and it is from this that much of modern magical work of this kind is taken. According to the writer Pico della Mirandola, there are two forms of magic: Goetia, which relies on contact with demonic forces and is essentially black magic; and theurgy, which is its opposite and relies on contact with divine forces such as archangels and gods.

The *Book of Simon the Magician* (Simon allegedly being a contemporary of Christ) also began to circulate, with a similarly 'ancient' history behind it. All of these grimoires were popular at the time of publication and all are still used by magicians today. We will now look at some of the best-known examples, including two later grimoires, *The Magus* and the *Books of Moses*, which date from the very early nineteenth and late eighteenth century respectively.

## *The Key of Solomon*

Solomon is the epitome of the magician throughout Western magic and acts as a kind of guarantee of efficacy. Texts bearing Solomon's name circulated throughout the Mediterranean region in the early centuries after Christ, and the power of his name continued into the Renaissance period. The *Key* itself probably dates to fourteenth- or fifteenth-century Italy before being translated into English, and it is likely to have been the inspiration for the seventeenth-century *Lesser Key of Solomon*. Jewish Kabbalism and Arabic alchemical practice feed into these texts, as do Graeco-Roman beliefs.

Divided into two books, the *Key* contains details of preparations for magical experimentation, but not – unlike some grimoires – the actual work of spirits. Rigorous preparation on the part of the magician is required, and it is made clear that any results take place through the intervention of God. Everything must be done at the appropriate planetary hour, using very specific materials, words and symbols. Following the instructions given, the practitioner is supposed to be able to perform such operations as becoming invisible, finding treasure (an enduringly popular experiment), summoning demons and more. The second book is also a how-to guide, containing information about which animals are to be sacrificed to the spirits and what magical tools one should use.

## *The Petit Albert*

The 'Little Albert' grimoire, a compilation from various writers (mostly anonymous, although Paracelsus is cited), is somewhat later than the *Key of Solomon* and became popular throughout France during the Enlightenment. As in Britain, this is most likely the result of the impact of affordable printing. The *Petit Albert* contains household tips as well as magical ones, but it also has instructions on how to make the infamous 'Hand of Glory': a dead human hand, taken from a hanged man, mummified in nitre and covered in wax, to be used as a sort of candle. Take it into a building, the spell says, and everyone in it will be rendered motionless. The opportunities for trying this kind of magic were limited, not to mention the questionability of its eventual efficacy, but such practices seeped out into the wider culture, ultimately to be popularized through horror films and novels.

## The Book of St Cyprian

There are a number of grimoires in several European translations attributed to the third-century St Cyprian, supposed to have been a pagan magician who converted to Christianity. These include a Scandinavian version – the 'Black Books' – which are unrelated apart from the story of their common origin. The other versions of the grimoire are comprehensive, containing details of love magic, luck, healing spells, exorcisms, treasure hunting, divination, conjuring demons – all the elements that we associate with the typical grimoire, in fact.

## The Dragon Rouge / Grand Grimoire

Also resulting from the growth in French grimoires following the arrival of affordable printing techniques, the 'Red Dragon' was popular throughout France and, like many other French grimoires, made its way into its African colonies: elements of French works seem to appear in contemporary Vodou. It claims to date back to the sixteenth century but probably derives from the nineteenth, and it also claims to be based on the writings of Solomon. Characteristically, it, too, contains details of how to summon a demon and force it to do one's will: a common goal in certain types of magical practice.

### The Sworn Book of Honorius

Honorius of Thebes is another ancient and probably mythical magician, like Solomon and Cyprian. The grimoire associated with his name contains instructions on gaining visions of hell, heaven and purgatory. It is genuinely old, being mentioned in a trial in 1347, and it is supposed to be the result of a group of magicians agreeing to pool their knowledge – a bit like an encyclopaedia. John Dee owned a copy of this work.

### The Fourth Book of Occult Philosophy

This grimoire draws on Renaissance polymath Heinrich Cornelius Agrippa's (1486–1535) great work, the *Three Books on Occult Philosophy*, but this particular text was written thirty years after his death and uses his name alone. It covers subjects such as geomancy (divination from the configuration of a handful of earth or random dots) and astrology, and some detailed instructions for conjuring spirits. It inspired Francis Barrett's *The Magus*.

## The Magus

Francis Barrett, a magician and balloonist, published this work in 1801. It relies heavily on *The Fourth Book of Occult Philosophy* and was a slow-burner in grimoire terms, being unsuccessful at the time but deeply influential on the occult revival nearly a hundred years later.

## The Sixth and Seventh Books of Moses

This was published quite late in the day in the eighteenth century but is hugely influential. As with other grimoires, it is supposed to have been written by an ancient figure and contains Talmudic references along with psalms and – also in common with many other texts – examples of seals that can be used to contact spirits. Each seal comes with an incantation. It draws on the work of Agrippa and the Kabbalah on the use of the psalms in magic. Deploying biblical scripts for magical purposes was common in British magical practice for centuries.

> Psalm 123.—If your servant or journeyman has run away from you, write this Psalm, together with his name, on a leaden or tin plate, when he will return to you.[9]

This grimoire spread from Germany to America via the Pennsylvania Dutch and was taken up by the African American community. This sort of cultural adoption and spread is what makes tracing the history of grimoire-based magic such a difficult and fascinating task: people exchange information and books across cultures, and practices that we tend to see as being original to a particular community – for example, the sacrifice of black cockerels in some forms of African magic – may actually be French, having come into the colonies from Europe. This particular grimoire was a founding text of Rastafarianism and a lot of Appalachian folk magic stems from it, too. In the 1920s the Nigerian press featured adverts for the *Sixth and Seventh Books*: seen as European magic, it was considerably popular. In Rastafarianism it is referred to as a famous Obeah book (Obeah is a kind of sorcery practised especially in the Caribbean). It might be argued that the grimoire has come full circle with the success of the *Books of Moses*: elements that stem originally from Egyptian papyri returning to Africa with the advent of the European printing press and the spread of grimoires via colonization.

$$))) \bigcirc (((\,$$

As we have seen from the examples above, much of the knowledge contained in grimoires is highly practical. It is designed to obtain certain things for the magician, wealth, power and sex being perennial favourites.

Reputable modern practitioners of this kind of magic generally take a particular attitude towards conjuration. Rather than the view that spirits, angels and demons are there to be summoned, they adopt the approach that conjuration is a working relationship. Modern conjuration is more like a business contract in which you make contact with a spirit and draw up a pact for a limited period, during which you agree to do certain mutual things. For example, if you need money, you can contact a spirit whose speciality is wealth and offer an exchange:

perhaps burning a candle and incense once a week, or making them a specific offering (this does not necessarily mean anything on the scale of animal sacrifice, by the way, and certainly not human sacrifice – several of the spirits of the grimoires require only a small piece of burned bread).

The idea behind this practice is that there is a kind of cosmological chain of command. God is at the summit of this, with the archangels and angels beneath and the cast-out demons and devils some considerable distance below. The angelic hierarchies are very extensive, encompassing thousands of entities – seraphim and cherubim, principalities and thrones, for example. Demonic hierarchies are similar in complexity to angelic hierarchies and vary according to which commentator you happen to read. In the nineteenth-century French *Grimorium verum*, the hierarchy is very similar to a system of line management, with Lucifer, Beelzebub and Astaroth at the top and everyone else divided into a series of lesser ranks – dukes, earls and so on – below them. Lucifer rules Europe and Asia, Beelzebub Africa and Astaroth the Americas. To an extent the grimoires are a mish-mash of different cultures and traditions and can sometimes appear oddly specific. The goetic demon Frimost from the *Grimorium verum*, for example, is said to attend 'the nocturnal assemblies of the Lebanese', which may refer to the influence of heretical sects such as the Druze.

Many people have understandable reservations about dealing with demonic spirits, equating it with Satanism. Theologically, this is not entirely correct, although demonology does come under the heading of 'black magic'. It has attracted an immense amount of negative press over the centuries, sometimes rightly, but a great deal of unnecessary sensationalism has become attached to the issue. Approached with care, demonology can be an interesting and, some argue, productive area of magic.

The classification of demons is itself old, dating back to the *Testament of Solomon* (first millennium AD), among other works. In the *Testament*, Solomon is aided in building his temple by summoning demons via a magical ring given to him by the Archangel Michael. There are numerous ways in which demons can be categorized: in terms of the four elements, the Seven Deadly Sins, the four directions, or by their actions, for instance. The idea of a magical servant who can run around the world doing work for you (bringing you money, finding you a sexual partner, cursing your enemies) is very appealing, particularly to the magician who has little material power. It is easy to see why grimoires were such big sellers, and why even members of the clergy are known to have studied them in secret: they have turned up in private clerical libraries and are documented as having been exchanged between clergymen. Perhaps for this reason, there are 'get-out' clauses in some grimoires: the idea, for instance, that it is not *you* doing the black magic, but the spirits – so they are in the wrong, not you, even though you are dealing with them.

To mitigate the dangers of dealing with demons, grimoires often provide safeguarding advice. Most suggest caution when one is engaged in conjuration. Unlike most modern ritual magic, where you draw a circle and work within it, conjuration typically involves two locations: a circle, in which you stand, and a triangle (perhaps drawn in chalk) a few feet away, in which the spirit is conjured. This is to protect you: if the neophyte magician wishes to conjure something large and scary, she does not want it to appear in the same space as herself. Thus a kind of magical containment field needs to be set up, in which the demon can manifest safely and with less risk to the magician. A 1665 anonymous addition to Reginald Scot's *Discoverie of Witchcraft* (1584, and an alleged account of witchcraft rather than a grimoire) tells us:

> Magitians, and the more learned sort of conjurers, make use of Circles in various manners, and to various intentions. First, when convenience serves not, as to time or place that a real Circle should be delineated, they frame an imaginary Circle, by means of Incantations and Consecrations, without either Knife, Pensil, or Compasses, circumscribing nine foot of ground round about them, which they pretend to sanctifie with words and Ceremonies, spattering their Holy Water all about so far as the said Limit extendeth; and with a form of Consecration following, do alter the property of the ground, that from common (as they say) it becomes sanctifi'd, and made fit for Magicall uses . . .
>
> Let the Exorcist, being cloathed with a black Garment, reaching to his knee, and under that a white Robe of fine Linnen that falls unto his ankles, fix himself in the midst of that place where he intends to perform his Conjurations: And throwing his old Shooes about ten yards from the place, let him put on his consecrated shooes of russet Leather with a Cross cut on the top of each shooe. Then with his Magical Wand, which must be a new hazel-stick, about two yards of length, he must stretch forth his arm to all the four Windes thrice, turning himself round at every Winde, and saying all that while with fervency:

I who am the servant of the Highest, do by the vertue of his Holy Name Immanuel, sanctifie unto my self the circumference of nine foot round about me . . . from the East, Glaurah; from the West, Garron; from the North, Cabon; from the South, Berith; which ground I take for my proper defence from all malignant spirits, that they may have no power over my soul or body, nor come beyond these Limitations, but answer truely being summoned, without daring to transgress their bounds: Worrh. worrah. harcot. Gambalon.

Which Ceremonies being performed, the place so sanctified is equivalent to any real Circle whatsoever. And in the composition of any Circle for Magical feats, the fittest time is the brightest Moon-light, or when storms of lightening, winde, or thunder, are raging through the air; because at such times the infernal Spirits are nearer unto the earth, and can more easily hear the Invocations of the Exorcist.[10]

If things do get out of hand, you can swiftly appeal to the archangel towards the top of the hierarchy. But you should also have a measure of control over the demon in any case, via its sigil or symbol. In most grimoires each demon has a sigil, which constitutes its name and enables you to contact it (a bit like an email address).

Some contemporary demonologists maintain that a demon can be tortured into doing your bidding, for example by setting fire to its parchment sigil. This is a minority belief and practice based on the idea that demons are fallen angels, and that torture is actually doing them good by humiliating them and thus making them more humble so that they can be rehabilitated by the powers of heaven. It is a view that many occultists find distasteful, however.

Something that often gets glossed over when people are discussing demonology is that in most grimoires the angelic powers are generally regarded as being more powerful than those of their opposite numbers. It is also worth noting that a number of contemporary practitioners find that the term 'demon' is too loaded and prefer simply to use 'spirit' instead.

I am going to give an example of a demon here, to illustrate how you are supposed to conjure them. Paimon is a spirit from the Goetia, that form of magical practice which includes demonic conjuration. He is a mediator; you might, for example, wish to conjure him in order to contact other spirits. According to the *Lesser Key of Solomon*, Paimon is a king of hell who governs two hundred legions, half of them from the Angelic Order and half from the Order of Powers. He appears as a man with a woman's face riding a dromedary, and is crowned with a headdress made with precious stones. If Paimon is evoked by sacrifice or libation, he may appear accompanied by Bebal and Abalam. Paimon has a curiously dual role, governing angels as well as demons, as he appears originally to have been one of the cherubim (Agrippa's apprentice, the Dutch occultist Johann Weyer, mentions this). The grimoire describes his summoning:

Note, that at the calling up of him, the exorcist must looke towards the northwest, bicause there is his house. When he is called up, let the exorcist receive him constantlie without feare, let him aske what questions or demands he list, and no doubt he shall obteine the same of him . . .

Looking in the direction of the northwest, a circle must be drawn and the words of the invocation must be spoken aloud in a clear, firm voice as follows:

'I conjure thee Paimon by the power of the everlasting virtue of the highest that thou shalt appear in my presence and do my bidding lest thee suffer the everlasting torment and suffering for thy disobedience.

'Let thee in my presence do no harm that no hair of my head or evil, bodily or ghostly befall me. Let thee in my presence allow no spirit take hold and linger beyond their calling so that thee may suffer for their trespass.

'I conjure thee Paimon that thou shalt act as mediator in my communication and that thou shalt now offer me access to the spirit (name the name of the spirit with which ye wish to communicate) so that I may learn of them and theirs. Fail not in this calling and in thy chains need be let them be bound that they may do what of them I ask and answer all of them that I ask.'[11]

This kind of conjuration is typical of grimoire-based demonology. It requires precise instructions and a magician following these would be familiar with the format of the invocation, the spiritual hierarchy that underpins it, and rules such as what to wear. He might need to take note of the timing (the conjuration might have to take place at a particular planetary hour, for instance). The magic of the grimoires can be complex and needs extensive preparation; as such, it can be contrasted with the simpler folk magic that we will be looking at later.

In closing our remarks on grimoire magic, we should finally note that some magicians may have used grimoires as theoretical as well as how-to guides. Not everyone practises: grimoires may be approached as an intellectual exercise as well as for practical interest.

## Rosicrucianism

We shall end this chapter with a brief excursion into Rosicrucianism. This Renaissance theology, based on an alleged secret society of mystics, holds the seeds of late nineteenth- and twentieth-century esoteric thought. It is based on a set of anonymous writings that appeared between 1607 and 1616, 'built on esoteric truths of the ancient past', which, 'concealed from the average man, provide insight into nature, the physical universe and the spiritual realm'.[12]

In later centuries many esoteric societies claimed to derive their doctrines from much earlier times, and Rosicrucianism was said to have links with Masonry. Several modern Rosicrucian societies that date the beginning of the Rosicrucian Order prior to its first appearance in the seventeenth century are also in existence. Rosicrucianism is said to have originated with a German doctor and mystic, Christian Rosenkreuz, who was apparently born in 1378. This man probably did not exist, but Rosicrucianism seems, from its content, to have been influenced by the work of John Dee, and its writings make reference to alchemical principles, Hermeticism and Kabbalah. In turn, Rosicrucianism inspired the seventeenth-century scientific club known as the Invisible College, of which member John Wallis writes:

> About the year 1645, while I lived in London (at a time when, by our civil wars, academical studies were much interrupted in both our Universities) ... I had the opportunity of being acquainted with divers worthy persons, inquisitive natural philosophy, and other parts of human learning; and particularly of what hath been called the New Philosophy or Experimental Philosophy. We did by agreements, divers of us, meet weekly in London on a certain day and hour, under a certain penalty, and a weekly contribution for the charge of experiments, with certain rules agreed among us, to treat and discourse of such affairs.[13]

We will visit Rosicrucianism again briefly when we come to look at the Masons in the next chapter. However, as a conclusion, we may note the sheer breadth and range of Renaissance magical practice in the British Isles at this time: from Hermeticism, to cunning practice, to grimoire-based demonic conjuration, to Christian mysticism of the kind found among the Rosicrucians. All of these elements continue to intertwine in the centuries that are to come.

# FIVE

# The Georgians

With the Enlightenment and the gradual rise of science, the downscaling (to an extent) of naval conflict with neighbours and the cessation of civil war, England of the eighteenth century was a rather different place to the previous couple of hundred years. It was more prosperous, more peaceful. There was more time for cultivating the mind, for learning, for the pastime that would, in later years, develop into historical research. We see in this period the emergence of embryonic archaeologists and historians taking the time to walk among the nation's landscapes, to wonder. Who *were* the people who built Stonehenge, they asked? Who *were* our ancestors, and the ancient Druids? Richard Polwhele's book on Dartmoor, *Historical Views of Devonshire* (actually written by the Reverend John Swete in 1793), mentions a 'stone row', one of the many which are found on the moor, and presents it as a 'druid way'.

Hermetic magic was still being practised by learned men, though it was somewhat on the wane. Disciplines were beginning to coalesce into more recognizable forms and science was definitely winning – not surprisingly. It is more reliable than magic, more predictable, and predictability and repeatability are the hallmarks of successful attempts to govern reality.

The 'low magic' of the cunning folk was, however, still going strong, in an age where medicine could be costly and ineffective and public services such as we know them were not yet in existence. We find this sort of magical practice throughout the Georgian period; for instance in a case of alleged witchcraft in Silsoe, Bedfordshire.[1] A report in the *British Mercury* newspaper claims that the daughter of a local farmer was found to have swallowed all manner of unsuitable objects, from a pincushion to multiple brass pins and a pair of scissors. Nowadays, this would be seen as a form of disorder, but the *Mercury* relates that it 'was by the ignorant attributed to the power of witchcraft' and a local gardener named Saunders was held responsible. He and his wife were ducked until they nearly drowned. The *Mercury* adds:

About a month since the above mentioned Saunders died, and Mr. Capon's daughter having, through the assistance of the Faculty much recovered in health, the ridiculous notion that her singular conduct was the effect of the super-natural agency of Saunders is amazingly strengthened; for though since April the child had been gradually recovering from a very ill state of health, the untaught multitude obstinately insist that the favourable change is but the natural consequence of the death of Saunders, who notwithstanding the strong prejudice against him was, by the more rational part of his neighbours always considered as an industrious, inoffensive man. Not only in Bedfordshire, but in many other parts of the Kingdom, the absurd notion of the power of witchcraft is as strongly prevalent as at Yatton, Bristol or any part of Somersetshire.[2]

Note that the language used here comes down strongly against any concept of the *reality* of witchcraft. By this time, it is presented as a belief held only by credulous peasants. But people were still being accused of witchcraft throughout the Georgian era, and being punished for it, too, even though the Parliamentary Acts regarding witchcraft were repealed in 1735. While the educated classes might have scoffed at a belief in magic, not everyone shared their view.

## The Return of the Druids

If the history of paganism were a TV series, the Druids would be a bit like *Doctor Who*: a lot of people knew about them, but (probably) no one thought they would ever make a comeback. But return they did, over a thousand years later than their last appearance in Tacitus, in the late seventeenth and eighteenth centuries. Why should a bunch of respectable Georgians suddenly decide to dress up in white robes, carry mistletoe and attend rituals at Stonehenge? William Stukeley (1687–1765) described himself as a Druid, writing a number of popular books about Stonehenge and Avebury, which he depicted as Druid temples. An unorthodox Christian, he suggested that the Druids had been monotheistic (which was almost certainly not the case) and that their beliefs had been very similar to Christianity.

This was also a time of gentlemen's clubs: young men in search of a tribe were looking for new ideas. Some of them found these in writings about ancient Druidry, such as Stukeley's own work, and set up a new group called the Ancient Order of Druids (various versions of this order are still going strong today). It had its first meeting in 1781 in a pub: the Old King's Arms Tavern on Poland Street in London. This was a lot more genteel than the alleged ancient practices of burning people alive or sacrificing them in bogs, of course. It was, in part, for fun. It was a homegrown answer to classical literature: 'Look!' the eighteenth-century Druids were saying. 'We have our own traditions and they are good ones.'

In addition, the Druids were popular with the poets of the era. James Thomson, Alexander Pope and William Collins all featured the Druids in their work, presenting them as children of nature, wise forest-dwellers who lived in harmony with the landscape: an early hippie ideal. Note William Mason's poem *Caractacus*:

> Hark, amid the wond'ring grove
> Other harpings answer clear,
> Other voices meet our ear,
> Pinions flutter, shadows move,
> Busy murmurs hum around,
> Busy vestments brush the ground;
> Round, and round, and round they go,
> Thro' the twilight, thro' the shade,
> Mount the oak's majestic head,
> And guild the tufted mistletoe.[3]

Written in 1759, this refers to an account given of Druidic practice by Pliny in which the writer describes how the Druids gather mistletoe from oaks with a golden sickle. Whether they actually did this or not is doubtful, but the images appealed greatly to the nature-revering writers of the day. In 1774 John

Fisher produced *The Masque of the Druids* and portrayed the eponymous priests as inhabiting an Arcadian paradise ruled over by the goddess Venus. In 1792 the Druids were portrayed as a 'foe to blood' by an anonymous writer and enshrined in Georgian history as gentle philosophers eradicated by the cruel Romans.

In 1772 Druids literally returned to their old stamping ground of the island of Anglesey with the establishment of the Druidic Society, a charitable organization that attracted a number of wealthy residents. The image of the Druid has proved enduringly popular among the Welsh, and the Anglesey society was not the only one to have been formed in the principality. The Society of the Druids of Cardigan was set up around 1779, with the aim of holding 'literary picnics'.

Once again the Druids were perceived through someone else's lens, according to someone else's agenda. This time, they were gentle and benign, devoted to high-minded philosophy and working in conjunction with the natural world. The concept of them in eighteenth-century thought was that of the 'noble savage', a type of person uncorrupted by wicked city ways and retaining an innocence that modern man would do well to emulate, regardless as to whether the 'savage' in question lived hundreds of years ago or on some remote South Sea island. The Druidic idyll was not to last, but it might be argued that it is a rather lovely image, and one which, three hundred or so years later, the Druids still have not quite shaken off.

It would be a mistake to regard the Druid revival as a primarily religious movement, although it did have a strong spiritual component. The interest taken in it was political and romantic: fuel for poetry and literature. And as a gentleman's society, Druidry provided a focus for music and basically having a good time. In Wales there was a distinctly nationalist element, which came to the fore some years later with the revival of the Welsh language event called the Eisteddfod (this is why, when we speak of contemporary Druids, we need to be careful about separating them into pagan Druids and Welsh-language Druids).

So when did the 'new' Druids become religious? For this, we can blame an eccentric individual called Iolo Morganwg (1747–1826). He was, as his name suggests, Welsh, although he was christened Edward Williams. Morganwg was inspired by the political example of the French Revolution and was strongly nationalist and anti-monarchist. On moving to London, he claimed to have been the inheritor of an ancient Druidic tradition originating in the Iron Age. I need hardly add that he made most of this up. However, what he also invented was a series of rituals, initially performed with friends on Primrose Hill on the autumn equinox, September 1792, with Iolo as the sole presiding Druid and the friends as lesser bards and ovates. Iolo proclaimed the 'Gorsedd of the Bards' (the word *gorsedd* means a 'mound' in Welsh) and a small stone circle was erected, with a sword being placed upon a central stone. There is currently a plaque at the top of Primrose Hill celebrating Iolo's achievement.

Iolo Morganwg's example inspired other Welshmen, including the later William Price (1800–1893). A doctor who suffered from a form of mental illness that sent him into frequent rages, Price believed that marriage enslaved women and embarked on a series of unmarried partnerships. Pictures exist of him wearing a bizarre range of costumes, including a sort of astronomical onesie. Price believed in vegetarianism and when his son died he had the boy cremated, in the first instance of anyone doing so in relatively modern times. Price declared himself explicitly to be a Druid.

Back in the eighteenth century, the city of Bath also played a key role in the history of Druidry. The architect John Wood the Elder, who was responsible for much of the spectacular pale-gold architecture for which the city is still famous today, was intrigued by theories about the Druids and incorporated many 'Druidic' elements into his buildings. If you visit Bath and look at the circular group of houses known as the Circus, you will see acorns and panpipes as well as Masonic symbols, and its measurements are allegedly based on the measurements of parts of Stonehenge. Wood's idea of the Druids was more fanciful than anything else, but he was committed to the idea of a pre-Roman culture. The Circus is said to represent the sun, whereas Bath's lovely Royal Crescent, constructed by Wood's son, is supposed to represent the moon. Wood the Elder visited the genuinely ancient stone circle of Stanton Drew, too, and took copious measurements. It was, he asserted, a Druidic university, and he wrote:

And since there is an apparent connection between the ancient works of Akmanchester (Bath) and those of Stantondrui (Stanton Drew), it seems manifest that the latter constituted the University of the British Druids; that this was the university which King Bladud, according to Merlyn of Caledon planted; that it was at Stantondrui the king feated his four Athenian colleagues and that they were not only the heads of the British

Druids in those early ages, but, under Bladud, the very founder of them.[4]

The enthusiasm held by both Woods, father and son, is charming, even if it bears little relationship to whatever the ancient Druids actually believed.

This is not the only time that the Druids made a reappearance. From the Georgian period onwards, societies dedicated to Druidic aims, and Druidic individuals, form a thread throughout British life and culture. Their beliefs and practices may not be pagan as we would describe it today, but these groups and people, from the eighteenth and the nineteenth centuries, form a kind of conceptual bridge between the ancient Druids and twentieth-century revivalists. We shall meet the Druids again later on. But they were not the only Georgian society to have a lasting effect on public views of paganism.

## The Hellfire Club

Whenever we think of the Hellfire Club, we tend to imagine eighteenth-century rakes in doeskin breeches, ravished maidens, a great deal of quaffing of red wine, unspeakably vile acts committed in sinister caverns beneath High Wycombe, and the kind of Devil-worship that would disgrace a Dennis Wheatley cover. I am going to spend some of this chapter looking at the Hellfire Club, because its own origins and practices impact upon the path known as Thelema in the twentieth century.

We begin by noting that there was more than one Hellfire Club. The first was started in London in 1719 by Sir Philip

Wharton, a man of letters and, at the same time, a drunkard and a rake. He had a reputation for horse racing and fighting and once nearly broke a priceless heirloom cup of magical relevance (the 'Luck of Edenhall') at someone else's house by throwing it into the air and failing to catch it.

The Hellfire Club was at this point not particularly sinister, just a men's club that was fairly typical of its time. Grand Tours of the Continent produced clubs devoted to Italian or Turkish culture – or rather, the eighteenth-century idea of those cultures. There were clubs for Tories, for newspaper enthusiasts (the Wet Ink club), for homosexuals and transvestites. There was the Beefsteak Club, which also acquired a dissolute reputation and accusations of Satanism. And of course there were the Druids.

Oxford University was home to the Appalling Club, whose number were held to be members whether dead or alive. It had seven members, all of whom died under tragic circumstances, and who are still said to carouse in Jesus College as ghosts.

Other clubs focused on politics or poetry. A number of them – Wharton's included – were set up as a joke. Wharton's club had the Devil as its president. This version of the Hellfire Club lasted until 1721, when one of Wharton's political enemies, Robert Walpole, put forward a bill against 'horrid impieties' and the club had to close. Wharton subsequently became a Mason and the Grandmaster of England.

> the members came to meetings in assumed characters
> . . . revered figures from the Bible, or saints . . . played
> for laughs. They staged mock rituals making fun of
> Christian dogmas such as the Trinity . . . the menu

included a drink called Hellfire Punch, and dishes
with names such as Holy Ghost Pie, Devil's Loins,
and Breast of Venus [constructed out of small chickens,
with cherries for nipples] . . .[5]

This version of the Hellfire Club came to an end, to be
resurrected some years later. One of its offshoots appeared in
Ireland in 1735, and another Hellfire Club set up home at the
George and Vulture pub in London in the 1730s. This latter
version boasted a remarkable lamp: a crystal globe with a golden
serpent, its tail in its mouth, and a pair of silver dove's wings. It
is Rosicrucian in origin. One of the members of this club was
a young baronet named Sir Francis Dashwood.

The Irish version was nastier and more violent than
Wharton's, and seems to have involved some kind of self-styled
black magic. It was noble – at least temporarily (one of its members murdered a footman and had his peerage revoked). It had
various venues and retreats in which members drank a potion of
whisky, butter and brimstone. Some of the meetings were said
to have been chaired by an enormous black cat of supernatural
origins, which was supposed to have been seen in the house in
question until fairly recently – it is the Killakee Dower House,
one of the most haunted houses in Ireland.

The person with which the Hellfire Club is most commonly
linked in the public mind is, however, Sir Francis Dashwood.
He was born in 1708 and gained his baronetcy when just
sixteen, on the death of his father. As a very young man, he
undertook the Grand Tour. It is probable that he became a
Mason during his Continental journey. He was taken to a variety of religious sites by his pious tutor, and apparently his usual

reaction to these was to laugh. He was involved in an episode in Rome where penitents came to a chapel service to flagellate themselves with miniature scourges; Dashwood strode up and down the church aisle with a horsewhip.

From accounts of the time, he was fairly representative of his day and age – cultivated and well-educated, but also jolly and prone to practical jokes, and a bit hapless. He certainly does not come across as sadistic or cruel, apart possibly from the horsewhipping episode. He had strong artistic tastes and an enthusiasm for women. He spoke plainly, confessed an inability to focus on difficult problems and said that mathematics defeated him.

In 1732, having returned to England, Dashwood set about enjoying London. He bought books on magic and possibly on sex from the notorious bookseller Edmund Curll. He set up the Society of Dilettanti, based around a common interest in Italy. This club met once a month and everyone dressed up in fancy costumes in which their portraits were painted. There was a certain amount of ceremonial regalia, including a staff wound about with serpents. In 1744 Dashwood founded the Divan Club, based on Turkish culture. The only criterion for membership of each club was that you had to have visited Italy or Turkey respectively.

Dashwood married Sarah, a rich widow, and became an MP in 1741. He was not a particularly successful politician, but his heart was in the right place: he tried to put through a bill of public works, for instance, to combat unemployment, and later provided funding for having the caves at West Wycombe excavated for a road-building programme. It is debatable whether the district needed it, but there was a lot of unemployment in the region and Dashwood was trying to provide some work for local men.

In 1751 he leased Medmenham Abbey on the Thames from a friend and had it rebuilt in a late Gothic style, popular at the time. The motto 'Fait ce que voudras' was placed over the door, taken from the sixteenth-century work *Gargantua and Pantagruel* by Rabelais. This motto has since become famous, or infamous, among ceremonial magicians after Aleister Crowley set up his own Thelemic Abbey with the mission statement 'Do what you wilt shall be the whole of the law / love is the law / love under will.'

Dashwood set up another club, the Brotherhood of Saint Francis of Wycombe, in 1752. It was not well attended, so they changed the name of the club to the Monks of Medmenham, again lampooning the idea of the closed, celibate austerity of a monastery. After this, the monks held regular meetings. They did not refer to themselves as the Hellfire Club, either at the time or later. The name, which comes from the earlier societies, came into use later via the popular press.

Membership varied, as with all clubs, but its core members were said to number thirteen, like a coven. They included Dashwood's brother, John Dashwood-King; John Montagu, Earl of Sandwich; satirical journalist John Wilkes; George Bubb Dodington, Baron Melcombe; Paul Whitehead; and a collection of the local lesser gentry and professional men. A lot of these people were in the public eye and scandal would have accrued to them, just as politicians attract rumour and scandal today.

One notable associate of the club, and a Mason, was Founding Father Benjamin Franklin. Along with Franklin,

Dashwood revised the Book of Common Prayer, which is an unlikely undertaking for an alleged Satanist (accusations of Satanism and orgies became attached to the Hellfire Club much later in the nineteenth century).

Apart from the aristocratic adventuress Lady Mary Wortley Montagu, women were not allowed as members per se, but they apparently did attend. There is a suggestion that the ladies dressed as nuns, which would obviously have been more shocking in that day and age than in this one. However, one contemporary account says that the monks were asked to bring along women 'of a cheerful and lively disposition, to improve the general hilarity'. Some may have been prostitutes – it is estimated that one in five women of the Georgian period worked in the sex trade in some capacity – but many may well have been friends or locals. A couple of the women were apparently the mistresses of noblemen and another was Lady Betty Germain, who owned one of John Dee's scrying stones, suggesting that she had at least a passing interest in the occult.

It is highly unlikely that the club worshipped the Devil, and there is no evidence of actual orgies. Horace Walpole, who did not like Dashwood, says that they worshipped Bacchus and Venus, but whether he means they actually venerated these deities or whether they did so metaphorically, in the sense that wine and women were frequent features of these events, is unclear. Dashwood had a number of statues erected in the gardens, including Venus and Bacchus, but also Daphne, Flora and Priapus. To Dashwood and his classically educated contemporaries, these would have been familiar figures. There is also a lot of evidence that Dashwood was taking things like sacred geometry fairly seriously, as his later building works show.

Harpocrates – the Egyptian god who entreats silence by placing a finger to his lips – presided over the refectory, and Dashwood may have encountered him on the Continent: a medal was struck which featured Harpocrates to celebrate the assumption of the Earl of Middlesex to the English lodge in Florence. Angerona, a Roman goddess, was at the other end of the dining room, making a similar gesture.

Radical journalist and politician John Wilkes, a member of Medmenham, wrote: 'No profane eye has dared to penetrate into the English Eleusinian mysteries of the chapter-room, where the monks assembled on all solemn occasions, the more secret rites were performed and libations poured forth in much pomp to the BONA DEA.'[6] Author Michael Howard has interpreted this mention of the Bona Dea, or 'good goddess', to mean that Dashwood practised Druidic rites, for which he was allegedly expelled from the eighteenth-century Druidic revival group An Ulieach Druidh Braithreachas in 1743.

So far it sounds like an informal coven, with Wilkes making explicit reference to the Eleusinian mysteries, the idea of which would have been familiar to anyone with a classical education. It is likely, though, that the spiritual allegiances of the Hellfire Club harked back to Masonry and the Templars. There is more than a whiff of ceremonial magic about their apparent undertakings: the library at Medmenham had a book on Kabbalism, so Dashwood would presumably have been aware of the basics of the Kabbalah.

The English author Nathaniel Wraxall writes in 1815 of black baptisms, the sprinkling of sulphur, inverted crucifixes, blood-red wafers and the like, but Wraxall was writing at a considerably later period. Geoffrey Ashe, in his history of the Hellfire Club, writes:

> The morbid or puerile anti-Christianity that goes in for Black Masses and deliberate evil seems foreign to the Medmenham kind and there is no hint of it in the more trustworthy materials. Members of a society that carried on where the Dilettanti left off may well have dabbled in Italianate sorcery, and may well have done so in the free milieu of the Abbey.[7]

By the 1760s the people involved in Medmenham were increasingly involved in the political affairs of the day and the Hellfire Club ran out of steam. A lot of its original members were old or dead. There is, however, a suggestion that the rites went on in the caves under High Wycombe. Commentators on the Hellfire Club have suggested that the caves are based on a Trionfi system, that is, on the Tarot trumps, so that in progressing through the caves, you move through the trumps of the Major Arcana and their various archetypes. The caves contain a banqueting hall said to have been lit by the Rosicrucian lamp that once hung in the George and Vulture inn, and which apparently made its eventual way into the hands of the founder of Wicca, Gerald Gardner. Running through the caves is a small rivulet, the Styx, which was once crossed by boat and whose name has obvious classical allusions.

The last we hear of public events at Medmenham was an episode in 1770 involving the Chevalier d'Éon de Beaumont, a transgender French secret agent who was purportedly involved with the Hellfire Club. Dashwood himself was moving on.

Medmenham was sold and Dashwood built a church at West Wycombe with a massive golden ball on top, which is still in place today. He also built a hexagonal mausoleum in which George Bubb Dodington's body was placed, and later that of Dashwood's wife Sarah. He improved his own gardens and opened them to the public, including a Temple of Bacchus, which was opened with a pagan rite. Members of the old club were gradually succumbing to mortality, including the steward, Paul Whitehead, who burned all his papers just before he died and gave instructions to Dashwood for his heart to be placed in an urn in the mausoleum. It used to be shown to visitors but someone stole it in the 1830s. Dashwood himself died in 1781.

## Freemasonry

The Hellfire Club is of interest, but it was not the only organization of its day to influence contemporary paganism: there was a group around at this time that had far greater reach and impact and which is still very much in evidence today. It is time for us now to look at Freemasonry.

Once again, we find ourselves examining a set of beliefs and practices that cannot be considered pagan, yet which substantially influence pagan and occult thought in our own day. The history of the Masons is an enormous subject, plagued with disagreement and rife with speculation. The likelihood is that it emerged from the stonemasons' guilds of the Middle Ages and developed into a gentlemen's organization during the early eighteenth century. There are early Masonic texts from the fourteenth century which suggest that the actual craft of Masonry began in Egypt with Euclid. Later texts link it to Solomon's Temple, and in the late 1700s William Preston claimed that it had Druidic roots. Masonry weaves in and out of esoteric British thought for hundreds of years, although in itself it is not a religious organization: it references a 'Great Architect' (God), but it is not supposed to discriminate against members' actual religions or to replace them, despite claims by Christian fundamentalists that it is a Satanic sect.

> English Freemasonry in the eighteenth century was frankly humanitarian and convivial. The degree work was comparatively insignificant. The passing from labor to refreshment was quickly accomplished, and the evening spent in hilarious good fellowship, during which innumerable churchwardens (the long clay pipes of the period) were smoked, and many bowls of bishop emptied; songs and glees were sung, and speeches made.[8]

William Hogarth, in his painting *Night* (1736), caricatures the results of these convivial habits of the brethren. The English Masons linked up the Craft with the ancient building guilds; the Continental brethren attributed the origin of the order to the Knights Templar, who went to Palestine to recover the Holy Sepulchre from the Infidels, and there became indoctrinated with the mysticism of the East; others contended that Masonry was derived from Rosicrucianism. The fraternity in France and Germany attracted many educated men who, having abandoned the dogmas of the historic Church, sought sanctuary for their philosophical tenets in Freemasonry. It was the Chevalier Ramsay, a Scotsman, who in 1737 first broached the Templar origin of Masonry, claiming among other things that the order was closely connected with the mysteries of Ceres at Eleusis, Isis in Egypt and Minerva at Athens.[9] Here, we begin to see Masonry linked to some very distant spiritual disciplines, and this association has been going on ever since.

Sir Philip Wharton became Grand Master of the Premier Grand Lodge of England in 1723, which is of note because, as we have seen, he was also the founder of a version of the Hellfire Club. He later joined an anti-Masonic group that parodied the practices of Masonry, though it is not clear what his motivations were. Benjamin Franklin – also associated with Dashwood's Hellfire Club – became a Grand Master in the U.S. (I would not be inclined to read anything too sinister into all this, by the way.)

Masonry has a grade system for its members. In the early 1700s its new constitution mentions the Entered Apprentice as being the first grade, followed by the Fellowcraft/Master. The third grade, or degree, was in place by about 1730. Nowadays, different Masonic systems have slightly different degrees but there can be a lot of them – all the way up to the 33rd degree.

This is important for us to know because magical lodges ever since have been basing their grade systems on that of the Masons. This does not mean that Masonry itself is a magical organization. But its structure was both a springboard and a model upon which people with an interest in the occult, mainly male, could base their own organizations, and it was not long before Masonry began to intertwine with magic. We have, for example, the curious case of the Count de Cagliostro, an Italian nobleman who arrived in London in 1776 with a lot of money and a countess in tow. He was supposed to be a Rosicrucian and an alchemist, and he managed to predict some winning lottery numbers by apparently Kabbalistic means, which brought him to the attention of the authorities. He was imprisoned for a short time and left England, but before he did so, he joined one of the London Masonic lodges.

Deeply immersed in mystical doctrines, Cagliostro determined to found an Egyptian Rite of Freemasonry upon the first three degrees of the Fraternity, in which magical practices were to be perpetuated. According to the Inquisition biographer he borrowed his ideas for the ritual from an obscure spiritist, George Coston, whose manuscript he accidentally picked up in a bookshop in London. But of this there is no evidence.

In his magical seances, Cagliostro made use of a young boy or young girl in the state of virgin innocence, to whom power was given over the seven spirits that surround the throne of the divinity and preside over the seven planets. The boy or girl would kneel in front of a globe of clarified water placed upon a table, covered with a black cloth embroidered with Rosicrucian symbols, and Cagliostro, making strange mesmeric passes, would summon the angels of the spheres to enter the globe; whereupon the youthful clairvoyant would behold the visions presented to his or her view, and often describe events taking place at a distance.

Many eminent persons testified to the genuineness of the feats performed. This is what is called 'crystal vision' by students of psychical research, although the object employed is usually a ball of rock crystal and not a globe of water, such as Cagliostro used. The Society for Psychical Research has shown that persons in a state of partial or complete hypnosis frequently develop clairvoyant and telepathic powers. The crystal is used to promote hypnosis, also to visualize the images that appear in the mind. Undoubtedly Cagliostro was an accomplished mesmerizer. He possessed remarkable psychic powers which he confessed that he did not understand. But, like many mediums who have such gifts, he sometimes resorted (if his enemies are to be believed) to trickery and sleight-of-hand to accomplish results when the real power was not forthcoming.[10]

After this, Cagliostro had an eventful career across Europe and was eventually brought to trial, claiming to have been an initiate of the Illuminati. And so a thousand Internet conspiracy theories were launched – their seeds go back to the eighteenth century and before.

Victorian Mason and occultist A. E. Waite, writing a century or so later, describes the Egyptian Rite thus:

Egyptian Masonry was . . . conferred upon both sexes – apparently in separate temples. It was intended to replace the Craft, which offered a vestige only of the true mystery and a shadow of the real illumination; but in order to secure the end more certainly, according to the mind of Cagliostro, the Masonic qualification was required of his male candidates . . . The statutes and regulations of the Royal Lodge of Wisdom Triumphing, being the Mother Lodge of High Egyptian Masonry for East and West, specify three grades as comprised by the system. These were Egyptian Apprentice, Egyptian Companion or Craftsman, and Egyptian Master. At the end of his experience the candidate is supposed to have exterminated vice from his nature; to be acquainted with the True Matter of the Wise, through intercourse with the Superiors Elect who encompass the throne of the Sublime Architect of the Universe. These intelligences are seven angels, who preside over the seven planets, and their names, most of which are familiar in ceremonial magic, were said to be as follows: Anael, the angel of the Sun; Michael, the angel of the Moon; Raphael, who was allocated to Mars; Gabriel, referred to Mercury; Uriel, the angel of Jupiter; Zobiachel, attributed to Venus; and Anachiel, the ruler of Saturn.

In the grade of neophyte, the candidate was prepared in a vestibule containing a representation of the Great Pyramid and the figure of Time guarding a cavern. He was introduced into the temple in virtue of his ordinary Masonic titles and as a seeker for the true Masonry possessed by the wise of Egypt. He knelt before Cagliostro, who posed as the Grand Copht, founder and Master of the Rite in all parts of the globe, and the Master . . . breathed upon him. This took place not only amidst the swinging of censers but the recital of exorcisms to effect moral regeneration. He was instructed in seven philosophical operations: (1) in connection with health and disease in man; (2) on metals and the medicines thereof; (3) on the use of occult forces to increase natural heat and that which the alchemists term the radical humidity of things; (4) on the liquefaction of the hard; (5) on the congelation of the liquid; (6) on the mystery of the possible and impossible; and (7) on the means of doing good with the utmost secrecy.[11]

Cagliostro seems to have been one of those types, part-charlatan, part-genius, whom we meet throughout magical practice across the centuries. Iolo Morganwg was another. They repeatedly pop up in the history of paganism and they are fascinating, perhaps because of the amount of dissent and chaos that they leave behind them. I am quoting A. E. Waite at length above because he was so enmeshed in the Golden Dawn, which we will look at in the next chapter. Cagliostro's Egyptian Rite shares a lot of elements with Golden Dawn rituals: the Egyptian focus, the admittance of women (which mainstream Masonry still does not allow), the working with angelic forces and the undercurrent of alchemy. Magical lodges based on forms of the Egyptian Rite are still around today, such as the Ancient and Primitive Rite of Memphis-Misraïm.

The founders of the Golden Dawn were all Freemasons and adopted some of the structure of Masonry, combined with Rosicrucianism and other forms of Hermetic magic. Aleister Crowley claimed to have attained the 33rd degree in Mexico, but he is not recognized as a Mason by the Grand Lodge of England (understandably). Nonetheless, the structure of Masonry found its way into the organization that he developed and which is still going strong today: the Ordo Templi Orientis.

Gerald Gardner was also a Mason and borrowed elements of it when he began to put modern Wicca together: blindfold-ing initiates, an emphasis on secrecy (which might just have been simple caution) and the degree system. Wicca has three degree grades, and so does contemporary Druidry, which has in turn borrowed heavily from Wicca. When my partner and I attended a Masonic dinner some years ago, we were amused and intrigued to find some familiar phrases in the accompanying literature. (As an aside, my partner was considered for Masonic membership but was blackballed by one elderly member of the lodge because of his associations with witchcraft – this is contrary to Masonic guidelines and several Masons left the lodge over it.) Both Masonry and Wicca employ tools: Masons use a compass to touch the chest of the initiate, Wiccans use a sword. Even one of the better-known Wiccan catchphrases, 'so mote [must] it be', probably comes from Masonry:

> Christ then of his high grace,
> Save you both wit and space,
> Well this book to know and read,
> Heaven to have for your mede [reward].
> Amen! Amen! so mote it be!
> So say we all for charity.

This little rhyme comes from the Halliwell Manuscript, probably written in the fourteenth century, which is described by some Masons as the oldest genuine record of Masonry that we know. It tells the story of the beginnings of Masonry (allegedly in ancient Egypt, as we have seen), and claims that the 'craft' came to England during the time of King Athelstan, during the 900s.

In researching this issue, I looked up some of the more sensational evangelical Christian sites online that purport to 'expose' links between Masonry and Wicca. Despite the lurid claims that some of these sites make, they are essentially correct: there is a connection and it comes via the number of Masons who went on to found their own orders and lodges, such as Gardner. Generally, if you are the sort of person who likes to belong to secret societies, you are the sort of person who likes to belong to several of them, and you may also be the sort of person who falls out with your original lodge and goes off to start something better of your own. This was certainly the case with Crowley, for instance.

However, the connections between Masonry and Wicca remain a thorny issue among some Masons and occasionally emerge as a controversy. One of the American Lodges issued a diktat against admitting Wiccans in 2012 (probably owing to a Christian bias on the part of the Grand Master), which elicited the following comment from Masonic writer Christopher Hodapp:

> A question that pops up from time to time on Masonic forums and in lodge has to do with the requirement of a petitioner to believe in a 'supreme being' and whether Wicca qualifies as such a belief. Undoubtedly, part of the trepidation by some Masons to accept Wicca as a religion has to do with seeing inverted pentacles drawn on floors by hooded devil-worshippers in too many old *Night Gallery* reruns. Curiously, these same brethren generally have no problem with the inverted pentacle of the Order of the Eastern Star.[12]

It is likely, however, that Freemasonry and the various pagan and esoteric paths that have based themselves upon it will continue to maintain their uneasy truce with occasional hostile outbreaks for some years to come.

Let us now look at some important individuals of the eighteenth century who have had an effect on modern practice. Of these, the foremost is William Blake.

## William Blake

Blake is highly regarded within the contemporary occult world and seen by many people as a true visionary. Born in 1757, he lived and worked in London and its environs, and his extraordinary paintings and verse continue to inspire us today. It is hard to classify him: William Rossetti refers to him as a 'glorious luminary' and it is accurate to say that Blake was a truly individual and independent thinker. He had his influences – the Hermeticist Emanuel Swedenborg was one – but he forged his own way in all matters, from art to poetry to religious thought, and he was himself an influence on younger artists and spiritual seekers, such as Samuel Palmer (1805–1881).

It should be noted that Blake was working within the Christian tradition. He was not himself a pagan, but neither was he an advocate of mainstream religion and some of his ideas derive from Greek and Norse mythology as well as biblical precedent. He did not agree with Newtonian scientific philosophy and his view of the world is that of the visionary: a world in which God and angels and even Satan himself are visible to those who are capable of seeing them. He had his first vision at the age of four, in which God looked in at the window, terrifying the infant Blake, and later, walking through Peckham, he claimed to have seen 'a tree filled with angels, bright angelic wings bespangling every bough like stars'. Also when he was four, he told his parents he had seen the prophet Ezekiel under the bed. He believed that his inspiration came from archangels, who subsequently enjoyed his works. In 1800 he wrote to his contact John Flaxman that

> Felpham is a sweet place for Study, because it is more spiritual than London. Heaven opens here on all sides her golden Gates; her windows are not obstructed by vapours; voices of Celestial inhabitants are more distinctly heard, & their forms more distinctly seen; & my Cottage is also a Shadow of their houses. My Wife & Sister are both well, courting Neptune for an embrace . . . I am more famed in Heaven for my works than I could well conceive. In my Brain are studies & Chambers filled with books & pictures of old, which I wrote & painted in ages of Eternity before my mortal life; & those works are the delight & Study of Archangels.[13]

One gets the impression that for Blake, the world was a magical place, full of wonders, and in ways he seems to have seen little difference between the angels he witnessed and the people whom he met in the streets; they were different in scale and nature, but both were equally real. In later years, W. B. Yeats was influenced by his work, and there is a sense that it infuses later occult writing and art: he influenced Crowley's work as well, and the woman who illustrated Crowley's Thoth Tarot deck, artist Lady Frieda Harris.

## Francis Barrett

Barrett (b. *c.* 1770–80) is regarded as one of the Georgian era's principal occultists. His book *The Magus*, that we considered in our section on grimoires, is still in print. It draws heavily from Cornelius Agrippa, developing his ideas for the nineteenth century. Barrett's aim was to establish an occult school, and he gave classes in magic from his flat:

> The Purpose of this school (which will consist of no greater number than Twelve Students) being to investigate the hidden treasures of Nature; to bring the Mind to a contemplation of the Eternal Wisdom; to promote the discovery of whatever may conduce to the perfection of Man; the alleviating the miseries and calamities of this life, both in respect of ourselves and others; the study of morality and religion here, in order to secure to ourselves felicity hereafter; and, finally, the promulgation of whatever may conduce to the general happiness and welfare of mankind.[14]

A bit more ambitious than Hogwarts, although you would be studying some of the same subjects if you passed your OWLS:

> Those who become Students will be initiated into the choicest operations of Natural Philosophy, Natural Magic, the Cabbala, Chemistry, the Talismanic Arts, Hermetic Philosophy, Astrology, Physiognomy, etc., etc. Likewise they will acquire the knowledge of the Rites, Mysteries, Ceremonies and Principles

of the ancient Philosophers, Magi, Cabbalists, and Adepts, etc.[15]

Some of Barrett's ideas about magic were relatively sophisticated and are still found within contemporary occultism, notably the concept of bringing about changes in reality in accordance with the will: 'The magical power is in the inward or inner man. A certain proportion of the inner man longs for the external in all things. When the person is in the appropriate disposition an appropriate connection between man and object can be attained.'[16] Barrett can be regarded as a link in the chain between the world of the Renaissance grimoire magician and the magical societies of the nineteenth century.

))○((

How might we sum up the eighteenth century in terms of paganism and magic? We find a substantial amount, still, of the cunning type of magic at the lower levels of society. Science is by and large becoming the dominant discourse, replacing religious views of the universe. Gentlemen are setting up and joining clubs, mainly for reasons other than the development of their spirituality, although some of these clubs have esoteric elements and, as we have seen, go on to influence the development of more overtly occult societies in later years. The continued rise of the printing press and published books make some unusual subjects, such as Kabbalism, accessible to a wider audience. Where magical practice does exist, however, it remains Christian in terms of its influences, with little if any trace of its pagan roots. But people are beginning to become more interested in our ancient pagan ancestors such as the Druids, and to revive their practices within a Christian context.

As a final note on this period, there is another type of magic that began to increase in popularity during the eighteenth century: stage magic, also known as conjuring. People had been doing conjuring tricks for hundreds of years, sometimes under the guise of 'real' magic, but in Britain conjurors such as Isaac Fawkes began to successfully present their tricks to fashionable audiences. Fawkes and others explicitly denounced the supernatural, asserting that their shows were for entertainment only. Fawkes, who performed in smart clothes and a powdered wig, made thousands of pounds from his trade. It is hard to see how he could have achieved this in an earlier age when the idea of real magic had not yet been challenged by science.

We may note, too, this proposed (and unsuccessful!) amendment to the Witchcraft Act, suggested in 1770:

An Act to protect men from being beguiled into marriage by false adornments. All women, of whatever rank, age, profession or degree, whether virgins, maids or widows, that shall, from and after such Act, impose upon, seduce or betray into matrimony, any of His Majesty's subjects, by the scents, paints, cosmetic washes, artificial teeth, false hair, Spanish wool, iron stays, hoops, high-heeled shoes and bolstered hips, shall incur the penalty of the law in force against witch-craft and like misdemeanours and that the marriage upon conviction shall stand null and void.[17]

This is almost certainly a droll snipe at the fashion industry rather than the figure of the witch, although it may arguably betray an underlying fear of female sexuality.

# SIX

# The Victorians

The general reader might not necessarily think of the Victorian period as being a significant epoch in the history of the occult, given popular perceptions of its staunch Christianity and puritanical attitudes, but this would be incorrect. It is possible to claim that the bulk of the twentieth-century pagan revival started in the nineteenth century, with pre-Victorian poets such as those within the Romantic movement, now-obscure writers like William Harrison Ainsworth and Charles Leland, and many who are still well known today, such as Charles Kingsley and Kenneth Grahame. It also saw the work of occultists such as Éliphas Lévi and that powerhouse of modern occultism, the Hermetic Order of the Golden Dawn. Revivalist Druids also made appearances throughout the Victorian period.

This was also the era of ideas coming from the East, brought in by people such as Madame Blavatsky. It was the century in which Aleister Crowley, 'the Great Beast', was born. One might argue that a combination of relative affluence, a reasonable amount of leisure time, colonialism and a reaction to Victorian religious repression all contributed to this outpouring of spiritual experimentation. Whatever the cause, several of the Victorian organizations that had a substantial influence on later occultism and paganism are still around today, such as the Theosophical Society, plus offshoots of the Golden Dawn itself.

I am going to look at these organizations shortly, but first I am going to devote some attention to an overview of the nineteenth century's early literary scene, with poets and popular novelists contributing to the emergence of what we might term a pagan sensibility. This is perhaps ironic since, as we have seen, the pagan societies of early Britain were mute in literary terms, but the people who later drew upon them for inspiration used literary forms as their principal means of expression. And of course, many of these writers carried on with the classical interests of the previous century, reframing the Greek and Roman gods and goddesses within a British pastoral context.

## The Romantic Poets

The Romantic poets were enthralled by the pagan deities of the classical world. (For a fuller account of this part of paganism's literary heritage, I would recommend Ronald Hutton's *Triumph of the Moon* of 1999, which explores much of the work of the late Romantics.) Stephen Hebron points out:

> In the Romantic period it was taken for granted that the intellectual and artistic achievement of ancient Greece and Rome was one of the foundations of western culture. The Classical world permeated almost every aspect of life, from political institutions and philosophical enquiry to scientific method and the basic forms of architecture. The classics of Latin literature,

such as Virgil's *Aeneid*, the *Odes of Horace* and Ovid's *Metamorphoses*, were standard texts.[1]

Samuel Taylor Coleridge was made a 'Grecian' scholar at school, having been found reading Virgil for fun, although according to Ronald Hutton he did not think it was particularly healthy to become too fond of classical paganism. Thomas Love Peacock signed off his letters 'in the name of Pan'. John Keats decided to translate the *Aeneid* into English at a similar age to Coleridge, and Shelley translated Plato's *Symposium* as an adult. Classical literature imbued the backgrounds of these people: relating one's own work to Greek or Roman preoccupations would have been second nature. After hearing Keats read from *Endymion*, William Wordsworth (who shared Coleridge's views on the matter) commented that it was 'a Very pretty piece of Paganism'.[2]

A review in *Blackwood's Edinburgh Magazine* was sarcastic, however:

> From his prototype Hunt, John Keats has acquired a sort of vague idea, that the Greeks were a most tasteful people, and that no mythology can be so finely adapted for the purposes of poetry as theirs. It is amusing to see what a hand the two Cockneys make of this mythology; the one confesses he has never read the Greek Tragedians, and the other knows Homer only from Chapman; and both of them write about Apollo, Pan, Nymphs, Muses, and Mysteries, as might be expected from persons of their education.[3]

So the use of classical inspiration was not uncontentious, but it was definitely a prevailing theme. Shelley's 'Hymn of Pan' is one example, written in 1820 as part of Mary Shelley's play *Midas*, but not the first: Thomas Taylor had already translated the Orphic 'Hymn to Pan' in 1792. Keats used supernatural entities freely throughout his own poetry; *Lamia* is one such example. His work is peopled with nymphs and dryads, the nature spirits of ancient Arcady, and we know that he read a copy of *The Examiner* in 1817 in which pagan religions were discussed, because he mentioned it in a letter to his friend Leigh Hunt, who was staying with the Shelley family at the time. Shelley himself had been engaging in some kind of informal cult of Pan and famously remarked in a letter to Thomas Jefferson Hogg:

> I hope you paid your devotions as usual to the Religio Loci, and hung up an evergreen. If you all go on so, there will be a hope some day . . . a voice will be heard along the water saying 'The Great God Pan is alive again', – upon which the villagers will leave off starving, and singing profane hymns, and fall to dancing again.[4]

Shelley also mentions raising a 'small turf altar to the "mountain-walking Pan"', in another letter from 1821.

It is hard to know to what degree these poets and writers actually believed in the old gods and goddesses, or whether, as is more likely, they regarded them as useful metaphors or charming conceits, but in a sense this does not matter to contemporary paganism, which takes a similarly loose ontological view. What does matter is that these ideas and images filtered into the culture of the nineteenth and twentieth centuries: most Britons over the age of thirty were taught the Romantic poets in school, for instance, and this is why so many people in the UK at least are familiar with some of the basic Greek myths. Most contemporary pagans do not, however, worship the Greek gods unless they themselves happen to be Greek, although there is an emerging Hellenic polytheistic movement in the United States at the moment and a couple of groups devoted to Hekate internationally. But what has been bequeathed to us by nineteenth-century literature is a particular sensibility towards the natural world.

## Leland and Ainsworth

We devote a section now to two Victorian writers: mid-nineteenth-century American folklorist Charles Leland and the popular novelist William Harrison Ainsworth. Very few people outside the esoteric world have heard of either man these days. They are writers who have largely vanished from the literary canon, and although many pagans are familiar with Leland, Ainsworth is still less well known. However, their work is important to contemporary paganism because a central part of Wiccan belief derives from them.

Charles Leland (1804–1903) was a Pennsylvania-born writer, humorist and folklore specialist who travelled extensively. His interest in magical practice began early: he related that after his birth his nurse took him up to the attic and performed a ritual involving a Bible, a key, a knife, lighted candles, money and salt to ensure that he would have a long life as a 'scholar and a wizard'. Given that he died at the age of 99,

I think we could say that the nurse knew her stuff – assuming Leland was not making this up. He studied Algonquin and Romany culture, becoming president of the English Gipsy Lore Society in 1888. Like many of the people whom we have considered, Leland's reliability as a historian and the rigour of his methodology are open to debate, but his influence is undoubted.

In Gardnerian Wicca, the Horned God is the consort of the goddess. But who are these deities? Like Herne the Hunter, the goddess of the witches also has literary origins, and some of them lie in Leland's work. Leland published *Aradia; or, The Gospel of the Witches* in 1899, and while some have questioned its legitimacy, it contains what he believed to be the religious text of a group of pagan witches in Tuscany, documenting their beliefs and rituals.

The text is composed of Leland's translation of an Italian manuscript, the *Vangelo* (Gospel), to which he claimed to have been alerted by a local expert on Italian witchcraft. He called this woman 'Maddalena' and described her as a witch. In addition, he did some of his own research into Italian folklore. Maddalena apparently told Leland about the *Vangelo* in 1886 but it was over a decade before he was able to get his hands on a copy, and then several years before he could publish it, after translating it.

*Aradia* is written in fifteen chapters that deal with Italian witchcraft and spells. It is named after the 'goddess' of the witches who comes to the mortal world to help the peasants fight their oppressors with magic. The book begins with the tale of Aradia's birth: she is the daughter of Diana and Lucifer, who is described as a god of the sun, the moon and of light. Diana tells Aradia to

. . . go to earth below
To be a teacher unto women and men
Who fain would study witchcraft.[5]

Aradia therefore comes down to Earth and makes a vow to
her followers that

ye shall all be freed from slavery,
And so ye shall be free in everything.[6]

Once she returns to her mother's realm, however, Aradia still
has the power to make spells come true, and thus witches can
appeal to her for help. A large part of the book is made up of
spells and rituals.

*Aradia* was not widely known until the 1950s, when it
was picked up by Gardnerian Wiccans. Is it really a part of
genuine Italian witchcraft? This is very hard to say. Aradia
herself may derive from a classical figure named Herodias,
originally Herod's wife and later one of the nymphs in the
train of the moon goddess Diana, who were said in folklore
to fly across Italy. 'Maddalena' herself seems to have really
existed under a different name: she was probably a fortune-
teller named Margherita. But whether she gave her friend
Leland a genuinely old text, or whether she invented
the whole thing – or indeed whether *he* did so on his own
initiative – is uncertain.

Part of the first chapter was adopted by Gardner and the
early Wiccans: the Charge of the Goddess, one of the main
texts in Wicca, contains the following words:

And as the sign that ye are truly free,
Ye shall be naked in your rites, both men
And women also: this shall last until
The last of your oppressors shall be dead.[7]

Gardner's priestess, Doreen Valiente, included this passage directly from *Aradia* when putting together the Charge of the Goddess. Literary invention or not, some contemporary pagans continue to worship this goddess as a deity and it is arguable that she is the basis for modern conceptions of the 'goddess', with several Wiccan traditions adopting the name 'Aradia' for a lunar goddess, the Great Goddess or other entities.

She has also become a central figure in Stregheria, a form of Italian Wicca introduced by American witch Raven Grimassi in the 1980s. Grimassi asserted that 'Aradia di Toscano' was the historical founder of a revivalist religion of Italian witchcraft in the fourteenth century. He has in addition claimed that Leland's *Aradia; or, The Gospel of the Witches* is a Christianized version of Aradia's story.[8]

In 1992 Aidan Kelly, co-founder of the New Reformed Orthodox Order of the Golden Dawn, proposed that both Aradia and Diana had been human priestesses.[9] Folklorist Sabina Magliocco says of Kelly's version of Aradia that she is 'a notably erotic character; according to her teachings, the sexual act becomes not only an expression of the divine life force, but an act of resistance against all forms of oppression and the primary focus of ritual'.[10]

We will be looking more closely at various archetypes of the goddess when we come to consider pagan belief in the twentieth century. But as we can see from the example of Leland's *Aradia*, some of the seeds of these are found in nineteenth-century literature and art; the influence of this work on contemporary Wicca is substantial. Leland, however, is not alone.

One of the figures from English folklore on whom Shakespeare draws in *The Merry Wives of Windsor* is Herne the Huntsman. The name 'Herne' first appears in connection with a fourteenth-century huntsman in Windsor Forest, who offers his soul to the Devil if he can bag a certain number of deer. The Devil accepts and Herne's ghost haunts Windsor Great Park as a result.

Herne later appears as a character in a novel by William Harrison Ainsworth (*Windsor Castle*, serially published in 1842) and this is principally where his modern incarnation comes from. The plot of *Windsor Castle*, a historical Gothic romance, centres around Henry viii's relationship with Anne Boleyn, but the villain of the piece is Herne. He is now an evil force, a soul-stealer, and Henry proves unable to stop him.

Ainsworth wrote a number of historical novels most accurately described as potboilers. Born in Manchester in 1805, Ainsworth lived in the city until he was nineteen. His father, a lawyer, took an interest in historical crime and regaled his young son with tales of highwaymen and swordplay, stories that fed naturally into his own later work (one might assume that the novels of Sir Walter Scott, which enjoyed a vogue at the time, also had their effect). Ainsworth wrote *The Maid's Revenge* and *A Summer's Evening Tale*, along with a book of poetry in 1822, which he dedicated to the Romantic essayist Charles Lamb. Via the *London Magazine*, to which both men contributed, Ainsworth became a correspondent of Lamb's and subsequently a friend. With his fellow clerk John Partington

Aston, he worked on a collaborative romance, *Sir John Chiverton*, which was (somewhat incestuously) published by John Ebers, the father of Ainsworth's new wife Fanny.

The romantic novel was a success. Walter Scott asked to meet Ainsworth, and Ainsworth's father-in-law asked that he take over his publishing house, although this did not entirely suit him and he went back into the law. His father's tales of highwaymen had evidently affected him: his novel *Rookwood* (published in 1834 and featuring Dick Turpin) was an even bigger success, setting Ainsworth firmly on his path as a novelist and bringing him to the attention of a fashionable group of writers known as the Fraserians (of *Fraser's Magazine*), who included Coleridge, William Makepeace Thackeray and Thomas Carlyle.

Ainsworth was instrumental in the early career of the young Charles Dickens, introducing him to his publisher, and he also entertained some of the up-and-coming men of the age, including Benjamin Disraeli. He proceeded to write almost forty historical romances, which remained popular, among which was *Windsor Castle*. But gradually Ainsworth's star waned. He moved to Brighton and then to Tunbridge Wells, dying in 1882. Unlike his friend Dickens, he is largely forgotten despite his voluminous output.

In the novel Ainsworth creates his own origin story for Herne: the hunter serves under Richard II as his forest-keeper. While hunting with Richard, Herne prevents the king from being killed but ends up dying himself. To rescue Herne's life, Richard and his party turn to a healer, who saves Herne but complies with the request of the hunter's rivals to remove Richard's favour. Herne is found hanging from a tree, but then disappears and returns in spectral form.

At this stage, Herne is still a ghost, not a god. With the emergence of Wicca in the 1950s, the figure of the Horned God starts to take his place as the principal male force of the Wiccan pantheon, depicted as an ancient Celtic god: Cernunnos. This is often held to be the antlered figure represented on the Gundestrup cauldron, dating from the first century BC and found in 1891 in a peat bog in Denmark. The enigmatic figure on the cauldron holds a serpent in one hand and a torc in the other, and is surrounded by animals. His name appears in the first-century monument known as the Pillar of the Boatmen. In this, the horned figure has torcs hanging from his antlers. The name may derive from the Gallo-Latin adjective *carnuātus* (horned) and may also be related to the epithet *Carnonos*, which is written in Greek on a Celtic inscription at Montagnac – the inscription refers to 'the God Cerunincos'. Although the name Cernunnos is itself used only once, on the Pillar of the Boatmen, it has become attached to representations of antlered male forms found throughout Europe.

Thus Cernunnos has become conflated with Herne to form the twentieth-century Horned God. We can see that rather than being a genuinely ancient Celtic figure, he derives from Shakespeare, and from a colourful nineteenth-century novel. Although Herne and Cernunnos have merged, the worship of the latter seems from the archaeological evidence to have been centred in early times around Paris, whereas Herne is a figure who is very much local to Berkshire. (It has been suggested that the name 'Herne' comes from the old Saxon god Woden, who was also called Herian, after his role as the leader of dead souls, the Einheriar, and of the Wild Hunt, the spectral group of hounds who chase the souls of the wicked across the sky.)

But the figure of Herne continues to inspire both pagans and writers. Susan Cooper's novel *The Dark is Rising* (1973) features him as a central figure and the epitome of 'wild magic' – neither good nor bad, but simply a powerful natural force. It is this kind of image that continues to inspire the pagan vision of this ghost-to-god. Herne appears in contemporary fantasy novels too, such as those by Jim Butcher and C. E. Murphy, and the Wild Hunt also feature in the work of Alan Garner, in his children's novel *The Moon of Gomrath* (1963).

Early twentieth-century writer R. Lowe Thompson makes the direct suggestion that Herne and other Wild Huntsmen in European folklore all derive from the early figure of Cernunnos, and this contention may have filtered into popular belief. He states:

> In any case the reader may also be prepared to recognize Cernunnos and the older magician, who emerge as the Wild Huntsman. My assumption is that these two forms have been derived from the same Palaeolithic ancestor and can, indeed, be regarded as two aspects of one central figure, will help us to understand the identification of Herlechin and Herne, whom I will take as the most familiar example of the huntsman.[11]

This is a big claim, and one for which there is no evidence. Yet references to Cernunnos and the Wild Hunt, combined with Ainsworth's novel and other literary references to Herne the Hunter, undoubtedly informed the development of the Horned God in the twentieth century.

## Edward Lovett

The folk magical practice prevalent throughout earlier centuries did not suddenly stop and become literary. The folk magic that many ordinary people relied upon for curing ailments, matters of the heart and attempts to become wealthier did not simply die out once the bells rang in 1800. For our knowledge of what people were actually doing in the nineteenth century in terms of magical practice, we are indebted to collectors and folklorists such as Edward Lovett (1852–1953), whose collection of charms and amulets gives an invaluable insight into nineteenth-century British superstitions. His close association with Henry Wellcome and the latter's museum resulted in the 'Folklore of London' exhibition, held at the Wellcome Historical Medical Museum in 1916. The Wellcome Collection says of Lovett:

> He worked for much of his life at the Bank of Scotland in the City of London, rising to the rank of Chief Cashier, but in his leisure time he took great pleasure in his collecting trips to the working-class areas of London. He acquired a wealth of material from sites such as herbalist shops, the barrows of costermongers [street sellers] and the city's dockyards, collecting from people neglected by most historians.[12]

Lovett himself does not seem to have been a believer in the power of the charms that he amassed, although he did make an amulet for his son when the young man went off to the Front in the First World War. Most of Lovett's collection came from his walks around London and Surrey, but an interest in alpine plants gave him an introduction: rather sweetly, he swapped tiny plants that he or others had grown in seashells for his contacts' amulets. The charms that he collected are varied: lucky left-handed whelk shells from sailors, for instance. He wrote:

> My own experience is that, at any rate for the seeker after amulets, there is no better hunting ground than the hawker's handbarrow in the poorest parts of slums of such dense aggregations of people as London, Rome, and Naples . . . For many years I have been in touch with some of the London street dealers in unconsidered trifles, and am much surprised to find how much they know as to the reasons for carrying certain amulets.[13]

He also tells us in another article (co-written with A. R. Wright, hence the use of the third person) that

> The stone amulets comprise the two most original forms of amulet still to be found in the British Isles, the naturally-perforated stone and the many objects known as 'thunderbolts' . . . The story of a beautifully polished green-stone celt shown illustrates the difficulty of obtaining such objects from their possessors. About twenty-five years ago, during a visit to Jersey, Mr. Lovett found this celt in a labourer's cottage, and much wished to add it to his collection of stone implements. The owner, however, would not part with it, saying that it was a thunderbolt and would save his family from sickness and harm. He was offered five shillings, and

a few days later ten shillings, but would not listen to the offers. The following year Mr. Lovett again called upon the owner of the thunderbolt, and offered him fifteen shillings for it, with no result. The bid was raised to twenty shillings, but without success. About eight months later a friend in the island wrote that the man who had the curious stone was 'hard up,' and had asked whether the gentleman from London would still be willing to buy it, so that only after two years did the stone change hands.[14]

We also have this:

When at the last British Association Meeting there, Mr. Lovett noticed in several fancy dealers' shops bundles of shell necklaces of identical pattern. When he came presently to another shop of the same kind in which there was an old woman, he went in and asked, 'What are these necklaces?' 'Three pence.' 'I mean, what are they for?' 'For visitors.' 'I will buy some. But why are they all made exactly the same way?' 'Because they are made by the fishermen.' 'Why do they make them in that particular way?' 'Because they have always been made in that way. I made them that way when I was a girl, and my mother used to make them that way.' 'But you can't have made them for visitors when you were a girl. There were no visitors. What did you make them for then?' 'Oh, just for fun.' 'No, you didn't make them for fun, – you made them for luck.' 'Who told you that? They said so, but that was silly.' Another old woman then came into the shop, and was presently asked by the shopkeeper to show the 'spider shell' in her pocket. This proved to be a pelican's foot shell, which she would not part with. It had been carried by her husband for thirty years, and was now carried by herself 'for luck.'[15]

Lovett spoke to all manner of people in his rambles: shepherds in Sussex, for example, who showed him examples of 'cramp nuts', or charms against spasms. A number of these amulets are not man-made but are taken directly from the natural world: woody accretions from beech or ash, fossilized shark's teeth, hag stones (stones with a natural hole running through them) and pieces of amber, carried as a cure for toothache. Lovett mentions little bags containing the forefeet of a mole, also to be carried against cramp. The curved appearance of these feet may be, Lovett speculates, a remnant of the doctrine of 'like curing like'. Presciently, Lovett notes that he doubts whether these old customs will last much longer, as the professions that handed them down to father and son – fishing, sheep-herding, costermongering – were already beginning to change.

Lovett faced the usual problems of the outsider investigating magical practice, including people's reluctance to talk, either because they did not trust him with the information or because, in what was becoming a fast-developing industrial age, they were ashamed of their own superstitions. What Lovett's work shows, however, is that there was still a strong streak of belief in magic throughout the Victorian period among ordinary people who would undoubtedly have described themselves as Christian.

His collection can be found in various museums: the Pitt Rivers Museum in Oxford and the Wellcome Collection. Much of the collection was held in the Cuming Museum in Southwark, now closed due to a fire.

Folk magic was not, however, the only form of magic practised in the Victorian period. We are now going to look at some of the personalities and organizations that have had such a crucial impact on the contemporary pagan and occult world.

## Blavatsky and the Theosophists

Helena Blavatsky, whose intense stare gazes out at us from photographs, was a founder of the Theosophical Society. A Russo-German aristocrat born in 1831, she grew up in Russia and travelled extensively in that country. Her travels were initially aided by her marriage, at seventeen, to Nikifor Vladimirovitch Blavatsky, the governor of Erivan province. She said she married him because of his belief in magic, showing an early dedication to the practice that she would make her life's work. The marriage did not last.

Because of the impenetrability of that vast land, and owing to missing records and a degree of autobiographical falsification on the part of Blavatsky herself, it is hard to prove whether or not she did as she claimed and travelled to Tibet, apparently on the instructions of a secret group of otherworldly beings, the Masters of the Ancient Wisdom. She alleged that when in Tibet she was trained in the development of psychic powers. Even if only a fraction of her exploits actually took place, Blavatsky led an exciting life, travelling with the Druze in Lebanon and in 1871 sailing to Egypt on a ship that blew up mid-voyage.

By the 1870s Blavatsky had come to Europe and was involved in the Spiritualist movement. Spiritualism was enjoying a considerable vogue in the latter half of the nineteenth century, and its impetus continued into the twentieth. On moving to the U.S. in 1873, Blavatsky became friendly with a man named Henry Olcott, a military officer, journalist and lawyer. In 1875 they formed the Theosophical Society and Blavatsky published her most famous work, *Isis Unveiled*, which draws on Hermeticism and Neoplatonism, and which claimed to reveal an 'ancient wisdom' underlying all of the world's religions. Having made this ambitious claim, Blavatsky and Olcott moved to India, where they converted to Buddhism and popularized Theosophy throughout the subcontinent, an endeavour that encountered a setback when Blavatsky was prosecuted for producing fraudulent psychic phenomena. She returned to London, where she died in 1891 after publishing more literary works, including the influential *The Secret Doctrine* (1888). The Theosophical Society did not fold on her death, however, but continues today; its headquarters are in Gloucester Place in London.

The Theosophical Society states on its website:

> Derived from the two Greek words, 'Theos' (a god, the Deity) and 'Sophia' (wisdom) . . . Theosophy may be defined as 'knowledge of divine things' or 'Divine Wisdom such as that possessed by the gods'. Its philosophy is a contemporary presentation of the perennial wisdom underlying the world's religions, sciences, and philosophies.[16]

Theosophy seeks to be a tolerant, non-dogmatic path that emphasizes peace and fraternity regardless of creed or colour, race or sex, strives to encourage the study of comparative religion, philosophy and science, and investigates the 'unexplained' laws of nature and the 'powers latent in man'. It does not matter what other spiritual path you might follow, as long as it is more or less in accord with the above.

Theosophy is not pagan. Yet it is important to our study of paganism because so many of the concepts that have been introduced under its aegis – psychic phenomena, telepathy, communication with hidden entities, astral travel – have made their way into contemporary spiritual thought. It would be unusual to find a pagan practitioner who has not encountered one or more of these practices and beliefs, which are also shared with many New Age paths. Nowadays, the Theosophical roots of these belief systems are found within a variety of paths that may not have a great deal to do with one another. There are many pagans who would consider themselves to be psychic and some who work with 'hidden masters'. Working with angelic powers is held in common between forms of ceremonial magic and the New Age, although the underlying theology may differ considerably. With the emergence of postmodernism and relativism, there is a smorgasbord of belief available to the contemporary spiritual seeker, and despite occasional disapproval, many people blend worship of pagan gods and goddesses with other forms of healing, the use of crystals and the practice of divination. In general, most pagans leave it up to the individual. There is a degree of internal inflexibility – for instance within some forms of Wicca – but overall, religious dogma is frowned upon. If you want to combine astral travel with a belief in fairies and the practice of Eastern forms of healing such as Reiki, many pagans would say that you can do so. And a number of these practices derive from these late nineteenth-century movements, such as Blavatsky's teachings.

The movers and shakers of the Golden Dawn as well as many Victorian writers began to take an interest in Theosophical thought. For instance, children's writer Edith Nesbit wrote to her sister-in-law Ada Breakell in 1884 saying that she was reading 'an intensely interesting book which Harry [Edith's brother] would like called Esoteric Buddhism by Sinnett'.[17] Sinnett was a disciple of Blavatsky, and his book drew heavily on her views.

In Nesbit's *The Story of the Amulet* (1906) the Bastable children visit the lost island of Atlantis prior to the Flood. Nesbit's version of the island owes much to its initial origins in Plato's *Critias*, but she seems also to have drawn inspiration from Ignatius Donnelly's *Atlantis: The Antediluvian World* (1882).

Atlantis enjoyed a mild vogue among late Victorian and Edwardian writers, cropping up again in C. J. Cutcliffe Hynes's *The Lost Continent: The Story of Atlantis* (1899) and David Maclean Parry's *The Scarlet Empire* (like *Amulet*, also published in 1906). The popularity of this lost world most likely stems from Donnelly's work. Donnelly held that a number of ancient civilizations – the Aztecs and Phoenicians among them – came from Atlantis and that the gods of the ancient peoples were the ruling classes of the island itself. His ideas were enthusiastically taken up by Blavatsky, who features Atlantis as the origin of one of the root-races in *The Secret Doctrine*; her theories, in turn, were developed by Theosophists such as William Scott-Elliot, whose work *The Story of Atlantis* was published in 1896 and further draws on the idea of Atlantis and its lost sister-world Lemuria as the origins of ancient humanity. Nesbit's Atlantean episode in *The Story of the Amulet* is therefore part of a nineteenth-century tradition of Atlantean narrative, both within fiction and – in the case of Donnelly, Scott-Elliot and Blavatsky – outside it.

Why is Atlantis so important? I mention it here because it has inspired a range of twentieth-century offshoots: the occult writer Dion Fortune draws heavily on the legends of Atlantis in her famous novel *The Sea Priestess*, which we will look at in more detail in the next chapter. Marion Zimmer Bradley's influential novel *The Mists of Avalon* also features Atlantis as an origin of the magical world of the Arthurian myth cycle, drawing partly on Fortune's work. There are lodges and organizations that work with Atlantean-inspired magic, and a kind of meta-belief is prevalent throughout some pagan and New Age thought that Atlantis inspired spiritual progress throughout the Western world, from the British Isles to Egypt.

## Éliphas Lévi

Born on 8 February 1810 in Paris, Lévi's birth name was Alphonse Louis Constant. Destined for the seminary, he fell in love instead with a girl named Noémie Cadiot, whom he later married, and had to leave his religious studies. But he remained a student of the esoteric and wrote a number of books that proved seminal in the development of ceremonial magic in particular. His work greatly influenced the occult society of the Golden Dawn and the ideas of Aleister Crowley.

Lévi's first published work was called *The Bible of Liberty* and was a manifesto of Christian socialism. It certainly made an impact, as copies of it were confiscated by the Paris police an hour after going on sale and Lévi was subsequently incarcerated. Lévi used his eleven months in prison wisely by reading the philosopher Swedenborg, and his studies continued after his release, when he turned to the work of Renaissance esotericists.

In 1854 Lévi visited England and met the novelist – and Conservative MP – Edward Bulwer-Lytton. Together, they devised the idea of writing a treatise on magic, which led to Lévi producing *Dogma and Ritual of High Magic*, written in French (it was later translated by A. E. Waite, co-creator of the Rider Waite Tarot deck). Lévi incorporated the Tarot into his own magical system and this is partly why the Tarot is such a major part of magical practice today. He also incorporated elements of the Kabbalah, correlating the cards of the Major Arcana in the Tarot with the paths of the 'Tree of Life' described in Kabbalism. We have noted that these systems can be linked, and this point in history is where much of this linkage originates.

Much of magical practice today comes from the work of Lévi. The use of the four 'quarters' in pagan ritual (that is, the format of a magic circle, divided into the four directions) is influenced by his writings, as he tied the four suits of the Tarot into the elements and used the four elemental quarters in his magical ceremonies, although their use dates from earlier centuries. Also, if you come across images of Baphomet – the goat-headed, hermaphroditic deity whom some people mistakenly think is a representation of Satan – this, too, comes primarily from the writings of Lévi.

Lévi was not part of any particular tradition, though he had an interest in the doctrine of Rosicrucianism. He did, however, subscribe to the idea that there are underlying principles to all magical practice. Lévi held that there is more than one level of existence, and other dimensions may be drawn upon to change our own reality. The 'astral light' is an aspect of this, which we need to contact in order to attain power.

He also stated that human willpower alone has the ability to change reality (this is a central tenet of current magic), and believed that we are a microcosm of the macrocosm – so we are a reflection in miniature of the universe itself.

> Behind the veil of all the hieratic and mystical allegories of ancient doctrines, behind the darkness and strange ordeals of all initiations, under the seal of all sacred writings, in the ruins of Nineveh or Thebes, on the crumbling stones of old temples and on the blackened visage of the Assyrian or Egyptian sphinx, in the monstrous or marvelous paintings which interpret to the faithful of India the inspired pages of the Vedas, in the cryptic emblems of our old books on alchemy, in the ceremonies practiced at reception by all secret societies, there are found indications of a doctrine which is everywhere the same and everywhere carefully concealed.[18]

## The Golden Dawn

The Hermetic Order of the Golden Dawn is still around, but like most occult movements it has split, reformed and changed over the 150 or so years since its inception. Formed in 1888 by William Woodman, Samuel MacGregor Mathers and William Westcott, the Golden Dawn was established to explore esoteric concepts such as the Kabbalah, divination, astronomy, alchemy, the spirituality of ancient Egypt and Christian mysticism. Based on the principles of a Masonic Lodge (and taking some key concepts from the Masonic tradition), the Golden Dawn was radical in that it admitted women on an equal basis, and some of the most influential occultists in it were female, in contrast to Masonry and the Rosicrucian orders of the day.

The founders of the order were Freemasons with interests in other esoteric paths such as Rosicrucianism, and the order came about after a set of coded manuscripts allegedly came into the hands of William Westcott. In deciphering them, he found that they contained the address of one Anna Sprengel, a German Rosicrucian countess who apparently had the ability to contact supernatural entities known as the 'Secret Chiefs' – a form of council that oversees human affairs and with whom magical lodges and orders ideally need to be in contact, so that they have proper guidance. Westcott got in touch with Sprengel, who said she had founded the Golden Dawn in 1886. She initiated him and in 1887 gave him permission to start a magical temple in London.

It has to be noted that the foundation story of the Golden Dawn is highly dubious and it is fair to say that most occultists today do not believe in the Sprengel narrative. The impetus behind the Golden Dawn is most likely to have come from a combination of the imaginative talents of Westcott and Mathers, with inspiration provided by Anna Bonus Kingsford, a vicar's wife. The last died just before the Golden Dawn came into being, but she had co-founded a group called the Hermetic Order in 1884, emerging from a schism within the Theosophical Society. Kingsford's brand of 'religious occultism' included Renaissance magic, Christian principles, Eastern mysticism and a kind of Victorian feminism, plus vegetarianism and a belief in animal rights. Kingsford, who was friendly with Mathers in Paris, died of pneumonia, contracted after she crossed the city in a rainstorm to place a curse on Louis Pasteur (she disapproved of his experimental practices). There is no evidence for the existence of anyone called Anna Sprengel and Westcott is generally considered to have made her up as justification for the founding of the Golden Dawn, and naming her after Anna Kingsford. Other antecedents include the Societas Rosicruciana in Anglia, and the Masonic and esoteric Christian order founded by Robert Wentworth Little in the 1860s. A. E. Waite suggested that the grade structure of the society came out of the Order of the Golden and Rosy Cross, an eighteenth-century German group.

In 1891 Westcott claimed that his correspondence with Sprengel had ceased, and that the Golden Dawn was to establish its own contacts with the Secret Chiefs. Mathers claimed that he had done so, and his power was further consolidated when Westcott withdrew from the order in 1896 or 1897 (he apparently left some papers linking him to the Golden Dawn in a hansom cab, and as he was a professional coroner as well as a doctor, awkward questions were asked about his connection with an occult group, precipitating his departure).

As an initiatory order, the Golden Dawn did not at first practice magic *per se*, but concentrated on meditation and philosophical enquiry. In 1892, however, its members felt that they had progressed far enough into their work to set up an 'inner', more advanced form of working to complement the 'outer'. Soon, the order expanded, with temples being set up in

Paris, Edinburgh and Weston-super-Mare. The order gained its rituals from those Secret Chiefs, who communicated their wishes through Mathers.

At its height, the Golden Dawn had around a hundred members. It attracted many people to its first temple, the London-based Isis-Urania, which ran from 1888 to 1902 in Fitzroy Street, not far from Tottenham Court Road. Needless to say, the order did not persist in its original form – occult societies are rather prone to schisms – and soon, disagreements between its members began to cause ructions. Challenges to the authority of Mathers arose, with members questioning why the Secret Chiefs communicated solely through him. Some took issue with his growing friendship with a contentious member of the order, one Aleister Crowley. Over time, the order fragmented and now there are several organizations claiming it within their own ancestry. And it was not solely a European order: temples were established in the U.S. early in the twentieth century, possibly earlier, and also in New Zealand.

The people who belonged to the Golden Dawn were varied, but they included some well-off members of society; broadly, those who had an interest in the arts and in radical thought – people who would today be termed as having 'alternative' interests, although many of them were ostensibly respectable members of society. A surprising number were Christian priests, including Alexander Ayton (vicar of Chalcombe, practising alchemist and Freemason); the Reverend Francis Heazell (secretary of a Church of England committee); the Bishop of Llandaff, Timothy Rees, and Father Charles Fitzgerald. The last two men, members of the Stella Matutina, took the Golden Dawn out to New Zealand.

Despite this clerical input, however, if Kingsford was an inspiration for the Golden Dawn, her interest in women's spirituality did the order a favour, for in addition to members of the clergy it attracted a number of unconventional and influential women. Born in London in 1860, Annie Horniman was one of these. She came from a privileged background: the family home looked out onto a 15-acre walled park. Her father, who founded the Horniman Museum, collected works of art from all over the world, resulting in an exotic domestic atmosphere. Like most middle-class Victorian girls, Annie was educated at home, but from an early age she had an independent streak and developed an enthusiasm for the theatre. Later, she took up smoking – almost unheard of for a young woman of her class and time. In 1882 she enrolled at the Slade School of Art, where she met a fellow student, Mina (aka Moina) Bergson. The two were to become friends. Nicknamed 'Tabbie' (after the cat), Annie embarked on a life of theatricality and art. She was introduced to Moina's boyfriend (later husband) Samuel Mathers, who in turn introduced her to astrology and, in time, to the Golden Dawn.

Horniman was initiated in 1890 and became a key member of the order. Independent and unconventional, she never married, and her private income went a considerable way towards funding the order's activities. Her path through it was not a smooth one, however. She seems to have had a considerable fear of sex, and this appears to have led to a nervous breakdown. In addition, she fell out with Mathers – possibly tired of being seen as a source of money – and at one point was expelled for insubordination. This was almost certainly Mathers's fault, as he became increasingly autocratic. Annie returned to her old love, the theatre, founding the Abbey Theatre in Dublin. Later, she also founded a repertory company in Manchester, her father's financial legacy allowing her to pursue her theatrical interests. In the 1920s she returned to esoteric pursuits and, with Mina, joined an organization called the Quest Society. She died in 1937.

Mina Bergson, born in Geneva in 1865, was the sister of the philosopher Henri Bergson (in adult life she changed her name to 'Moina' to sound more Celtic). As we've seen, she attended the Slade School of Art with Annie Horniman, and judging from her drawings she was a talented illustrator. In 1887 she met Samuel Mathers in the British Museum, and that was that. 'I won't marry him,' she reassured Annie – but she did.

In 1892 Moina and Samuel moved to Paris, where Moina had been brought up after the family moved from Geneva. Mathers began to demand oaths of loyalty from order members and expelled those who resisted. Moina remained loyal to him. In 1918 she was widowed when Mathers died in the great flu epidemic, and she later became the leader of an organization known as the Alpha et Omega, a successor to the Golden Dawn. She died in 1928.

We come now to a third important female member of the order, Florence Farr (1860–1917). The daughter of a doctor, she was named after Florence Nightingale, whom her father knew and respected. From her namesake, Farr took the idea that women could be independent and professional, but her own talents lay in a direction other than medicine. Strikingly beautiful, she attended Queen's College in Westminster and later became an actress, working closely with George Bernard Shaw. Farr was a free spirit and early feminist who believed in free love and had numerous affairs (with Shaw and allegedly

W. B. Yeats, among others), as well as a marriage that ended in divorce.

She was initiated into the Golden Dawn in 1890 by Yeats and taught Tarot, scrying and Enochian magic. She wrote extensively on the occult and became head of the order in Britain when Westcott resigned. However, she herself resigned from the order in 1902 after a row between Mathers and various other members (Mathers expelled her from her position as head) and a scandal involving associates of Mathers who turned out to be con artists.

At Annie Horniman's Abbey Theatre, Farr produced a number of plays, including some by Yeats and Shaw, and in the 1900s toured the u.s. to introduce America to the 'new Irish theatre'. She met Pamela Colman Smith, who became her stage manager for a time and who illustrated the Rider Waite Tarot deck. In 1912 Farr gave up her career as an actress and left Britain for India, and became the principal of a Hindu girls' college in Ceylon. She died there in 1917 of breast cancer ('I became an Amazon,' she wrote bravely of the amputation of her breast, but it was too late: the cancer had already spread).

Edith Nesbit, writer, socialist, Christian and esoteric explorer, was also an alleged member of the Golden Dawn (there are rumours but little evidence). Nesbit ticks a lot of early twentieth-century boxes for 'outright troublemaker', and this tendency emerges in her subversive, often anarchic children's fiction.

Nesbit probably joined the Isis-Urania first, but the Surrealist artist Ithell Colquhoun mentions Nesbit's further involvement in the Stella Matutina, the order founded by Robert Felkin in 1903 after a schism in the Golden Dawn.

In her history of the Golden Dawn, *The Sword of Wisdom* (1975), Colquhoun cites James Webb's work *The Flight from Reason* (1971) as the origin of the claim of Nesbit's involvement.

When the Golden Dawn initially split, it did so into two organizations: the Alpha et Omega, and the Hermetic Society of the Morgenrothe. It is possible – and here I am speculating – that Nesbit joined the latter and stayed with it when it became the Stella Matutina; those who remained were more interested in occultism than mysticism. Jack Sullivan suggests that Nesbit's 1911 novel *Dormant*, which involves the search for an elixir of immortality, might have reflected alchemical work within the Golden Dawn.[19]

Perhaps the most famous woman in the Golden Dawn outside esoteric circles was Maud Gonne. Born in 1866 in Surrey, Gonne became an iconic figure of Irish womanhood. Her family moved to Ireland in 1867. In 1889 she met W. B. Yeats, beginning one of modern poetry's most famous one-sided love affairs. Like a number of the women of the Golden Dawn, Gonne was both beautiful and a free spirit, and in 1890 she had a child with the French political activist Lucien Millevoye. The boy later died of meningitis, in 1891, and in the same year Gonne was initiated into the order. She and Millevoye had another child, Iseult, in 1894, when she began to speak publicly about the Irish and Ireland.

In 1898 she underwent a 'spiritual marriage' with Yeats, which was unconsummated, and she legally married John McBride, whom she later divorced. A fierce nationalist, she became a figurehead for Ireland and died near Dublin in 1953.

The women of the Golden Dawn are justly famous for their participation in one of Western magic's most powerful engines, and we have mentioned only a few. The men, however, are equally as interesting. Known or alleged members included novelists such as Algernon Blackwood, Arnold Bennett and Arthur Machen, cinematographer Charles Rosher, and, of course, Yeats.

Yeats himself remains one of the greatest poets in the English language. He was committed to the cause of Irish literature throughout his life and was fascinated by Celtic legends: his research on Irish folklore and early verse contributed to what is known as the Celtic Twilight. He was also involved in the theatrical life of Dublin. Throughout his life he was interested in the occult and was widely read on different esoteric systems, including Theosophy. In 1923 he was awarded the Nobel Prize in Literature. He died in 1939.

Arthur Edward Waite (1857–1942) was an American-born writer and occultist. He is best known today for his part in the creation of the Rider Waite Tarot deck, still one of the most popular forms of the Tarot owing to its remarkable depth of symbolism. R. A. Gilbert, Waite's biographer, writes that

> Waite's name has survived because he was the first to attempt a systematic study of the history of western occultism – viewed as a spiritual tradition rather than as aspects of proto-science or as the pathology of religion.[20]

Waite was influenced by Éliphas Lévi, and was drawn to psychical research after the death of his sister (this is not uncommon: Arthur Conan Doyle also became interested in spiritualism partly as a result of the death of his son). Waite joined the order in 1891 but left in 1893. Like many members, he proceeded to duck in and out of various versions of the order, and Freemason and Rosicrusian groups, and was well connected with the London literary scene: he was friends with supernatural writer Arthur Machen, among others. Crowley referred to him unkindly as 'dead Waite', but throughout the early years of the twentieth century he wrote a number of texts on magic: *The Book of Ceremonial Magic* (1911), *The Holy Kabbalah* (1929) and an encyclopaedia of Freemasonry.

$$\mathrm{)) \bigcirc ((}$$

The Golden Dawn was a ceremonial magical lodge specializing in long, complex rituals requiring a considerable amount of discipline and preparation. These were based on a variety of spiritual traditions, such as Celtic and Egyptian mythology, and particularly the Kabbalah. Members were expected to be able to remember long screeds of ritual and to make their own robes and regalia: Yeats's meticulously prepared magical items can still be seen in the National Library of Ireland in Dublin. The order was also experimental, investigating the use of sound, art and poetry to produce spiritual effects in its members.

The structure of the order was based on grades, very similar to those found in Freemasonry and in particular to those of the Societas Rosicruciana in Anglia, and members progressed from grade to grade via an initiation in which they were traditionally blindfolded, questioned and challenged, after which they would be expected to undertake a course of study. It was deeply hierarchical. Initiates would be expected to study the elements of Hermetics with which we have become familiar

– astrology, the Kabbalah, the Tarot and divination – as well as the Hebrew alphabet, evocation, the creation of talismans and geomancy. They would be expected also to build up a working knowledge of the mythologies of the Western tradition and the various angels and archangels. The Golden Dawn's teachings were complex, eclectic and diverse.

Members had access to the Westcott Hermetic Library, which contained a wide range of alchemical texts, and people such as A. E. Waite wrote widely on the subject. Order members such as Allan Bennett and William Alexander Ayton, to name but two, had a background in chemistry and would have had little difficulty in putting alchemical principles into practice had they so chosen. In *Rosicrucian Alchemy and the Hermetic Order of the Golden Dawn* (1996), Jean-Pascal Ruggiu pinpoints the Mason and Societas Rosicruciana in Anglia member Frederick Hockley as the prime mover of an alchemical tradition within the Golden Dawn; whether other members had access to this as well is not known. Ruggiu also states that 'Alexander Ayton, the alchemist of the Golden Dawn, told W. B. Yeats that he made an elixir of life that he shewed to "a French alchemist", probably Éliphas Lévi himself when the latter visited England in 1861.'[21] He goes on to suggest that this alchemical strand survived the 1903 split and continued in the Stella Matutina.

Members of the Golden Dawn used meditation and visualization to contact other worlds: Florence Farr, for instance, used scrying to communicate with her Egyptian priestess contact, Nem Kheft Ka. Farr's separate group, the Sphere, which operated within the Golden Dawn with a particular focus on Egyptian magic, apparently worked with Nem Kheft Ka through her sarcophagus in the British Museum.

Edith Nesbit's *The Story of the Amulet* is dedicated to E. A. Wallis Budge, keeper of Assyrian antiquities at the British Museum and the translator of the Egyptian Book of the Dead, whom Nesbit met when she was researching the book. It does not seem as though Budge had formal connections to the Golden Dawn itself – there is no record that he was a member – but he was friendly with some of its personnel (Farr, for instance, who worked with him on her interests in Egyptology). There is speculation stemming from an implication in Ithell Colquhoun's *Sword of Wisdom* (1975) that the Golden Dawn carried out some of their ceremonies in the British Museum; this would presumably have been with the connivance of Budge. Colquhoun would not have been directly involved with the Golden Dawn itself, owing to her age, but she did belong to the Stella Matutina. Her cousin Langford Garstin was a member of the Alpha et Omega temple, and may well have given her information. A. E. Waite conducted a great deal of his esoteric research in the British Museum.

$$))\ \bigcirc\ ((($$

But what sort of magical practice did the Golden Dawn undertake? We might look briefly here at one of the basic rituals, known as the Lesser Banishing Ritual of the Pentagram or LBRP, which is often conducted at the beginning and/or end of magical rites. You would begin with the Kabbalistic Cross: drawing your hand down from your forehead (intoning the word 'Ateh' – 'thou art') to your groin (the word 'Malkuth' – 'the kingdom'), then to your left shoulder (the word 'Ve-geburah' – 'the power') and your right shoulder ('Ve-gedulah' – 'and the glory'), followed by clasping your hands in front of your chest

('Le-Olahm' – 'amen'). (Many people will recognize this as the first part of the Lord's Prayer, in Hebrew.) You would then 'draw' a series of pentagrams in each of the four directions with your hand, visualizing white light emanating from your hand and intoning four of the names of God. You would ask the four archangels for their protection: Raphael before you in the East, Gabriel behind you in the West, Michael to your right in the South, and Uriel to your left in the North. The ritual is completed with a phrase along the lines of: 'For about me flames the pentagram, and in the column shines the six-rayed star.'

The LBRP is still common practice today; it is one of occultism's many legacies from this influential ceremonial magical order. Most occultists and a number of pagans will come across it, or shortened versions of it, at some point in their magical careers. I use it on a fairly regular basis as a 'space clearer': the idea behind it is to remove any spiritual influences from the room or area in which you are going to work, to provide a clean slate for your own practice. A Druidic group to which I belong did a series of Golden Dawn rituals some years ago, following in the modern pagan tradition of eclecticism and borrowing other people's magical practices. These were based on a celebration of the Egyptian deities. We found them of interest, but very long and prone to a sonorous Victorian tone that would possibly have seemed more natural at their time of writing, but which to a modern audience came perilously close to turgid. What cannot be denied, however, is that a lot of our contemporary practice derives from the experimental and inclusive approach of our late nineteenth-century forebears.

## The Fabian Society

The Fabian Society was not an occult group, but a political one. I mention them here to give an example of how intertwined some of these late nineteenth-century organizations were, and how many of the principal figures of the day moved in and out of them: a relatively small group of people, mainly middle- or upper-class, with similar worldviews.

In his article 'The Hermetic Order of the Golden Dawn, 1888–1901', Dennis Denisoff writes:

> Due, in part, to its emphasis on the role of the imagination in human development, writers and artists had a particular affinity with the Golden Dawn. For Alex Owen, late-Victorian occultism 'owed as much to the *modernité* of Baudelaire or "the decadents" as it did a particular socialist tradition or the rationalized components of modern Western society'. Four known members of the Golden Dawn – Farr, Nesbit, Machen, and Sharp – contributed to publisher John Lane's Keynote Series, best known for its decadent and feminist works.[22]

Nesbit's husband Hubert Bland was at the founding meeting of the Fabian Society on 4 January 1884. Nesbit started work on the society's pamphlet committee and soon became co-editor of its journal, *To-day*. Eleanor Marx, daughter of Karl, also joined, and so did Annie Besant, H. G. Wells, George Bernard Shaw and Florence Farr. This is one of the nexus points of the literary and esoteric worlds of late nineteenth-century London. While the connections between the Fabians and the Golden

Dawn may seem anomalous to anyone versed in strict contemporary Marxism, which frowns on the superstitious, these twin threads of the political and the esoteric were to remain entwined throughout the end of the century and beyond, with a number of free-thinkers and radicals being engaged with both.

The late nineteenth century was an age in which the rapid changes caused by industrialization and urbanism, the expansion and secularization of education, led to widespread questioning of the whole gamut of traditional values. Socialism was the defense of the oppressed poor against the indifference or worse of the dominant Conservative and Liberal parties. Spiritualist mediums, and the more academic and credentialed Society for Psychical Research, proposed and carried out empirical research into the claims of traditional scriptural religion that there was some kind of afterlife. Both currents were looked on in their day as the epitome of modernism.[23]

Edward Pease and Frank Podmore, two of the Fabian founders, also had significant esoteric concerns. In *The History of the Fabian Society* (1916), Pease wrote:

In the autumn of 1883 Thomas Davidson paid a short visit to London and held several little meetings of young people ... I attended the last of these meetings held in a bare room somewhere in Chelsea, on the invitation of Frank Podmore, whose acquaintance I had made a short time previously. We had become friends through a common interest first in Spiritualism and subsequently in Psychical Research, and it was whilst vainly watching for a ghost in a haunted house at Notting Hill – the house was unoccupied: we had obtained the key from the agent, left the door unlatched, and returned late at night in the foolish hope that we might perceive something abnormal – that he first discussed with me the teachings of Henry George in 'Progress and Poverty,' and we found a common interest in social as well as psychical progress.[24]

Podmore, meanwhile, wrote a number of books on psychic phenomena, notably *Phantasms of the Living* (1886, co-authored by Frederick Myers and Edmund Gurney), *Studies in Psychical Research* (1897), *Modern Spiritualism* (1902) and *The Newer Spiritualism* (1910). Another Fabian, Oliver Lodge, conducted experiments on telepathy in the 1880s, and despite being a physicist was the president of the Society for Psychical Research from 1901 until 1903.

## Aleister Crowley and Thelema

Alongside Yeats, one of the most famous members of the Golden Dawn was Aleister Crowley. In contemporary occultism, one often hears the name of Crowley not infrequently coupled with the curious word 'Thelema' (or 'Thelemite'). Before we explore the life of the 'wickedest man in the world', I am going to digress a little bit and look at the origins of this word.

In François Rabelais' classic sixteenth-century work *Gargantua and Pantagruel*, the giant Gargantua grants the enterprising Friar John an abbey on the banks of the Loire.

The Abbey of Thélème is hexagonal and built according to very precise measurements, hinting at a possible interest in sacred geometry. It contains huge galleries and libraries. There are gardens and a scented swimming bath, tennis courts, stables and 9,322 rooms for the inhabitants. Over the door is that famous motto – 'Fay ce que voudras' (Do what you will).

Women are admitted if they are beautiful and sweet-natured. Men must also be of a noble calibre. The Thelemites learn languages, disport themselves about the picturesque grounds and love one another. They are allowed to leave – it is not a cult – but the suggestion is that they will not want to. Rabelais believed that vice occurs only because people are forbidden to do things, and that if you allow them to do things, they will behave themselves accordingly. He takes this from Erasmus, surely one of the nicest philosophers to grace the planet.

The Thelemites are so in accord with one another that they act as a single body. If one of them wants a drink, they all do. If one of them wants to play in the fields, they all go along. The abbey is also aristocratic. The inhabitants do not do their own washing up. There is an army of servants in the background who keep the place running smoothly.

Crowley adopted some of the concepts of this imaginary lifestyle, but he was not the first: the Abbey of Thelema was also an inspiration for Dashwood's Hellfire Club, over a hundred years before Crowley's birth in 1875.

Raised in a family who belonged to the Plymouth Brethren, Crowley bestrides British magical practice like a colossus. His mother referred to him as 'the Beast' whenever he did something of which she disapproved, a nickname that stuck. Crowley attended Cambridge and, owing to a generous inheritance, did not initially have to worry about money. He originally intended to study the moral sciences, but switched to English literature. He seems also to have discovered an omnivorous sexuality at this stage.

Joining the Hermetic Order of the Golden Dawn via a meeting with Samuel MacGregor Mathers, Crowley had a contentious relationship with pretty much everyone involved in it, including Yeats, Waite and eventually Mathers himself. He seems to have had some respect for Dion Fortune (whom we will talk about later), although she clearly caricatures him as the repellent fawning villain of her novel *The Winged Bull* (1935). He also features in W. Somerset Maugham's *The Magician* (1908) as the sinister Oliver Haddo: Maugham knew Crowley reasonably well, as a friend of the painter Gerald Kelly. Crowley had been at Cambridge with Kelly and had married his sister Rose in 1903. Maugham's sister-in-law Beldy was a close friend of Rose's.

After a mystical experience in Egypt in the early 1900s, Crowley founded the magical system known as Thelema, the principles of which are laid out in his work *The Book of the Law* (1904). Crowley claimed that these were given to him by an Egyptian entity named Aiwass. They are a mixture of beliefs, drawing from, among others, the work of Empedocles, the Book of Revelation, Rabelais and Nietzsche. His next decades were passed in Europe (his version of the Abbey of Thelema was founded in Crete in 1920) and the u.s., and he took a succession of both male and female lovers, plus several wives. His inheritance gradually ran out, but he continued to be supported by a number of his Thelemic followers.

As formidable a chess player and mountaineer as he was a magician, and the possessor of a strong if sometimes cruel sense of humour, Crowley's influence on British magic is hard to overestimate. Certainly much of his practice and behaviour were unpleasant, including an alleged cat-killing. He died a heroin and cocaine addict, in penury in Hastings (though it is worth noting that the heroin was prescribed by his doctor to treat an asthma condition), leaving an outraged society and a great many literary works (poetry, fiction and non-fiction) behind him.

The nickname of the 'wickedest man in the world' came from L. Ron Hubbard, science fiction writer and the founder of the Church of Scientology. But despite his unpleasant conduct, Crowley was a committed, sincere and experienced magician who continues to exert an influence upon modern magic, via the organization with which he is most closely associated, the Ordo Templi Orientis, or OTO.

His legacy in popular culture has been contentious. Crowley is often associated in the public mind with sex magic, and his heritage, as far as groups like the OTO are concerned, still features this type of practice in various forms. Crowley engaged in sexual acts with both men and women that had a magical component: the idea behind this is that sex and orgasm involve the release of energy that can be harnessed to magical ends. Crowley was not the first magician in the West to address this issue: the nineteenth-century occultist Paschal Beverly Randolph wrote about it in *The Mysteries of Eulis*. The American sex reformer Ida Craddock published a series of pamphlets in the late nineteenth century – *Heavenly Bridegrooms* and *Psychic Wedlock* among them – which Crowley reviewed. Crowley claimed that his work *The Book of the Law* solves the sexual problem completely. Each individual has an absolute right to satisfy his sexual instinct as is physiologically proper for him. The one injunction is to treat all such acts as sacraments. One should not eat as the brutes, but in order to enable one to do one's will. The same applies to sex. We must use every faculty to further the one object of our existence.[25]

For the OTO, Crowley associated different sexual techniques (such as masturbation, heterosexual intercourse and anal intercourse) with different initiatory grades. Some of his considerable body of work on sex magic was made public, but some was available only to initiates.

The results of Crowley's interest in these practices might be best described as unfortunate: his relationships with women usually ended badly. One of his order – modernist writer Mary Butts – commented on his lovers' addiction issues, constant pregnancies and suicide attempts, and was critical of the peculiar rituals that Crowley imposed on his adherents, including dietary constraints.[26] A central figure of Thelema is the image of Babalon, the Scarlet Woman, a goddess based on the woman who rides on the beast in the Book of Revelation. To Crowley, she was the Sacred Whore and, to a lesser extent, a fertility figure. Crowley believed that human women could become her avatars on Earth and encouraged his lovers to see themselves in this light. But despite this emphasis on the goddess, Crowley remained firmly in charge.

The Thelemic Gnostic Mass itself leans heavily on its origins in Freemasonry and is carried out before a naked priestess who sits on the altar, following the pattern of a Christian Mass to some extent. Participants take a sacrament in the form of a 'cake of light', a wafer containing menstrual blood (this is minimal: the blood is mixed into a cake that is then charred, and the charcoal-like fragments are used in making the wafers, so the amount of organic material that participants in the Mass are ingesting is close to homeopathic).

In a Gnostic Mass that I attended in 2017, the priestess was concealed behind a veil. This was before an audience who were mostly not OTO members and who had not been to a Gnostic Mass before. It was explained to us that the sacrament contained blood, and after a pause, a rather nervous voice asked, 'Where does the blood come from?' 'From the priestess,' came the reply, and there was another pause while everyone worked this out (I should perhaps not have added, 'She is free range.') In this event, some of the cakes of light were also gluten-free: a nod to modern dietary requirements. The Mass itself consists of a series of poetic invocations to the sun, the moon, the Lord and Lady, birth, marriage, death and other concepts, with prayers to some of the Egyptian deities: Nuit (Nut), the goddess of night, and Hadit (Horus of Behdet), the infinitely condensed centre of all things.

The Gnostic Mass itself has sexual overtones (the initial path taken by the priestess is meant to invoke kundalini, the sexual power that resides at the base of the spine in Hinduism), but its public performance does not involve actual sex. Neither does the Minerval, the pre-grade initiation which interested parties can undertake to get a flavour of Thelema and see if it is for them. Members of the OTO are known to practise sex magic, although the order also states that this is not compulsory. Recently, however, the OTO has fallen foul of a changing cultural climate in the wake of the #MeToo movement, with allegations of unaddressed sexual abuse. Babalon Herself has been critiqued as a representation of another form of misogyny: the woman who is perceived as liberated only if men can engage with her sexually. In this form of Thelema, the woman remains passive, not active.

The issue of sex magic within Western occultism and paganism is one that we will revisit when we look at the twentieth century, in the work of writers such as Dion Fortune, and in Wicca.

## Spiritualism

It might seem curious to have a section on Spiritualism in a book on the origins of contemporary paganism, but the kind of Spiritualism that flourished in the Victorian period has ramifications for modern occultism. The idea behind Spiritualism is that there is an afterlife; the spirits of those whom we have loved are there within it but can return to speak to us, usually through a medium during a séance or a device such as a ouija board. Some Spiritualists also believe in a 'spirit guide', an entity more advanced than humans who can guide the medium on ethical and other issues. Here, we return again to the ideas of Helena Blavatsky and the 'hidden masters' whom she claimed had guided her.

Spiritualism has its origins in the works of writers such as Franz Mesmer (1735–1815) and Emanuel Swedenborg (1688–1772). A respected scientist, Swedenborg claimed to have communicated with spirits who reside in a sort of hierarchical afterlife. Mesmer pioneered the techniques behind hypnotism, including putting subjects into a trance. We find influences of this not only in Spiritualism, but in later aspects of the pagan movement of the twentieth and twenty-first centuries. Spiritualists often date the origins of their practice to the late 1840s, when the Fox sisters in New York claimed to have made contact with a spirit, a murdered pedlar who communicated through rapping noises. The sisters were befriended by a Quaker group and thus began a crossover between Quakerism and Spiritualism.

The movement grew in popularity from the 1840s onwards and by the late nineteenth century there were estimated to be around eight million people interested in Spiritualism in the UK and USA. In the UK it was primarily Christian in form and many practitioners were women, often those who were interested in other radical movements such as the abolition of slavery and women's suffrage. It is often seen as a movement that gave women a wider role than they might have had within conventional society, and in this it bears a resemblance to the Golden Dawn.

However, Spiritualism suffered badly from instances of fraud. The manifestation of a substance called ectoplasm – a sort of vapour said to indicate the presence of spirits – was often in reality caused by lengths of muslin, part-swallowed by the medium and regurgitated, or secreted about the body. Intimate details revealed to members of a séance and alleged to derive from the spirits of lost loved ones were all too often gained by looking through personal belongings and sometimes questioning servants. However, although Spiritualism declined in popularity, it did not die out altogether: it enjoyed resurgence after the First World War (we have mentioned that Arthur Conan Doyle, creator of Sherlock Holmes, was a proponent, after the death of his son in the flu pandemic of 1918–20). And there are still Spiritualist churches in many towns throughout the UK today. I attended a Spiritualist service in Brighton in the 1990s: it resembled a nonconformist Christian service until the point where messages (sometimes accurate, sometimes not) were received from the dead and relayed to members of the congregation.

## The Celtic Revival

Antiquarian researches into Celtic culture and the history of Great Britain and Ireland began in the late seventeenth century. Manuscripts were located and translated, monuments identified and published, and other crucial work undertaken in recording stories and music. The work of that contentious Welsh antiquarian and author Iolo Morganwg led to a growing interest in Celtic studies. Gaelic culture had undergone a Renaissance during the late eighteenth century. James Macpherson's work *Ossia* was influential and so were the novels of Sir Walter Scott. Byron's Irish friend Thomas Moore was also well known for his poetry and songs. Studying folklore became a popular hobby. Even Beethoven was commissioned to produce a set of arrangements of Scottish folk songs.

In the mid-nineteenth century this revival showed no signs of slowing down. Folk tales and folklore continued to be an object of study and inspiration to the emergent Arts and Crafts movement. Queen Victoria wore jewellery inspired by Celtic motifs and in Scotland the artwork of the ancient Celts influenced everything from architecture to stained glass, from metalwork to book binding.

It was in this context that the 'Celtic Twilight' emerged – a group of writers who harked back to the legends of Ireland, Scotland and Wales, deriving inspiration from earlier folklore. They include Yeats, Arthur Machen and Lord Dunsany. And occultists such as the Golden Dawn's Samuel Mathers became obsessed with their Celtic heritage: Mathers even invented an ancestry that made him a Scottish nobleman, added MacGregor to his name, and cycled around Paris in a kilt.

A major influence on Celtic-inspired paganism in the twentieth- and twenty-first centuries has been the seminal collection of Welsh legends known as the *Mabinogion*. These tales are an example of early prose literature in Britain, featuring heroes and heroines and supernatural figures. Lady Charlotte Guest was the first publisher of these tales, although Welsh antiquarian and grammarian William Pughe had presented translations of some of them in the late eighteenth century. An aristocrat and the wife of a wealthy Welsh industrialist, Lady Charlotte spoke seven languages, including Welsh, and began work on translating the *Mabinogion* in 1837. The *Mabinogion* consists of four story cycles, or 'branches': Pwyll, Prince of Dyfed; Branwen, daughter of Llŷr; Manawydan, son of Llŷr; and Math, son of Mathonwy. King Arthur appears in some of these stories, along with his knights. The translation was published between 1838 and 1845, and republished in three volumes in 1849. It is unclear what the name 'Mabinogion' actually means, although Guest did not introduce it: the word was apparently in currency in the late seventeenth century.

Where did these tales come from? The origins of the *Mabinogion* are obscure and subject to much speculation. Scholars used to believe that they represented the legacy of an early Celtic oral tradition of myths and legends, but they are now seen as having been written in Middle Welsh in the twelfth or thirteenth centuries as a distinct set of tales that may or may not contain remnants of earlier legends.

To consider their history, we return briefly to the 1800s, when a woman named Augusta Waddington moved to Monmouthshire. In 1819 she held a series of cultural talks and learned of a Welsh folk hero named Twm Sion Cati; she paid a writer to make up stories around this figure and published them in 1828. In addition, she devised a Welsh national costume and bought Iolo Morganwg's library, which she gave to the Welsh nation. She also met Lady Charlotte Guest and tasked her with collecting Welsh stories, beginning with the *Red Book of Hengest*. This set of stories was written sometime between 1382 and 1410 in the area around the Towy Valley, and includes some of the tales of the *Mabinogion*.

The four branches are unusual: there are few details of combat, instead focusing on family life (albeit with added supernatural elements) and children. They also contain details about royal courts and the kingdoms of Gwynedd and Deheubarth. The original Welsh used a word for 'king' that was in currency after 1093 but before 1150. This suggests that the *Mabinogion* dates from this period, and Ronald Hutton asserts that we can most profitably look at the court of Gwenllian, the niece of Princess Nest, somewhere between 1110 and 1135. He suggests that Gwenllian commissioned the *Mabinogion*, possibly as a literary way of bringing North and South Wales together. These were troubled times, with unrest throughout the province and considerable friction not only between different Welsh princes, but between the Welsh and their new Norman overlords.

The *Mabinogion* may contain elements of older folk tales, but Hutton's claim is that it is primarily medieval and post-Norman in origin, commissioned by a brave princess (Gwenllian herself died in battle) in an endeavour to unite a fragmented country.

Whoever wrote it originally, many of the stories and characters of the *Mabinogion* have found their way into contemporary paganism. Rhiannon, Arawn, Gwydion and Blodeuwedd are treated as minor deities, rather than the heroes and heroines of the original work. Other Welsh legends, such as the story of Taliesin, which dates from the fourteenth century (possibly earlier), have become part of the contemporary 'Matter of Britain'. Taliesin himself, the famous bard, might be genuinely old as he is mentioned in Saxon genealogies; there is a suggestion that he dates from as far back as the sixth century.[27] The people in these tales became deified as a result of suggestions that they were originally gods and goddesses, lingering in oral folk tales until presented as human beings or supernatural figures in mythological stories.

Rhiannon, for instance, appears in the *Mabinogion* as a woman from the Otherworld. Pursued but never caught (until she chooses it) by the warlord Pwyll, she has magical powers that do little to help her in the human world. She is nearly forced to marry another warrior, and once she is Pwyll's wife is falsely accused of killing their infant son and sentenced to a lengthy punishment. Since, as we have seen, early Celts were not literate, we have no indication beyond surmise that Rhiannon really was an ancient goddess. Her curious ability to ride in a calm, unhurried way, yet never be caught, indicates to some that she is beyond mortal and has a link with horse goddesses, but this metaphor also appears as an erotic narrative device in medieval love poetry.

The Celtic revival of the nineteenth century is worthy of note because it influences the Druidic revival of the twentieth. Later adherents of Druidry picked up on nineteenth-century ideas from literature and art (sometimes presenting them as historical fact) and carried them forward to shape modern Celtic-inspired paganism.

$$\mathcal{DD} \bigcirc \mathcal{CC}$$

The nineteenth century is the period when major shifts in the esoteric landscape occur. Many of these movements, the Golden Dawn, Theosophy and Spiritualism among them, continue into the twentieth century, when the shape of contemporary paganism and magic begin to take the forms that we know today. Our examination of the Edwardian era forms a bridge between the late nineteenth-century and the mid-twentieth-century developments of Wicca, Druidry and other groups. The Celtic revival had a major impact upon the development of modern paganism, and so did the Golden Dawn; there is a direct line of descent from that order into both Wicca and Druidry, as well as the more obvious lineage of ceremonial magic. It is in the twentieth century that many of the strands of belief and practice that we have been looking at, already coalescing in some areas, really start to cohere into the tapestry of contemporary paganism and magical practice. We have seen, over the previous few hundred years, paganism going largely into abeyance: apart from the Druidic revivals of the eighteenth century, magical practice has been firmly embedded in a Christian context.

This starts to change towards the end of the nineteenth century and, as we shall see, by the end of the twentieth, paganism and magic are closely intertwined once more. Modern paganism, already firmly in bud at the end of the nineteenth century, blossoms in the next.

SEVEN

# Modern Magic

The twentieth century is an exciting time for the student of paganism. Esoteric practitioners such as Dion Fortune dip their toes into the literary world; thriller writers such as Dennis Wheatley and Marion Zimmer Bradley return the compliment, with novels that have inspired generations of occultists and pagans. By the turn of the century, modern Druids have become a familiar sight at Stonehenge solstices; at its end, Wicca is close to being a household name thanks to TV shows such as *Charmed* and *Buffy the Vampire Slayer*. This century sees paganism going mainstream in the UK for the first time in a thousand years and, now the genie is out of the bottle, it is unlikely that it will be put back in it any time soon.

Conversely, the twentieth century sees much magical practice continue to decline in the UK, although it does not wholly disappear. I am referring here to folk magic. Ceremonial, Hermetically influenced magic has already been swept up into the big orders such as the Golden Dawn and remains under their wing as the twentieth century progresses, along with many individual practitioners. But the traditional content of cunning practice – healing, finding lost objects and cursing – is subsumed into non-magical organizations, such as the NHS, the police force and the legal system. If you have a problem with your marriage, you are more likely to make an appointment with a lawyer and seek a divorce than curse your spouse (although you might be tempted). If you have a wart, your first thought is probably to go to the doctor. The odd man out is divination, since we still do not have a reliable method of foretelling the future, and Tarot reading, crystal-ball gazing and palmistry continue to be popular throughout the century, given a little extra help by the repeal of the 1735 Witchcraft Act in 1951.

The last person to be imprisoned for witchcraft in Britain was Helen Duncan, who was sent to jail in 1944. Duncan was a fraudulent medium, but where she fell foul of the law was in holding a séance in 1941 in which it was revealed that the British warship HMS *Barham* had been sunk. This was true, but the news had not yet been broken to the public and there were fears that Duncan had leaked classified information (in fact, letters of condolence had already been sent to the families of the dead seamen, and it is estimated that some 9,000 people were aware of the fact that the ship had gone down. Duncan may have picked up this fact from a naval family member). She was made an example of by being imprisoned for nine months, although many people felt this was excessive, and Winston Churchill complained to the then Home Secretary, Herbert Morrison, that the charge was obsolete. After this, no further person was prosecuted and the Act was repealed.

That cunning craft was still practised to some degree throughout the twentieth century is evidenced by many anecdotal accounts of people visiting fortune-tellers, who often had booths at the seaside, and references in popular culture (for example, in Dorothy L. Sayers's novel *Strong Poison* (1930),

Peter Wimsey asks a manicurist to obtain a suspect's nail clippings to demonstrate that the man has been accustoming himself to taking arsenic, but the girl immediately asks him if he is going to use them for a spell and says that she wants no truck with anything 'occult').

I have said that folk practice tends to go onto the back-burner in the early decades of the twentieth century. However, we might argue the case for its return in a somewhat different form at the end of the century, when healing practices such as Reiki and energy work become increasingly popular. Because of constraints of space, we will not be devoting a great deal of time to the New Age, which has become particularly popular in parts of the United States – California, for example – but aspects of the New Age are also the inheritors of magic. Writers like Doreen Virtue, who started their careers in teaching about angels, are in essence harking back to older forms of magic, and so are the authors of works such as *The Secret*, which relate to the manifestation of wealth and other desired outcomes through the focus of the will.

In this chapter, as well as some important literary influences, we are going to look at the main trends within paganism in the UK over the course of the twentieth century and into the twenty-first, which we first encountered in our Introduction. The history of British paganism and magic as we move from the nineteenth century into the twentieth becomes a series of intertwined strands that by now will be familiar to us from the late Georgian and Victorian periods: a combination of literary fiction, cultural organizations, and magical and religious societies, plus the remnants of grass-roots folk practice and superstition. The twentieth century brings a novel element to the mix in the form of new media: film, television and the work of the tabloid press.

〉〉○《《

In the previous chapter we considered a number of popular nineteenth-century works that are not well known today, but which have nonetheless influenced contemporary paganism. Ainsworth and Leland were not, however, the only Victorian writers to explore ideas that subsequently became part of twentieth-century movements. H. Rider Haggard, author of the novel *She* (1886), stated, 'I have a respect for Thor and Odin. I venerate Isis and always feel inclined to bow before the moon.'[1] He evinced an interest in magic – as Ronald Hutton writes: 'This rich and idiosyncratic cocktail of beliefs is implicit in the plots of many of his novels, and contributes to their allure.'[2] In the same book, Hutton considers the work of Rudyard Kipling and Kenneth Grahame, whose novel *The Wind in the Willows* (1908) contains the chapter 'The Piper at the Gates of Dawn', which alludes to the re-emergence of the god Pan – an eerie and evocative passage:

> and then, in that utter clearness of the imminent dawn, while Nature, flushed with fulness of incredible colour, seemed to hold her breath for the event, [Mole] looked in the very eyes of the Friend and Helper; saw the backward sweep of the curved horns, gleaming in the growing daylight; saw the stern, hooked nose between the kindly eyes that were looking down on them humourously, while the bearded mouth broke into a

half-smile at the corners; saw the rippling muscles on the arm that lay across the broad chest, the long supple hand still holding the pan-pipes only just fallen away from the parted lips; saw the splendid curves of the shaggy limbs disposed in majestic ease on the sward; saw, last of all, nestling between his very hooves, sleeping soundly in entire peace and contentment, the little, round, podgy, childish form of the baby otter. All this he saw, for one moment breathless and intense, vivid on the morning sky; and still, as he looked, he lived; and still, as he lived, he wondered.[3]

In Grahame's novel, the animals live above the ruins of a great city, something which it is easy to miss on a quick read. Maybe it is Roman – or perhaps London, fallen at last? It is significant, though, suggesting a longing for a purer world, an Arcadia without human interference. We have met this type of idyll before, in the longings of the later Druids.

Pan was a popular god among the late Victorians and Edwardians, and his ancient influence pops up later in the twentieth century, too, in some surprising places. W. Somerset Maugham, Saki, D. H. Lawrence, Arthur Machen, E. M. Forster, Algernon Blackwood, Robert Louis Stevenson – all of these authors and more have a Pan moment somewhere along the line. A character in Saki's story 'The Music on the Hill' (1911) informs his wife calmly that

the worship of Pan never has died out . . . he is the Nature-God to whom all must come back at last. I've been a fool in most things . . . but I'm not such a fool as not to believe in Pan when I'm down here ... if you're wise you won't disbelieve in him too boastfully while you're in his country.[4]

His arrogant wife does not believe this and removes a bunch of grapes on the altar of a small temple that she finds on the estate, containing a statue of Pan. When she tells this to her husband, he replies: 'I don't think you were wise to do that ... I've heard it said that the Wood Gods are rather horrible to those who molest them.'[5] He's quite right: shortly after this, his wife is gored to death by a stag.

In E. M. Forster's 'The Story of a Panic' (1904), a group of English tourists encounter that sinister sense of a terrifying presence in the Italian countryside, and it affects one of their party, a young boy, to a remarkable degree:

Eustace Robinson, aged fourteen, was standing in his nightshirt, saluting, praising, and blessing, the great forces and manifestations of Nature. He spoke first of night and the stars and planets above his head, of the swarms of fire-flies below him ... of the great rocks covered with anemones and shells that were slumbering in the sea. He spoke of rivers and waterfalls, of the ripening bunches of grapes, of the smoking cone of Vesuvius and of the hidden fire-channels which made the smoke, of the myriads of lizards who were lying curled up in the crannies of the sultry earth, of the showers of white rose-leaves that were tangled in his hair. And then he spoke about the rain and the wind by which all things are changed, of the air through which all things live, and of the woods in which all things can be hidden.[6]

Pan is not perhaps so strange a god for the British to adopt when one considers the repressive elements of Victorian society, both social and sexual. There was perhaps an emergent feeling that in the recent industrialization and urbanization of the nation, some connection with the wild natural world had been lost – a feeling that continues to draw many people to paganism today. After the First World War, too, there may have been a reflection on the darkness of human nature. And the developing discipline of psychology was beginning to investigate the powers of the subconscious mind. Dion Fortune's occult hero Doctor Taverner is a psychologist as well as an occultist, for instance, and Fortune studied psychology herself. As Richard Stromer says in his thesis on Pan:

> Considering all of these factors, it hardly seems surprising then that a deity such as Pan – a rambunctious, instinctual, libidinous god of all things and places wild – should have become a cultural icon presaging cataclysmic social and cultural changes lurking just over the historical horizon.[7]

Helen Law, in her work on Greek references in English poetry, notes 106 citations of Pan, one-third of them in the late nineteenth and early twentieth centuries.[8] Sometimes Pan is the kind guardian of the woods, protector of straying otter babies, and sometimes he is a sinister force, the generator of panic out in the wild world.

Pan is not the only deity to have been adopted by the Edwardians, and the classical world is not the only influence. We have seen Egyptian themes in the work of late Victorian occultists, but many esoteric writers and practitioners had already been looking closer to home, to the works generated by the Celtic revival. Anthropologist James Frazer had produced an influential work, *The Golden Bough*, in 1890 and this was reprinted in the early 1900s. Frazer himself was emerging from a background of a growing British interest in folklore (an interest that was influenced in turn by German Romanticism and the work of Wilhelm Mannhardt). He drew on myths and beliefs to put forward the idea that ancient religions were primarily fertility cults, based around the sacrifice of a 'sacred king' (Dionysus, Osiris, Adonis, Tammuz and even Christ being examples). *The Golden Bough* scandalized Victorian society when it came out, owing to Frazer's comments about Christ, but the book's impact on anthropology was shown over time to be less marked than its literary heritage and, through this, its substantial effect on paganism. Frazer's work influenced Yeats, Fortune and, later, the poet Robert Graves. Crowley referred to Frazer as 'the only man worthy of note' in the field of religion and believed that *The Golden Bough* was invaluable.[9] The work also influenced Wicca: Gerald Gardner took on many of Frazer's ideas, and Gardner was another who described Diana as 'queen of the witches'.

This is ironic. As Hutton and others have pointed out, Frazer was an atheist from a radical Free Church of Scotland heritage whose aim was to discredit Christianity by including it within a range of ancient superstitions. Frazer did not do this explicitly, but there is a general consensus among historians that this was his intention. Mary Beard suggests that Frazer sought to compare the folk rituals of the British countryside with those of a savage antiquity, and thus discredit all of them, along with Christianity itself. But Frazer's presentation of Christ as one in a long line of nature gods achieved an effect contrary to the one he originally intended, by drawing people's attention to the old pagan religions in a new and stimulating light. Hutton states: 'Frazer arguably did succeed in doing further damage to the status of Christianity, but fostered not so much an enhanced respect for rationalism and progress as a delight in the primitive and unreasonable.'[10] Thus, if you are to trace modern paganism back, the majority of its most significant paths can be shown to have deep roots in *The Golden Bough*.

## The Inklings and Dennis Wheatley

Fantasy fiction as a genre has been around for some time, arguably ever since Homer composed the *Odyssey* and the *Iliad* in the late eighth century BC. In Britain, fantasy fiction's first proponent is Mary Shelley, the teenage author of *Frankenstein* (1823). But it is in the twentieth century that fantasy literature really starts to make its mark, along with genre films and television. One of the greatest works of British fantasy is surely J.R.R. Tolkien's saga *The Lord of the Rings* (1954), based on Saxon and Norse lore. Tolkien's friend C. S. Lewis's novels about the imaginary land of Narnia have also inspired generations of children to look more closely into magic and the pagan world.

Both Tolkien and Lewis were members of the Oxford literary group known as the Inklings. This discussion group met throughout the 1930s and '40s. All members were Christian, and yet their novels continue to have an effect upon modern paganism: although Narnia, for example, is a Christian allegory, the number of pagan allusions within it is so great that many children (including me) totally failed to realize that it was a story about Christ, and fell in love with the magic realm and the talking animals. The recent filming of Tolkien's and Lewis's novels has brought their work to an even wider audience.

The number of novels that feature magic, witches and wizards is too great for us to provide an overview here. The twentieth and twenty-first centuries have seen a plethora of them, from Sylvia Townsend Warner's 1920s feminist classic *Lolly Willowes*, in which the protagonist enters into a relationship with Satan, to the works of the Inklings and the occult thriller writers, all the way through urban fantasy to J. K. Rowling. The Harry Potter books are among the most popular novels ever written in English, introducing a generation of children to magic school, but Rowling draws (at least in terms of literary heritage) on the works of Ursula K. LeGuin, Diana Wynne Jones, Susan Cooper, Lloyd Alexander and many more. The subject of magic is perennially popular in fiction and shows no signs of going away any time soon. I would venture the suggestion that when many adults who come to paganism for the first time make the often repeated assertion that it is 'like coming home', it is possible that they do so because the way that pagan movements approach the world is reminiscent of the magical realms they encountered in children's fiction. This is not to make an ontological claim; and it is not to say that the deities within paganism are purely fictive. Who knows but that the gods have chosen to make themselves known through popular narratives?

'People who live in miserable rows of grim little houses don't want to read about other people who live in miserable rows of houses,' said Dennis Wheatley.[11] His novels are sensationalist, escapist and fun. Like Ian Fleming's Bond books, they are full of fine wines and glamorous lifestyles.

In the 1930s Wheatley conceived a series of whodunnit mysteries, presented as case files, with testimonies, letters and pieces of 'evidence' such as hair or pills. But after these early ripping yarns, he set out to write a novel about black magic, possibly after getting to know a neighbour, Tom Driberg – an upper-middle-class champagne socialist and committed Christian who had a habit of cottaging. Driberg, psychiatrist Anthony Storr remarked, was the only person he had ever met who could genuinely be described as 'evil'. He had in his youth been a follower of Aleister Crowley, but this gradually changed as Crowley became poorer and Driberg more powerful – the former complaining in his diary that 'Tom Driberg's unforthcomingnesses are really unschooltiesome'.[12]

Wheatley met Crowley in the 1930s. Of Crowley, his biographer Phil Baker says, 'people meeting him for the first time often feared that he would make indecent advances, but in practice he was more likely to borrow a fiver.'[13] Wheatley took Crowley to lunch but never spoke much about it afterwards. Crowley did not mention the lunch in his notes either, although he did give Wheatley a copy of his book and recommended that he invoke the 'Hymn to Pan' at midnight.

More influential on his writing was Wheatley's meeting with Montague Summers, a dubious clergyman obsessed with the idea that occult orders were criminal and political conspiracies. It is this idea that seems to have fired up Wheatley's imagination. 'The cult of the Devil', said Summers, 'is the most terrible power at work in the world today.'[14] Summers was, however, a Satanist himself when young. Wheatley and his wife Joan went to stay with him and were placed in a room infested with spiders. There was also a large toad, which Summers explained was the reincarnation of a friend of his, saying: 'I'm just looking after him.'

The visit ended in disaster when Wheatley declined to buy a book that Summers offered him. The benign old clergyman became apoplectic and hurled the book to the floor. Wheatley and Joan made their excuses and left. Summers did, however, admire Wheatley's novel, *The Devil Rides Out* (1934), which was by then fast becoming a bestseller. Wheatley also became friendly with occultist Rollo Ahmed (who claimed to be both Egyptian and from Guyana), and they got on well – Ahmed had served time for fraud, and there seems to have been something in Wheatley's character that was drawn to men of dubious character.

By the end of the 1930s, Dennis Wheatley was one of the most popular writers in the UK. His success was not regarded kindly by the literary establishment. At a party, literary critic James Agate discussed Wheatley with another guest who said that Wheatley had told him his novels had been translated into every language except one, although he could not remember which, to which a passer-by replied, 'English'. Wheatley probably did not care given how much money he was making, which he was determined to keep it out of the hands of the taxman. He spent lavishly on wine, food and antiques, particularly Chinese pieces, and also set up a company from which the books were written – part of what his autobiographer Phil Baker describes as a guerrilla war with the Inland Revenue.

Two weeks before his death in November 1977, Wheatley received conditional absolution from his old friend Cyril Eastaugh, the bishop of Peterborough. He was cremated in Tooting. As Baker writes: 'Nothing could have been more in tune with his beliefs than to rise up towards the radiance and be welcomed by some really top chaps in the field.'[15]

So what sort of a man was he? Dennis Wheatley was popular and well-liked throughout his life. He was quintessentially English. His work is regarded as something of a joke these days, but a great many occultists were inspired by reading Wheatley, and many retain a considerable affection for him. Though there is no evidence that he practised magic himself, Wheatley is one of a number of writers of occult thrillers – like Harrison Ainsworth – who have nonetheless served a role in feeding into a contemporary religious movement. And on a final note, occultist William Gray once claimed to esoteric writer R. J. Stewart that Wheatley's novels were a plot by British intelligence, who had recruited him to discredit the occult.

## Dion Fortune

Dion Fortune is one of the major figures of the history of paganism in the twentieth century, but there are still many people who have not heard of her.

Fortune – whose birth name was Violet Firth – was particularly connected with London and Glastonbury. Her book *Avalon of the Heart* (1934) describes a long love affair with the Somerset town. Much of the magical practice that she employed during her 'war work' was built on images of Glastonbury and of the Tor, but it dealt with Christian as well as Arthurian and

Celtic heritages: she combines a number of influences within her work.

Fortune has left a wide-ranging legacy, including a literary one, and this is perhaps best borne out in the writings of another female writer who has made a significant mark on paganism, particularly in the UK and USA: Marion Zimmer Bradley, author of *The Mists of Avalon* mentioned earlier. The Atlantean background from which the Arthurian characters of Bradley's novel emerge is directly inspired by Fortune's writings on Atlantis in her novel *The Sea Priestess* (1938).

Fortune was born in Llandudno, North Wales, on 6 December 1890, the daughter of parents with an active interest in the Christian Science and Garden City movements and who were involved in the running of hydrotherapeutic establishments. Her interest in occultism was sparked in 1916 when, as a psychotherapist, she came across the startling work of Dr Theodore Moriarty, who became her first esoteric teacher and inspired her series of short stories, *The Secrets of Dr Taverner*. Fortune claimed that a great deal of the background material of those short stories was not only true, but downplayed, as no one would believe her if she told them what really happened.

Having embarked upon the occult path, Fortune became a member of the Theosophical Society and the Alpha et Omega temple of the former Golden Dawn, followed by the Stella Matutina, and also the Cromlech Temple. But she became disillusioned with these groups and set about founding her own.

Fortune's group was based in an old officers' mess hut erected at the foot of Glastonbury Tor, named Chalice Orchard. It became the first headquarters of the Community (later

Fraternity and then Society) of the Inner Light. Soon afterwards the group acquired a house in the Bayswater district of
London that was big enough to accommodate some members
as well as to contain office facilities and a magical lodge. The
Fraternity soon became an initiatory school of high calibre.
Members attracted during the 1930s included Establishment
figures such as W. E. Butler, Colonel C.R.F. Seymour and the
author and literary agent Christine Hartley. Working in trance
mediumship, Fortune claimed to have made contacts with certain inner plane adepts, or Masters. She is thus set firmly within
the milieu of early twentieth-century occult practice with its
links to Theosophy and Helena Blavatsky.

During this period, Fortune wrote several esoteric novels
to illustrate the practical applications of her textbooks and the
articles in her house journal, the *Inner Light Magazine*. She
pioneered the popular exposition of the Kabbalah as a key to the
Western Mystery Tradition with her book *The Mystical Qabalah*
(1935), which is still one of the best texts available on the subject.
Her other important work, *The Cosmic Doctrine* (1966), which
was apparently mediumistically received early on in her career,
was at first reserved for senior initiates; its text is abstract and
difficult to follow and is intended for meditation rather than
as a straightforward guide.

During the Second World War she organized her own contribution to the war effort on a magical level, with an extended
meditation group, and continued to operate in the midst of the
Blitz despite a bomb bringing down the roof of her London
headquarters in 1940. Her meditational work included a series
of weekly and then monthly letters to students, later published
as *Dion Fortune's Magical Battle of Britain*.

In early January 1946 Dion Fortune returned from Glastonbury feeling tired and unwell, was admitted to Middlesex Hospital in London and died a few days later from leukaemia, at the comparatively young age of 55. She is buried in the municipal cemetery at Glastonbury, with the remains of her close friend and colleague Charles Thomas Loveday close by.

The Society of the Inner Light (the name was changed for legal reasons) continued to operate as an initiatory school for some years after Fortune's death, under the leadership of Margaret Lumley Brown. A number of writers and practitioners, such as Gareth Knight and Dolores Ashcroft-Nowicki, were trained under its aegis and are still working today.

*The Sea Priestess* is arguably Fortune's greatest work of fiction. Some of her earlier occult thrillers contain episodes of unintentional hilarity – an episode in *The Demon Lover* where the villain shocks and appals the heroine by driving her at nearly 60 mph on a motorcycle, for instance – but these must be seen in their context and period. In some, the prose is very purple indeed. But by the time of *The Sea Priestess*, Fortune's writing has hit a high mark of fluidity and humour.

Her hero, Wilfred, is a young estate agent whose world is changed by the appearance of an elderly property client, Vivian Le Fay Morgan, who is restoring a ruined fort at the end of a nearby headland. Gradually she introduces him to more ancient beliefs, for Wilfred is linked to the lunar feminine and is powerfully affected by the tide and the moon. Out on the headland, he starts to have visions of a former life in which refugees from Atlantis come to the West Country and establish a cult. They call their new land after the names of the old – the 'Naradek' river, for instance, becomes the 'Narrowdick'.

A number of the place names that subsequently turn up in Marion Zimmer Bradley's *Mists of Avalon* emanate from this earlier novel: the river Naradek, for instance – although this may be an element of existing mystery school tradition rather than having been invented by Fortune. If it is, it possibly comes from the Golden Dawn. Esotericist and writer Dolores Ashcroft-Nowicki, in her workshops on Atlantean magic, apparently was directly inspired by Fortune's novel, and a lot of her mystery teachings come from Fortune's own work.

Morgan herself turns out to be the reincarnation of the sea priestess, summoned from drowned Atlantis in order to save another drowning land, this time the Levels of the West Country. Wilfred, too, is a reincarnation – of the original Sea Priestess's sacrifice. There are shades here of Frazer's *The Golden Bough*, and the novel contains themes that are common throughout Fortune's writing: lunar and water magic, polarity between male and female, the return of the old gods and powers. In the sequel, *Moon Magic* (published posthumously in 1956), Fortune leaves the West Country as a setting for her other great esoteric landscape love, London, and we see Somerset no more. The book is said to have been finished by Fortune after her death. Whether she actually channelled it through a medium, or whether someone else simply picked up on her notes and her intuition, is not for me to say, but finished it was.

Glastonbury artist Yuri Leitch has suggested that Morgan might be based on sculptress and writer Katharine Maltwood, who was glamorous and wealthy, and who seems to have had a substantial occult background. Maltwood and Fortune appear to have fallen out at some point, as Maltwood talks disaparagingly about 'pretend occultists' in Glastonbury (she lived nearby) at the time that Fortune was working there. Writer Alan Richardson suggests that Morgan may also be based on Golden Dawn and Cromlech Temple member Maiya Tranchell-Hayes, who was a contact of Fortune's. The Cromlech Temple was part of the Holy Order of the Sun (an analogous order to the Golden Dawn).

Whatever the case, Fortune's literary descent lives on in *The Mists of Avalon*. There seems little doubt that Marion Zimmer Bradley was directly inspired by Fortune's works. Bradley's inheritor and sister-in-law Diana Paxson has stated in a letter that Fortune's Vivian Le Fay Morgan was both the progenitor and descendant of the Morgaine in the *Mists* novel. They are not very similar characters: Fortune's Morgan is probably Dion as she would have liked to have looked, whereas Bradley's Morgaine is described as small and plain. Appearance is nonetheless important, because to her half-brother Arthur, with whom she inadvertently mates under tribal law, Morgaine is darkly bewitching, much in the manner of her literary progenitor.

*The Mists of Avalon* began something of a feminist pagan revolution. It is somewhat fashionable now to disavow the novels as being so influential, partly because of recent revelations about Bradley's alleged abuse of her own children, but most roads in the contemporary Goddess movement lead back to this novel. There has been a lot of contention about just how much of a pagan Bradley herself actually was, and the answer seems to be that she was not perhaps a committed one, since she died a Christian, although she and her husband did form a ceremonial lodge in the 1960s called the Aquarian Order of the Restoration. However, Bradley has said explicitly that the priestess training in *Mists* comes from the writings of Starhawk, founder in 1979 of the Reclaiming witch tradition, and thus you have here an instance of fantasy literature and contemporary magical practice influencing one another. This explains, I think, why the magic in the *Avalon* books feels so American. Whether it realizes it or not, u.s.-based Wicca draws much more heavily on Christian practice. There is nothing wrong with this as such, but reading Bernard Cornwell's Arthurian novels, in which the magic is heavily founded on folklore and shamanism, highlights the difference. Whether she was a long-term practitioner or only dabbled, Bradley certainly had the ability to tap into a particular sensibility. In this she shares the ability of other fantasy writers who seem able to convey an inspirational mood, such as Robert Holdstock.

In the case of *Mists*, I am also intrigued by the parallels between a writer who starts a story about two sisters and then hands over the rights to the series to her sister-in-law, who is herself a priestess: Diana Paxson practises the modern version of the Norse divinatory art of seidr, which we visited in Chapter Two.

I ought to add that Bradley's work is not the only contemporary fantasy series to have been inspired by the work of Dion Fortune. Fantasy writers Katherine Kurtz and Deborah Turner Harris also draw on her writing in the Adept series. Kurtz's novel *Lammas Night* (1983) is directly inspired by Fortune's *Magical Battle of Britain*, and the events of the Adept series, which take place much later (the 1990s onwards), are drawn from Fortune's own brand of visualizatory magic. I know of at least one form of ceremonial magical practice that was adopted from Kurtz's *Lammas Night*, by someone who works closely with Dolores Ashcroft-Nowicki, so here again we have fantasy literature both emerging from esoteric practice and feeding back into it.

Aleister Crowley's order was not the only magical group in the UK to address sex magic. Dion Fortune writes extensively about it in her novels as well as her non-fiction works: the energy of magic comes from the polarity between male and female (non-heterosexual sex is not addressed here). Her 1924 work *The Esoteric Philosophy of Love and Marriage* is directly concerned with sexual energies, and it seems likely that she was influenced by the magical teachings of the Cromlech Temple. Moina Mathers accused Fortune of 'betraying' secrets concerned with sex magic, and from new research by James North, it appears that this material came from the higher grades of the Cromlech Temple.

Fortune's approach to this issue was much more concerned with ethics and responsibility than Crowley's. It is possible now to take issue with Fortune's heteronormativity and also with the lack of agency displayed by some of her female characters (Ursula in *The Winged Bull* is manipulated for his own magical ends by her much older brother, who is presented as one of the good guys, with little regard for her own wishes), but I do not consider this to be unusual for the time in which she was writing. Morgan Le Fay in Fortune's novel *Moon Magic* also deploys sexual tension for magical purposes, but she is definitely in the driving seat where the power dynamics of the novel are concerned. Note, though, that Fortune is concerned more with sexual energy in magic than she is with sexual practice in magic.

With comments such as 'Orgasm earths the force; so does a properly worked magical ceremony,'[16] it is clear that this form of magic is central to Fortune's practice and it is still considered to be of significant interest to modern occultists. Much Wiccan symbolism is based around fertility and sex – Gardner conceived of Wicca as a fertility cult, after all. The blade dipped into a chalice at the culmination of some Wiccan rites is an obvious analogy to the sexual act and some covens do still make sex part of initiation rituals.

$$ )) \bigcirc (( $$

It was not just the written word that influenced magical practice over the course of the twentieth century. Few people know much about Austin Osman Spare today outside occult circles, and his name will even be unfamiliar to many pagans. However, interest in this artist and occultist is beginning to be revived, with a television documentary in 2017 and London exhibitions of his work in Southwark and at the esoteric Atlantis Bookshop.

Hailed at the beginning of his career as the next Aubrey Beardsley, Spare was born in 1886 in London. Following a spell at the Royal College of Art, he was one of the youngest entrants into the Royal Academy summer exhibition in 1904. He was a friend of Aleister Crowley and also produced a series of his own grimoires: *Earth Inferno* (1905), *The Book of Pleasure* (1913) and *The Focus of Life* (1931). He made a number of drawings for Crowley's magazine *The Equinox* and was paid with a ritual robe. He joined Crowley's magical order Argenteum Astrum but was not a full member and later fell out with Crowley – like so many people. There was a suggestion that Crowley had tried to seduce him, while Crowley himself claimed that Spare had been overly interested in black magic and had been held back from full membership of the order as a result.

Later in life, Spare claimed to have been seduced by an older woman named Witch Patterson, one of the descendants of the

Salem witches who taught Spare how to practise magic, but there is little evidence for her existence. He was, however, a close friend of suffragette Sylvia Pankhurst while at art college, so may have had sympathies with unconventional and strong women. Inspired by Symbolism and Art Nouveau, his disturbing and beautiful artwork continues to be sought by collectors. John Singer Sargent and Augustus John both praised his draughtsmanship.

Spare lived in poverty in Southwark, undertaking paintings of local people in exchange for beer and cat food (he adopted a large number of stray cats). He died in 1959, but his work was rediscovered in the 1970s when interest was taken in him by musicians such as Genesis P-Orridge, a founding member of COUM Transmissions, Throbbing Gristle and Psychic TV. Occult writer and Thelemite Kenneth Grant also kept his legacy alive.

Spare's principal influence on the practice of magic in the twentieth century was through his use of sigils. In this, he may in turn have been influenced by the Golden Dawn, although sigils appear in many of the grimoires and we came across them when we looked at demonology. A sigil is a magical symbol containing different elements, and is composed of, for example, a fusion of letters. Once you have created the sigil, you need to destroy it so that it enters into the unconscious mind: your subconscious will then set to work upon it and manifest whatever the sigil holds. Spare's work has thus fed into the creation of chaos magick, a contemporary form of magical practice that also uses sigils, among other elements.

Having looked at some of the influences on mid-twentieth-century pagan and esoteric practice, it is now time to consider some of the groups themselves. We will begin with the largest modern pagan movement in the UK: Wicca.

# Wicca

Wicca is the most public of all the pagan paths, though not the most notorious. Its personalities, whether living or not, continue to influence paganism, for there is a case to be made that Wicca involves an element of the personality cult. This is not necessarily a bad thing but it is in evidence, and is partly a result of the way that Wicca is structured.

But before going into the history of some of the personalities around Wicca, I shall give a brief overview as to what Wiccans believe and practise. In general, although there may be differences between groups (and there are some fierce, if to the outside eye minor, doctrinal issues between Wiccan paths), Wiccans follow what has become a standard set of practices. These include:

- Following the 'wheel of the year': the four 'sabbats' (Samhain (31 October), Imbolc (1 February), Beltane (1 May) and Lammas (1 August)) and the four cross-quarter days (winter solstice (*c.* 21 December), spring equinox (*c.* 21 March), summer solstice (*c.* 21 June) and autumn equinox (*c.* 21 September)), which all fall six weeks apart and which are celebrated. The cross-quarter days, being astronomically based, might vary slightly as to the calendrical date.
- The lunar cycle: holding rituals according to the phases of the moon.
- Honouring the gods and goddesses, which might be Celtic, Saxon, Norse, Egyptian or other.
- Spell work: some Wiccans do practise 'actual' magic; others don't, and prefer to worship instead.

◖ Initiation. This is the single biggest issue that divides Wiccans from other pagan groups. In Wicca your joining of a particular path – Gardnerian, Alexandrian or other – depends on who initiates you and who initiated them. It is a bit like the papal lineage and is taken very seriously. Quite often people are described as 'not proper Wiccans' because they haven't been initiated by the right person or because someone disagrees with another group's doctrinal practice – for example, whether women can initiate other women, or men other men (standard practice is that women initiate men and vice versa).

◖ Some Wiccans worship other entities, but the typical deities of contemporary Wicca are the Horned God and the Great Goddess. We have explored the origins of the Horned God in our previous chapter, and we are going to be examining the origins of the Goddess – sometimes presented as a triple figure of Maiden, Mother and Crone – a little later in this chapter, when we come to investigate the Goddess movement.

While other pagan groups are initiatory, for example some Druidic organizations, they do not attach nearly as much importance to the initiatory line and they tend to look askance at Wiccans for being so obsessed with it. American Wiccans in particular take lineage very seriously. A senior Wiccan friend was once asked, in the U.S., 'which number' he was. He eventually worked out that the person meant the number of initiations he was from Wiccan forefather Alex Sanders. The person who asked him turned out to be 36 or so initiations down the line;

my friend was number two and was treated with great respect correspondingly.

Wicca has contributed greatly to British paganism, and it has spread across the world, too: North America, the Antipodes, Europe and elsewhere. Its popularity with young women, in particular, goes in waves; every generation seems to discover it anew, with its emphasis on the divine feminine.

So what is the difference between Wicca and witchcraft? *Is* there a difference? The people we looked at in our earlier chapters may have been witches, but they certainly were not Wiccans. Wicca itself started primarily with Gerald Gardner. However, not everyone practising witchcraft – and what that is is often self-defined – would identify themselves as Wiccan. A lot of people do not want to work in a group, such as a coven. They are termed 'solitaries', although they may dip in and out of other people's groups from time to time or attend public ceremonies. They may follow the wheel of the year and do magic according to the phases of the moon. However, they are unlikely to get caught up in Wiccan politics and they may or may not be initiated: you do not *have* to be an initiate to practise magic. 'Hedgewitch craft' is still popular, with people doing what they have been doing for centuries – mixing up healing herbs in their kitchens, making their own incense and candles, and generally practising low-key, private witchcraft that is no one's business but their own. It is hard to know how many of them there are, but apart from the fact that they tend to practise privately, they bear most resemblance to the old cunning folk whom we looked at in previous chapters.

So where did Wicca itself begin? One of the most influential people in the course of twentieth-century magical practice was its founder, Gerald Gardner. The son of a timber merchant, born in 1884, Gardner was asthmatic as a child and received no formal education. His governess took him abroad for the sake of his health, so the young Gerald gained a wide experience of the world, and in 1900 he headed for Asia, where he became a rubber and tea planter. His working life was therefore spent in Malaysia and India, with occasional visits to Britain, until he retired. With his wife, Donna, Gardner returned to London and subsequently bought a house in the New Forest. Here, he was to meet a group of people who would change the course of his life.

They were known as the Crotona Fellowship, a Rosicrucian group. Gardner, who had had a lifelong interest in magical practice, claimed that some of the group had associations with a local coven that practised a form of witchcraft that had endured for hundreds of years, although it is by no means clear that this was the case.

One of the instigators of the concept of an ancient witch cult that has lasted secretly through the ages was the so-called 'Grandmother of Wicca', Margaret Murray. A respected Egyptologist unable to return to Egypt during the First World War, Murray concentrated on researching her belief that the witch trials were an attempt to stamp out a pre-Christian pagan fertility religion in Britain and Europe that worshipped the Horned God and a moon goddess. Her 1921 study *The Witch-cult in Western Europe* was hugely influential: many of its claims have passed into popular belief. But, as Hutton says, it 'rested upon a small amount of archival research, with extensive use of printed trial records in nineteenth-century editions, plus early modern pamphlets and works of demonology'.[17] Murray's research is now substantially discredited and regarded with deep suspicion by academic folklorists, but it is likely that the Crotona Fellowship, among others, adopted her speculations as historical fact and hence regarded themselves as a continuation of an ancient witch cult: 'Murray may have seemed the ideal fairy godmother, and her theory became the pumpkin coach that could transport them into the realm of fantasy for which they longed.'[18]

One of the Crotona Fellowship was a woman named Edith Woodford-Grimes, a pillar of the local community and a private elocution teacher from a strongly Christian family who assisted Gardner in drawing up a modern form of witch-craft – what would become modern Wicca. Author Philip Heselton has done a comprehensive job in researching the roots of Wiccan practice, which seem to come mainly from the Golden Dawn, Aleister Crowley, British folklore, Gardner's own enthusiasms (which included naturism), and possibly more curious origins such as variations on the Scout movement like the Kindred of the Kibbo Kift (a back-to-the-land youth move-ment established after the First World War, which drew on esoteric thought to perform their own rituals) and contem-porary children's literature. Gardner was, from the accounts of those who knew him, an endearingly enthusiastic man, and with the help of various women friends – such as Edith, and his coven member Doreen Valiente – penned a number of the texts and rituals that we associate with Wiccan practice. He was also often mischievous, and somewhat prone to exaggeration, so some of his claims about the origins of witchcraft need to be taken with a pinch of salt.

Gardner can truly be called the 'father' of modern Wicca, and his influence – often criticized – is difficult to overestimate.

He was a remarkable individual and however much of the Wicca he developed came from external, old sources, and however much he might have made up, what he presented to the world over a number of years is now one of the world's fastest growing religions. But Gardner was not the only personality involved in the promotion of Wicca.

Alex Sanders was the founder of the form of witchcraft known as Alexandrian Wicca, now one of the best-known forms of the Craft. An erudite publicity-seeker, Sanders did a great deal in the late 1960s and early '70s to publicize Wicca. Born on 6 June 1926 in Liverpool, Sanders came from a Welsh background and claimed to have been initiated into witchcraft by his grandmother, a Mrs Bibby.

> One evening in 1933, when I was seven, I was sent round to my grandmother's house for tea. For some reason I didn't knock at the door as I went in, and was confronted by my grandmother, naked, with her grey hair hanging down to her waist, standing in a circle drawn on the kitchen floor.[19]

It is difficult to know just how many of his claims are true, as – not unlike Gardner – Sanders had a trickster-like aspect that frequently led him to embellish the facts. The priestess Patricia Crowther says that she had letters from Sanders in the early 1960s in which he made no mention of this familial initiation, and he claimed subsequently to have been initiated by a woman in Nottingham. However, in later biographies his wife Maxine stated that he came from a highly psychic family, and that this fuelled his interest in the esoteric.

Sanders worked as a stage medium for a while, but he also had more conventional employment, including work in a pharmaceutical factory, during which he met Maxine's mother. She was a woman who had strong spiritual interests and they became friends, though Maxine's father, by all accounts, did not like him. Sanders worked with a number of covens, most of which seem to have been Gardnerian, but despite his relatively novice status, he was already courting the media interest that would become a hallmark of his later magical career.

In 1965 Sanders handfasted – a non-legal form of pagan marriage – Maxine, who, though a very young woman at the time, had already been involved with a magical order associated with the Egyptian mythos. Sanders's behaviour towards his glamorous young partner was often questionable: he arranged for naked pictures of her to be published in a local newspapers, resulting in not just embarrassment but persecution from Maxine's shocked neighbours in Manchester.

The relationship continued, however. Sanders made Maxine his High Priestess and they moved from Manchester to London in 1967, where Maxine gave birth to their child Maya. In 1972 she had a son, Victor, but by this time the couple had separated, partly, it seems, because Sanders had strong homosexual leanings and had an affair with a young man in the coven.

From reading Maxine's early autobiography, *Queen of the Witches*, and her more recent *Firechild*, it appears that Sanders was an abusive and manipulative individual, however talented he may have been in terms of magical practice. His love of publicity and relationship with the *News of the World* tabloid brought the Craft into the public eye, sometimes in a most sensationalist manner, and it is debatable whether Sanders really did the movement any favours by this. Nonetheless, Sanders's magical practice resulted in the Alexandrian movement, spawning hundreds of covens across the UK and U.S. Alongside Gardnerian Wicca, it is one of the major movements in witchcraft today.

Sanders died in 1988. Maxine, however, continues to teach and run covens of her own. *Firechild* is well worth reading as it gives a good sense of what the Craft scene was like in the 1960s and '70s – rather more colourful than it is now, it must be said. An early piece of film footage exists of Sanders performing a ritual dance in an Aztec loincloth. Halfway through, he sets it on fire, then nonchalantly beats it out and continues with the performance.

From the point of view of the more established and sophisticated Craft today, it is perhaps too easy to smile at some of the more theatrical aspects of the early Wiccan movements. But what is beyond question is that people like the Sanderses brought Wicca into the public eye, and although a number of their rituals may seem questionable, this public focus did eventually serve to popularize this particular spiritual path. Alexandrian Wicca also gave rise to other influential Wiccans.

Born on 28 June 1916, Stewart Farrar was one of those people and was instrumental in bringing modern witchcraft to a wider audience. He graduated from University College London with a degree in journalism in the 1930s and went into the army, and after the war he returned to Britain to work as a journalist. In 1969, while working for a paper known as *Reveille*, he was sent to cover a press screening of the film *Legend of the Witches*, where he met Alex and Maxine Sanders. Invited to interview Sanders, the two got on, and Sanders in turn invited him to attend an initiation ceremony. This gave rise to Farrar's book on Wicca,

*What Witches Do* (1971), and sparked a lifelong interest in the craft. During one of the meetings, he met his future wife, then Janet Owen, and they were initiated by the Sanderses.

After their marriage, Stewart and Janet moved to Ireland and went on to publish a number of highly regarded and influential works on witchcraft. They were subsequently joined by Gavin Bone, who married Janet after Stewart's death in 2000.

Born in 1950, Janet Farrar grew up in London, where she worked as a model and receptionist. She began attending Sanders's rituals after she went along to 'rescue' a friend. She has subsequently become one of the best-known faces of modern paganism, featuring in many photographs of Craft practices. She currently lives in Meath with Gavin, and continues to write on paganism and witchcraft. Her openness, tolerance and sense of humour make her one of the most accessible people from the early years of the modern Craft and her ability to conduct profound rituals while puncturing pomposity is sadly rare. Gavin Bone himself was born in 1964 and grew up in Portsmouth. He is a registered nurse with a particular interest in healing, and he has publicized the role of healing within modern witchcraft and written a number of works on the ways in which energy is channelled. With Janet, he runs a progressive coven in Ireland called the Coven Na Callaighe, and holds workshops and talks throughout the world. Together they take a straightforward and sensible approach to witchcraft, preferring to refer to it as 'progressive' rather than adopting one of the more loaded hereditary titles such as 'Alexandrian'.

These are not the only influences. Born as Roy Bowers in 1931, the young man who called himself Robert Cochrane proved influential within a strand of witchcraft now known as the Clan of Tubal Cain. Like others, he claimed to have been born into a family of hereditary witches whose origins went back to the sixteenth century, but there seems to be no evidence for this and his family denounced these claims, stating that they were all Methodists. A working-class boy from West London whose charisma and imagination were undoubted, Cochrane seems in fact to have become interested in the occult after attending a lecture held by the Society for Psychical Research in Kensington. After a failed stint in the army (he was arrested for going absent without leave), Cochrane worked for some time as a blacksmith (hence his adoption of the biblical blacksmith Tubal Cain as a patron) and as a bargee, collecting what may have been authentic folklore from these traditional occupations. But he was also influenced by Robert Graves, advertising in the newspaper for anyone who had read *The White Goddess* to contact him.

Taking a combative attitude towards Gardner and Wicca, Cochrane nonetheless became well connected within contemporary paganism, becoming a friend of ceremonial magician William Gray and of Doreen Valiente and other Gardnerian initiates such as Eleanor Bone and Lois Bourne. Valiente described him as a remarkable man, but he was also troubled, and committed suicide on Midsummer's Eve 1966 by ingesting a combination of belladonna and Librium. The offshoots of the Clan of Tubal Cain nonetheless continue today.

Marian Green is a British author who has been working in the fields of magic and witchcraft since the early 1960s. In addition to the Quest conference – the longest-running pagan conference in Britain if not the world – she has edited the magazine *Quest* since founding it in 1970. She was previously a council member of the Pagan Federation and the editor of *Pagan Dawn*. Her books include *A Witch Alone*, *Everyday Magic*, *Magic in Principle and Practice* and many more.

The seeds of Quest began at a dinner, entitled the Pentagram Dinner, at the Rembrandt Hotel in London in 1964. Doreen Valiente and other pagan personalities of the 1960s were in attendance. In 1965 the dinner was held again, with William Gray demonstrating some of the connections between various paths in paganism at the time. The dinner became a conference in 1967 and moved to the Ivanhoe Hotel near the British Museum, charging half a crown as an entry fee. Occultist and writer Elizabeth St George (1937–2007) also attended. Eventually it moved to the Kenilworth Hotel but continued to be regularly attended by esoteric luminaries.

St George, a student of William Gray's who also worked for the London bookshop Atlantis, was in possession of a duplicating machine and thought it would be nice to have a newsletter in between meetings. The name *Quest* was chosen. A small press was started, publishing the works of more obscure writers who did not want to be in the public eye.

The Quest conference celebrated its fiftieth anniversary in 2017. It is now held in the Southville Community Centre in Bristol and features speakers from across the pagan community. Marian Green also still publishes the *Quest* quarterly journal, containing material on magic, witchcraft and practical occultism, along with personal experiences and reviews. It has been published four times a year since its inception, and is one of the longest-running regularly published magazines in Britain. Esoteric practitioner Pamela Couchman says:

I think I have been attending the Quest conference for twenty years, although I have missed the odd one here and there.

When I first starting attending it was before my own Internet days and social media was in the realms of ... pea soup. I can remember my excitement and nervousness on my first venture into the Quest conference, which was then being held in the Round House in Bristol.

My overriding feeling about my years at Quest [is that they] are really like a quest, the knock of change. In fact when I have physically opened the door of the venue and entered, I have often opened the door to change in my own life and spirituality. The people I have met, the spoken words in some of the amazing talks . . . But in truth the wealth of knowledge that Quest has held in its arms over the years is just awe-inspiring and has been the gateway to so many realms over the years.[20]

Conference attendee Lynda Woodhead comments:

It would [have been] around 1985–6. I was working in London – at that time, information on pagan moots or events [could only be found] via the various publications available. Trying to remember my first point of contact is difficult but I must have purchased one of them from a bookshop – I think Quest had its own publications out, as did The Cauldron, and through them I joined the Pagan Federation in about 1985. They were fab – lots of really good articles, and also 'real' magic – stuff that you live, which is part of everyday life – not just a hobby.[21]

Green's longstanding influence on contemporary paganism is undoubted, and she remains a champion of individual witchcraft practised away from the coven structure.

If you are interested in finding out more about Wicca and the history of magic, then one of your first stops should be the museum at Boscastle in Cornwall. This is one of the oldest occult and magical museums in the world and is well known to the majority of British pagans. Cecil Williamson originally founded it in Stratford-upon-Avon, but local opposition obliged him to move the museum (then the Folklore Centre of Superstition and Witchcraft) to an old windmill at Castletown on the Isle of Man in 1948. It was renamed the Museum of Magic and Witchcraft in 1951 as a result of the repeal of the Witchcraft Act in that year. Gerald Gardner was on board as the resident witch; the two men had become friends after a meeting at the Atlantis Bookshop in 1948. Williamson himself had first encountered magical practice in Devon in 1916, intervening to defend a woman who was being accused of witchcraft by locals, and was subsequently introduced to African magic in Rhodesia. A friend not only of Gardner but of Crowley, Williamson is said to have been hired by British Intelligence in 1938 to investigate the occult interests of the Nazis.

Williamson later sold the Isle of Man museum to Gardner, who invented a more exciting history for it and ran it for the rest of his life. Ownership passed to Monique Wilson after Gardner's death in 1964, but this version of the museum closed in the 1970s and the collection was sold to the Ripley's Believe It or Not! organization.

Meanwhile, Williamson moved his own version of the museum to the mainland. It was located in Windsor, where

Williamson once more encountered local opposition, and then Gloucestershire, where it was subjected to an arson attack. The museum ended up in Boscastle in 1960. Williamson stated:

> Three miles away from this spot you can find this pre-historic maze stone carved into a living rock face, proof that from ancient times man and his magic making with the world of spirit were active in this area. The centuries have passed and times have changed and yet all around us in this quiet corner of England there is a strange feeling that we are not alone and that the shades of persons passed on and over into the world of spirit are very close. That is why this Museum of Witchcraft is located here. One is standing on the edge of the beyond.[22]

Graham King bought the museum in 1996, taking ownership at midnight on Halloween, and ran it for many years despite a crisis in 2004, when a huge flash flood swept through the town, devastating local properties and washing cars out to sea. King saved many objects from the museum and earned the respect of the town by assisting coastguards in their efforts to make sure that everyone was safe (no lives were lost in the flood, although a waxwork figure of a crystal-ball reader was found in the wreckage and initially assumed to be a human body!).

King's efforts after this catastrophe led to the further development of the museum, and on his retirement, on 31 October 2013, he gifted the museum and its contents to Simon Costin, director of the Museum of British Folklore. With over 3,000 objects and 7,000 books, the museum is not only the repository of a significant collection of magical artefacts, but a major resource for academics and amateur researchers alike. It is invaluable to anyone who is interested in the beliefs and practices of cunning folk.

## Modern Druids

We have visited the Druids before: in ancient times and then more recently, in the Georgian period. But the Druids did not stop there. The 'friendly' societies and fraternal brotherhoods with a smattering of spiritual practice we met in the eighteenth century continued through Victorian times into our own day, and they are very much alive and kicking now. This is primarily due to one man – a gentle poet and naturist called Ross Nichols. But we shall begin by looking at his early twentieth-century forbears.

Modern Druidry owes much to George Watson MacGregor Reid and his son Robert, although neither are household names among Druids themselves, let alone the wider pagan field. Reid Senior was a combative, apparently somewhat overbearing man whose order – the Universal Bond – carries the dubious kudos of having been the last set of the Druids to be massacred. Nineteen of them went out to Libya in around 1913 to lend their support to an Islamic movement, the Senussi. This was during the Italian colonization of the region and the poor Druids died alongside the Senussi, under the fire of Italian guns. Reid was not among them, but he did go into battle of a different kind: against British bureaucracy, over the right to gather at Stonehenge (which local people had been doing for generations). Reid was no diplomat and he upset a great many people, eventually falling out with his own son Robert, a civil servant who nonetheless took up the mantle of his father's order on Reid Senior's death.

George Reid devoted his cause to many issues that are dear to the hearts of contemporary pagans today:

> health reform, back-to-nature, natural health and anti-vaccination movements; food reform, vegetarian and anti-vivisection movements; political reform, feminism, anarchism and socialism; religious reform, theosophy and mysticism, Celticism and anti-imperialism – all these were live issues then as now. They were the ideals of the counter-culture, and George Watson Reid was right in the thick of it.[23]

He was also highly visible in the media of the day: a big man with wild ideas and a huge presence. People flocked to hear what Adam Stout, in his Mount Haemus lecture quoted above, refers to as his 'magnificent rantings'.

Reid's son Robert was a very different type of person: a bridge-builder rather than someone who drops social bombs. He was well connected in the esoteric world, being a friend of occult scholar Lewis Spence and Gerald Gardner, and he was familiar with the rites of the Golden Dawn. His version of the order held midsummer rites at Stonehenge, but also celebrated the equinoxes at Tower Hill in London, starting in the 1950s. It is under Robert Reid's aegis that Druidry shows signs of the concepts that are familiar to students of it today: the four elements, self-development, a focus on the astronomical features of the year, and a focus also on King Arthur as a figure to be revered. The Tower Hill rituals contained the following vow, which is still an integral part of the rites of the Order of Bards, Ovates and Druids:

> We swear, by peace and love to stand
> Heart to heart, and hand in hand;
> Mark! O Spirit, and hear us now,
> Confirming this, our sacred vow.

Robert Reid died unexpectedly in 1964, and the Order of the Universal Bond was taken over by a natural health practitioner named Thomas Maughan, who pipped to the post a man named Philip Ross Nichols.

Born in 1902, Nichols was a friend of Gerald Gardner and the two men exchanged perhaps more information and ideas than many Druids or Wiccans are aware of. An academic, historian and poet (he was a contemporary of Auden and Eliot), Nichols was a member of the Ancient Order of Druids, but founded his own order – the Order of Bards, Ovates and Druids – in the 1960s. Today OBOD is the largest Druid order in the world, under the chieftainship of Philip Carr-Gomm, a student of Nichols, although the post will pass to Irish Druid Eimear Burke in 2020, thus giving OBOD its first female chief.

Nichols was perhaps less flamboyant than Gerald Gardner, but shared some of his interests, including naturism. Both he and Gardner were members of the nudist colony known as Spielplatz, and Nichols passed this interest into the wider order (generally, Druids do not work 'skyclad', or naked, as Wiccans often do, although they can if they choose. For public ceremonies, they wear a variety of robes, usually white, like the Romantic perception of their ancient forbears).

OBOD member and author Adele Cosgrove-Bray mentions a meeting between Ross Nichols and a Canadian friend of hers:

> I met a wonderful man named Philip Ross Nichols, sometime in the early 1970s. He was the Chosen Chief of the Order, and lived in a large Victorian house in the London W14 area. He was a small man, very elderly yet as agile as a little monkey. He wore delicate leather sandals and possessed the most exquisite feet I have ever seen![24]

Philip Carr-Gomm says:

> He was a teacher to me – not a guru. He didn't try to be a guru, and later – when I followed one for a while – I realised the difference. Ross offered culture rather than charisma. My guru offered plenty of charisma, but precious little culture, and although charisma may be superficially more appealing, in the end it is the culture in a person that endures. And it is the gifts of their culture that become their contribution to the world that outlasts their mortal lives.[25]

Known as Nuin (the ogham word for the ash tree), Nichols remains a largely unknown poet. He died in 1975.

Today, there are many ways of being a Druid. Some are environmentalists who champion tree-planting programmes. Some are writers, poets or novelists. Some are activists: protesting fracking is popular among contemporary Druids and they were very visible in the road protests of the 1980s and '90s.

Many of them do celebrate at Stonehenge; others are more at home at a rave or in the pub or in a historical lecture. Like all modern pagans, they are varied and diverse.

My own first experience of a Druidic ritual at Stonehenge was around the winter solstice in the late 1990s. I had become a member of OBOD some years earlier and our own group (I was based in Brighton) used to hold its rituals, based around the festivals of the wheel of the year, at the Long Man at Wilmington. The Stonehenge ritual was bigger and involved Druids from all over the country, but was not the main solstice gathering itself. Owing to demand, English Heritage stacks up groups of Druids, rather like incoming planes, in the days surrounding the solstices. We met towards sunset on a day when – unusually before Christmas – there had been quite a heavy snowfall and the stones stood with their feet covered. The sky was cloudless, with a red sun sinking over Salisbury Plain in the west and a full moon rising in the east. It was an exceptionally atmospheric, if exceedingly chilly, ritual, beginning with the casting of a sacred circle (someone walked around the perimeter of the stones with a wand), the calling of the four quarters, and then a celebration of the solstice itself, with reference to the shortness of the day, the full moon and a request for peace and healing for the earth.

There are too many Druidic orders to list here – which in itself shows how popular this nature-based spirituality has become. When I last checked with the press officer of the OBOD, the total number of people who had enrolled in the order's correspondence course was in the region of 36,000. And this is just one of the Druidic orders around today. Why is it so popular? I think this is due to the fact that it dovetails with a number of issues: it is anti-dogmatic, environmentalist and not seen as sinister (a reputation with which witchcraft, Wicca and ceremonial magic still struggle to some degree). It is favourable to feminism and concerned with green political issues. Although it is rarely party political, and you certainly get right-wing Druids, it seems tailor-made for many of the causes that are currently associated with the alternative left in the UK. Yet it is not doctrinaire. There are plenty of Druids who do not consider themselves political, and there is no pressure that I am aware of to become an activist. It is a spiritual path that leaves ethics up to the individual, and although there are often heated debates online and in person, there is no top-down attempt at control.

In religious terms, Druidry is also eclectic: you do not get followers of the goddess Rhiannon attacking adherents of the goddess Ceridwen. Which deity, or deities, a modern Druid chooses to follow is up to them, and it would be considered seriously bad form to try to proselytize on behalf of one particular god or goddess. The possible exception is the (small) number of Druids who adhere to far-right political paths – there are a few, and they tend to hang out with Norse brethren of similar political leanings. This is a problem we'll be looking at when we consider Heathenism below. But attempts to attach race or 'racial purity' to Druidry are extremely unpopular: Druidry is regarded as a set of spiritual practices, not as something that's intrinsic to a particular ethnic identity. There are Jewish Druids, Buddhist Druids and Christian Druids, including a couple of Church of England vicars. Celtic Christianity is seen as compatible with modern Druidry, with its emphasis on nature and personal spiritual improvement. Despite the activism and deeply held political opinions among some of its members, British Druidry in the twenty-first century resembles nothing more closely than the Anglican Church: mild-mannered, tolerant, often vaguely eccentric and earnestly encouraging to anyone who genuinely seeks to develop their spiritual interests.

## Heathenism

Remember the Saxons and the Vikings? Like the witches and the Druids, they too make a return appearance once the twentieth century gets going – at least in terms of their perceived religion. As we have seen, we have a certain amount of information regarding the religions of the Vikings and Saxons, and this has been revived by modern pagans. Like Druidry and Wicca, Heathenism's practices follow a similar sort of core, but this spiritual path has its own flavour as well.

People who follow this path fly under a number of banners: Asatru, the Northern Tradition, Odinism, Forn Sed and Germanic Pagan Reconstructionism. Heathenism is a nationally recognized, official religion in Iceland. The term 'Odinic' was used in the first half of the nineteenth century, by Thomas Carlyle among others.[26]

Modern Heathens, or practitioners of the Norse paths, worship the Saxon and Norse gods. They may hold 'blots', or meetings, and many follow the wheel of the year and other familiar pagan festivals. They look back to the ethical systems described in old Saxon and Norse texts, and a lot of modern Heathens put a great deal of work and study into the runes. There are, however, elements that are not shared by other forms of paganism, such as the Nine Noble Virtues, drawn up by the organization of the Odinic Rite in the UK in the 1970s and taken from the Hávamál:

- ☾ Courage (Valiance)
- ☾ Truth (Sincerity)
- ☾ Honour
- ☾ Fidelity
- ☾ Discipline
- ☾ Hospitality
- ☾ Self-reliance
- ☾ Industriousness (Diligence)

Unlike most text-based religions, Heathenism usually leaves ethics up to the individual, with many Norse practitioners using the Nine Virtues or similar lists of qualities as a loose basis.

There is no one central authority in Heathenism, an aspect common to most forms of paganism. While there are heads of orders, there is no one organization that dominates pagan groups in the same way that, for example, the Vatican dominates Roman Catholicism. And there is considerable acrimony among different Heathen groups, which are mainly split down political rather than doctrinal lines. Heathenry's big problem is Aryan nationalism and the far right, which is not entirely surprising given the Nazi Party's interest in the old Germanic religions. However, there are a great many Heathens who distance them-selves from these extremist views: a lot of groups stand explicitly with Declaration 127, which dissociates Heathen organizations from the Asatru Folk Assembly's stance against membership by non-white or LGBT Heathens, and which has now been signed by some 180 Heathen groups across the world. For instance, the organization Heathen Women United states that it 'has strict membership policies that hold a "zero tolerance" stance for racism, "white pride," or any form of homophobia or bigotry'.[27]

I do not want to overemphasize the role of the far right in contemporary Heathenry, as I believe it to be outnumbered by members of the community who do not hold its discriminatory views and, indeed, who strive to combat them. In the main, Heathenry is embraced as an ethical religion with some valuable contributions, such as runic lore, to paganism as a whole.

## Chaos Magick

Along with Wicca, I believe chaos magick to be one of the most original gifts that contemporary British paganism has given to the world. It is debatable whether it should even fall under the banner of paganism; perhaps, like other organizations that can loosely be described as 'occult', it is more of a fellow traveller. Chaos magicians might not worship pagan gods, although they may work with them, and they may not identify as pagan. If there is such a thing as the 'average' chaos magician, they tend to be creative, enquiring, experimental, often politically active, independent and also often alternative. Chaos magick is sometimes associated with drug use and indeed there is a strand of experimentation (usually responsible) with entheogenic substances within this particular path. Chaos magicians also tend to be more interested in cutting-edge science than other pagans: for instance, quantum mechanics and artificial intelligence.

The underlying principle of chaos magick is that techniques are more important than symbols, and that belief is what really fuels magical work. The latter idea is common to a lot of pagan and occult magical practice. However, many chaos magicians are agnostic over the exact nature of magic: whether it is an actual force that we do not yet understand, or whether it is a psychological mechanism, for instance.

So what do chaos magicians do? I shall give an example of a project in which I was tangentially involved. This took place in the early 2000s and the aim of it was to give the members of the project more time – literally to extend the hours in the day. In order to achieve this, a series of rituals were conducted in order to create a servitor: a magical entity that operates a little bit like a computer program. One of the ideas that has come out of chaos magick is that the universe possesses a basic operating system that can sustain different programs. For instance, Wicca might contain one of these programs, and so might Druidry. The magic undertaken in these paths is perhaps analogous to Word or Excel, with one operating system running beneath. But according to chaos magick, you can 'reprogram' the universe by devising a little program, via a ritual, that will alter reality to your requirements.

Whereas most strands of paganism usually stick to one particular group of gods and goddesses, chaos magick is much more prone to mixing and matching: it is very eclectic. One ritual might include deities from several different traditions – Ceridwen, Loki, Hindu deities such as Kali, or African deities such as Yemaya. Chaos magick also encourages experimental approaches, such as the use of sigils. The sigil might comprise the initials of the words in a statement of intent (for 'I wish for a more fulfilling job' you would take IWFMFJ and make them into an abstract symbol, a bit like a monogram). The system owes a lot to the work of the late esoteric artist Austin Osman Spare, whom we looked at earlier.

Chaos magick does not always invoke gods in its rituals. A chaos magician could write a ritual that employed four of the incarnations of the Doctor in *Doctor Who* in the quarters of a magic circle. I know of at least one that used characters from *Buffy the Vampire Slayer*: Willow in the east, representing air and the intellect; Buffy in the south, with powers of fire and the warrior; Xander in the West, representing water and the heart; and Giles in the north for stability and groundedness. This might come across as silly or irreverent – and chaos magicians do often rely on humour in their work – but it does have a serious side: the amount of energy that people invest in fandom can be seen as a magical act in itself, and the characters in popular TV shows are to an extent archetypes, just as the gods and goddesses are.

Chaos magick is inspired by the work of Peter Carroll (b. 1953) in the UK, and in the U.S. by that of science fiction writer Robert Anton Wilson (1932–2007), who described his work as an 'attempt to break down conditioned associations, to look at the world in a new way, with many models recognized as models or maps, and no one model elevated to the truth'.[28] It is well worth looking into his writings if you want to know more about chaos magick.

## Satanism

Satanism is the thing that comes to many people's minds when they hear the word 'paganism' – which is ironic, because the two paths have almost nothing to do with one another. Contrary to the 'Satanic panics' that were endemic throughout both the UK and the U.S. in the 1980s and early '90s, Satanism is neither a popular nor very common path. You do get teenagers messing about with ouija boards and – if they're ambitious – trying to summon the occasional demon, but this is not hardcore Satanic practice: it is a matter of experimental stupidity, and they usually manage to frighten themselves out of it at some point.

The sort of Satanism that is depicted in popular films and fiction is highly sensational and rarely practised. It is presented as the obverse of Catholicism: crucifixes turned upside down, the Mass reversed. However, there is a clear illustration in this – it is the reverse of a Christian worldview, not a pagan one. The Devil, Satan, is a Christian construct, not a pagan god.

Far more common than this kind of Catholicism-turned-upside-down are more modern forms of Satanism such as the Satanic Temple, whose witty billboards across the USA are a deliberate piece of political activism. The Satanic Temple is a political movement, however, not a religious one.

If the reader is interested in contemporary Satanism, I would direct them to the work of American writer Anton LaVey (1930–1997). It is hard to give an account of LaVey's history because he appears to have made so much of it up, including a background as a carnival showman and an affair with the then unknown Marilyn Monroe. What is incontrovertible is that LaVey became a doyen of the Californian occult scene from the 1960s onwards and produced a number of books in which Satanism is presented as a kind of Nietzschean philosophy, highly individualistic and unapologetically self-centred. LaVey is extremely entertaining but does not exactly come across as a nice guy – no surprises there, really, given his choice of religion. LaVeyan Satanists continue to practise across the world.

So what are the precepts of Satanism? LaVey drew up eleven 'rules' for guidance:

☾ Do not give opinions or advice unless you are asked

☾ Do not tell your troubles to others unless you are sure they want to hear them

☾ When in another's lair, show him respect or else do not go there

☾ If a guest in your lair annoys you, treat him cruelly and without mercy

☾ Do not make sexual advances unless you are given the mating signal

☾ Do not take that which does not belong to you unless it is a burden to the other person and he cries out to be relieved

☾ Acknowledge the power of magic if you have employed it successfully to obtain your desires. If you deny the power of magic after having called upon it with success, you will lose all you have obtained

☾ Do not complain about anything to which you need not subject yourself

☾ Do not harm little children

☾ Do not kill non-human animals unless you are attacked or for your food

☾ When walking in open territory, bother no one. If someone bothers you, ask him to stop. If he does not stop, destroy him

Ashley Palmer of the Church of Satan says:

> The main and most persistent misconception about Satanism and Satanists is that we believe in and worship an anthropomorphic or spiritual being known as 'Satan'

or the 'devil'. This is false. We Satanists are atheists who adopt 'Satan' as a symbol of passion, pride, liberty, and heroic rebellion in the tradition of the proto-Satanic themed poetry and writing of Giosuè Carducci, Lord Byron, John Milton, Benjamin DeCasseres, Mark Twain, and others that pre-date the founding of the Church of Satan.

Stating that one is an atheist leaves a lot of room for belief in a myriad of other spooky delusions unrelated to the existence of god(s) that are also regularly incorrectly packaged with Satanism, so I shall further clarify that as I apply the tool of scientific scepticism to critically analyse and question all things. I therefore reject all forms of pseudo-science, New Age spirituality and the supernatural, including, but not limited to: the occult, magick, Ouija boards, tarot, psychic divination, ghosts, immortality, astral projection, chakras, faith healing, astrology, and conspiracy theories. All of this is as ridiculous to me as praying to Jesus or Shiva.[29]

## The Goddess Movement

Included in the varied and diverse mix of modern pagan paths in Britain is the Goddess movement. It has been part of the UK scene since the 1960s, although it has its origins in the late Victorian period. The Goddess movement has proven popular, particularly among feminist pagans, and in some circles its theology is treated as a given, despite a substantial lack of evidence. Elements of it are found in Wicca and Druidry, too – the concept of a threefold goddess, Maiden, Mother and Crone. But was there such an ancient deity, and who worshipped her? We'll take a look now at where she comes from.

Contrary to popular belief, true triple goddesses are not that commonplace in the ancient world. Hekate, the Greek goddess of the underworld, has a threefold aspect, and there are the mysterious Celtic deities known as the Matres, or Matronae. These appear on votive offerings across Northern Europe and Gaul, sometimes Germanic, sometimes Celtic. They are female figures, one with her hair loose, and are accompanied by representations of sacrificial offerings, such as pigs, fruit and incense. The Greek Fates, or the Moirai, also come in threes. Few classical representations of them survive, but later European art portrays them in a way that has become familiar: Klotho is young and lovely, Lachesis is middle-aged and Atropos is ancient (the carved relief on Alexander von der Mark's grave by Johann Gottfried Schadow illustrates this nicely, as does Paul Thumann's late nineteenth-century painting *The Three Fates*). The other triplicity in Greek legend, the Graeae, are all depicted as ancient, sharing one eye and one tooth between them. Medusa's sisters, they encounter the hero Perseus and are bested by him. They are very similar to the triple Norns in Norse legends, whom we met earlier. However, none of these triplicities are explicitly referred to as Maiden, Mother and Crone. This concept really gained momentum with the publication in 1948 of Robert Graves's work *The White Goddess*. Graves, in turn, was influenced by Frazer's *The Golden Bough* and by Victorian academic Jane Ellen Harrison. Mary Beard comments that Harrison 'changed the way we think about ancient Greek culture – peeling back that calm, white marble exterior to reveal something much more violent, messy and ecstatic underneath ("bloody Jane" they called her, for more reasons than one, I suspect)'.[30]

Harrison, who read Classics at Newnham College, Cambridge, in the mid-1870s, was something of a celebrity in her day: 1,600 people came to one of her talks in Glasgow. She was theatrical and craggily glamorous, with a compelling personality, and was one of the first women in England to have a professional academic career. An atheist, she was nonetheless a member of the Ritualists group at Cambridge, a gathering of academics who sought to explain myths and classical drama as having their origins in ritual. She was also a pacifist and a feminist, attitudes that made her unpopular with many mainstream Victorians, but which led her to adopt a particular slant towards the classical world. Harrison believed that her research bore out the presence of an ancient matrifocal society, one in which women were predominant and that formed an alternative to the notion that the ancient world was violent, warlike and dominated by men. This concept was not original to Harrison, but came from ideas voiced among male academics in the last decades of the nineteenth century: Sir Arthur Evans, initially sceptical, came around to the idea that a single Great Goddess had been worshipped in Crete during his excavation of Knossos in 1901, for example, and we have already noted the influence of Frazer.

Harrison also subscribed to the idea both of a single Great Goddess, an Earth mother, and of the triple goddess concept – the latter deities being aspects of the Great Goddess. This is a viewpoint that is now commonplace among pagans, as in Dion Fortune's statement that 'All gods are one God, and all goddesses are one Goddess, and there is one Initiator.'[31]

Harrison named two of the deities the Maiden and the Mother, but did not expand on what the third entity might be. By 1910, fuelled by the work of people such as Frazer and other anthropologists such as Edward Tylor, the idea of a single Great Goddess, from the Near East or the Balkans, had become something of an orthodoxy in archaeological circles.

Harrison's book *Themis: A Study of the Social Origins of Greek Religion* (1912) hypothesized that the culture had projected a spirit, the 'year god' who dies and is reborn every year. Drawing on *The Golden Bough*, Sigmund Freud and new anthropological theories, Harrison suggested that the year god is the son of the great Earth Goddess and that the earliest Greek religion was matrilinear. According to this theory, the goddess Hera is a holdover from that early religion; her husband Zeus represents the patriarchal takeover of the earlier matriarchal society (according to Harrison, this is one reason why Zeus and Hera have such a difficult relationship!). Zeus is an 'archpatriarchal bourgeois', Harrison claimed, seemingly firmly on the side of Hera. She wrote indignantly that 'she who made all things, gods and mortals alike, is become their plaything, their slave, dowered only with physical beauty, and with a slave's tricks and blandishments.'[32]

Harrison's male colleagues were often uneasy with assertions such as these, claiming that they marred her scholarship and were overtly subjective. She in turn accused them of clinging to patriarchal notions as a result of 'emotion'. This is a difficult issue to address because, while many of Harrison's critics were clearly motivated by old-fashioned sexism, some of her theories do lack a sound evidential basis, and the notion of an ancient matriarchy is one of them. However, Harrison's big idea of an ancient matriarchy did not go away. We have seen that Margaret Murray also adhered to this theory and that Robert Graves took it up and ran with it in the course of *The White Goddess*.

Graves was born in 1895 and is perhaps best known as a novelist and poet, but his contribution to contemporary paganism is substantial. He was the son of an Irish poet, Alfred Graves, who was a key figure in the Celtic revival and who introduced his son to Irish mythology, an interest Robert retained for the rest of his life. *The White Goddess*, published in 1948, is a poetic examination of Celtic and classical mythology with some idiosyncratic interpretations. It is a work of artistic genius, but many of Graves's historical claims need to be taken with a pinch of salt. As a work of poetic inspiration, however, *The White Goddess* is fascinating. Part of Graves's intention was to make explicit what Frazer had hinted at in *The Golden Bough*: he commented that Frazer was able to keep his position in the heavily Christian era in which he wrote only by skirting around his subject. Graves wanted to take Frazer's ideas further, stating that Christianity is just one of a series of 'barbarous' religions, and that Judaeo-Christian belief, with its relegation of the Goddess to a minor role, is the cause of many of the world's problems. Graves went on to produce a retelling of the Greek myths, and again, while there is general agreement that he was an outstanding writer, classical scholars took issue with his interpretations. Graves fought his corner, insisting that academics were too 'prose minded' to appreciate 'ancient poetic meaning'. This sort of debate – poetic claims versus historical facts – is still ongoing within pagan circles. However, some of the concepts that Graves proposed within *The White Goddess* have become part of mainstream pagan thought.

These include the two supernatural entities represented by the summer king and the winter king, who battle for supremacy at the solstices. However, there is no evidence that this was a historical myth at any point. Similarly, the 'tree calendar' outlined in Graves's work – which links the old Irish 'alphabet' of the ogham to different trees – is a system that was substantially constructed by Graves himself, including his revisions of the work on ogham of his grandfather Charles Graves (Robert cut down the number of symbols from twenty to thirteen, for instance, to enable it to fit the calendrical system that he had developed).

One of the central ideas in *The White Goddess* is that of the triple goddess as the Bride, the Mother and the Layer-out. This has become a staple within modern paganism, and it is sometimes accompanied by a male equivalent for those who like balance. But it is important to reiterate that this is not an ancient concept. A number of Celtic scholars felt that Graves 'misled many innocent readers with his eloquent but deceptive statements about a nebulous goddess in early Celtic literature, on which he was no authority'.[33]

Hungarian academic Károly Kerényi also posited the idea of an ancient triple lunar goddess in the 1960s, and Lithuanian American archaeologist Marija Gimbutas put forward the notion of a prehistoric matriarchy that was in place until overrun by nomadic, male-dominated 'Kurgan' tribes. Gimbutas's *The Prehistory of Eastern Europe* (1956) is fascinating, but there also seems to have been an element of seeing what she wanted to see: for instance, she relates that early Egyptian figurines of women holding their breasts clearly relate to fertility issues, but authorities state that this was an Egyptian form of mourning.

She also seems to have accepted wholesale the idea that the witch trials were a war on women and that millions died, which, as we have seen, was not the case.

Although an element of interpretation is necessary with regard to historical artefacts, so too is a degree of caution, and that caution is not always in evidence with regard to Gimbutas's theories about early matriarchies. Ruth Tringham, professor of anthropology at the University of California at Berkeley and a researcher of the same period and area as Gimbutas, has expressed substantial doubts about Gimbutas's conclusions. Evidence of fortified sites and weaponry throughout Europe cast doubt on the 'peaceful society' hypothesis. In an interview in the *Whole Earth Review*, Gimbutas commented that her approach to research 'has to do with your intuition and experience. Just like an art creation you must feel that you are right in what you are saying.'[34] But this is not a viable position to take when considering the archaeological evidence. Many researchers were reluctant to criticize Gimbutas, however, because of sympathy for the relevance of her views to feminism. 'Whether or not the world she describes existed, her advocates feel as if they've glimpsed it, and long for its return.'[35]

One such was Riane Eisler, whose work *The Chalice and the Blade* (1987) drew heavily on Gimbutas's ideas and promoted the notion of a peaceful, woman-led society to which we should seek to return. The appeal of Gimbutas's and Eisler's ideas is a political one: the concept of an alternative to late twentieth- and early twenty-first century, male-dominated capitalism. However, Sally Binford, a Marxist-feminist anthropologist, suggests in refutation of the view that there is a conspiracy against Gimbutas's theories that if male anthropologists discovered significant evidence for an early matriarchy, they would publish their findings, either because of innate intellectual honesty or, more cynically, because such evidence would suggest that those matriarchies possessed innate flaws which led to their downfall and subsequent dominance by men.

> I can find no valid reason for the need to believe in a golden age of matriarchy. Certainly, if we did once live in matriarchal societies, we blew it by letting the patriarchs take over. How did this happen? One of the most intriguing 'explanations' is offered by Elizabeth Gould Davis: Because of their carnivorous diet, men grew enormous penises, and women were so turned on that they voluntarily surrendered their power. I cannot accept this as a serious piece of history.[36]

It is worth noting that some of the most severe criticism of Gimbutas's ideas has come from feminist archaeologists, who take issue with her methods, but also with her ideological stance of feminist essentialism (the idea that a society run by women would necessarily be nicer and more nurturing than one run by men).

Despite the serious arguments against the case for an ancient matriarchy, the idea is still prevalent among feminist spiritual circles. As a poetic metaphor it has merit, but I think we have to discount it as historical fact until more evidence is forthcoming. Likewise, the idea that ancient societies worshipped a triple goddess also needs to be taken with a pinch of salt. The use of poetic metaphor is not a valid form of historical enquiry.

Although our ancestors may not have worshipped a triple goddess, such devotional practice is definitely the case now. In several hundred years' time, if paganism is still extant in Britain, scholars will be entirely correct in stating that 'the ancestors' worshipped a triple goddess.

We have noted that Wicca appealed to many women because of the emphasis on female power and authority, but it retained an element of sexism (abusive behaviour by high priests, for instance), and in the 1960s and '70s this was unacceptable to some u.s. feminists, who decided to make a clean break. Thus began what is known as 'Dianic witchcraft' in the u.s.

Dianic witchcraft currently follows two distinct strands: the version founded in Texas in the 1960s by Morgan McFarland and Mark Roberts ('Old Dianic'), which views the Horned God as the consort of the Goddess (which, as we have noted, is a common pairing throughout modern Wicca itself) and which allows men to participate, and the separatist tradition founded by writer Zsuzsanna E. Budapest, who with three friends started the Susan B. Anthony Coven in 1971. It is a combination of Wicca, the form of Italian witchcraft known as Strega, folk magic and feminism. Budapest wrote:

It's the natural law, as women fare so fares the world, their children, and that's everybody. If you lift up the women you have lifted up humanity. Men have to learn to develop their own mysteries. Where is the order of Attis? Pan? Zagreus? Not only research it, but then popularize it as well as I have done. Where are the Dionysian rites? I think men are lazy in this aspect by not working this up for themselves. It's their own task, not ours.[37]

Whereas an ancient alternative to male-dominated religion may not have existed, at least not in the form envisaged by Gimbutas, Dianic Wicca does provide such an alternative. Budapest supported the idea of 'Mother Nature', the Great Goddess in her guise of the natural world. It is a gynocentric path that often follows the wheel of the year and the ritual format of contemporary paganism, but covens differ. Dianic witchcraft is currently working out its various positions regarding trans women, with some covens insisting on excluding them and others preferring inclusivity.

There are also a growing number of Goddess Temples throughout the Western world: the Goddess Temple in Glastonbury, founded in 2000; a temple dedicated to Sekhmet in the Mojave Desert; and temples in places as diverse as Bristol and Mount Shasta. Each of these tends to have their own culture, and they are dedicated to a wide variety of goddesses.

One of the most prominent figures to emerge from the American feminist Wicca of the 1970s, and indeed someone who has significantly shaped the subsequent course of paganism, is the American writer Starhawk. Born in 1951 as Miriam Simos, she has written some of the most influential works, both theoretical and practical. Her book *The Spiral Dance* (1979) has led many people to paganism, and she combines her writing on ritual and goddess worship with a commitment to ecological and feminist principles and radical political action. Putting her money where her mouth is, Starhawk has been instrumental in picketing the sites of nuclear plants, demonstrating at G8 summits and taking an active part in the direct action movement.

Starhawk is a co-founder of the Reclaiming movement, a series of covens that are linked to ecological principles. Members say that it has four main roots: the Anderson Feri tradition of witchcraft, anarcho-politics, eco-feminism and psychotherapeutic growth movements.

As a speaker, Starhawk is laid-back but inspirational. She continues to inform the modern pagan movement and although many object to her linkage of spirituality with politics and with a strongly feminist ethos, others see this as crucial to the future of the movement and of the planet: our spirituality informs our politics, and vice versa, they say, and the two cannot be easily separated. This holistic view of human principles means that we cannot use our spirituality as a means of escape from real-world problems. Below, Starhawk subscribes to the view of an ancient matriarchy, but takes it a step forward into contemporary political activism, the recreation of what she believes will be a kinder world.

The symbolism of the Goddess has taken on an electrifying power for modern women. The rediscovery of the ancient matrifocal civilizations has given us a deep sense of pride in woman's ability to create and sustain culture. It has exposed the falsehoods of patriarchal history, and given us models of female strength and authority. Once again in today's world, we recognize the Goddess – ancient and primeval; the first of deities; patroness of the Stone Age hunt and of the first sowers of seeds; under whose guidance the herds were tamed, the healing herbs first discovered; in whose image the first works of art were created; for whom the standing stones were raised; who was the inspiration of song and poetry. She is the bridge, on which we can cross the chasms within ourselves, which were created by our social conditioning, and reconnect with our lost potentials. She is the ship, on which we sail the waters of the Deep Self, exploring the uncharted seas within. She is the door, through which we pass into the future. She is the cauldron, in which we who have been wrenched apart simmer until we again become whole. She is the vaginal passage, through which we are reborn.[38]

As an example of goddess worship closer to home, we might take a look at Olivia Melian Robertson, one of British and Irish paganism's most enduring figures and the head of the long-standing Fellowship of Isis. Olivia was often seen around and about in London and Glastonbury, as well as her native Ireland and the u.s. She was not only a priestess but a writer and artist. She published six books and her first novel was based on her experiences working with the poor in Dublin's tenements (she had volunteered as a nurse during the war). She had her first exhibition of paintings at the age of 21.

Born on 13 April 1917 in Reigate, Surrey, Olivia and her clergyman brother Lawrence moved to the four-hundred-year-old Huntington Castle (known to the Fellowship of Isis as Clonegal Castle) in Ireland when her father inherited it from her grandmother in 1925. 'The IRA had occupied the castle, and treated it very well,' Olivia recalled, 'although they locked the cook in the dungeon, and court-martialled the butler.'[39]

Olivia's childhood was spent at the castle, where her family entertained a number of early twentieth-century luminaries, including her cousin Robert Graves and W. B. Yeats. Perhaps inspired by this early exposure to the Celtic revival, Olivia experienced a number of visions, including that of the goddess Isis ('a cross between a queen, a ballet dancer and a gym mistress . . . We had a long conversation, but afterwards I couldn't remember any of it'[40]) and both she and her brother became convinced that the goddess was a power in the world. This was somewhat embarrassing for a member of the clergy – Lawrence offered his resignation to his bishop, but was told there was no need. Over the years that followed, Olivia and her brother turned the castle cellars into a series of temples and shrines.

In 1976 Olivia, Lawrence and his wife Pamela set up the Fellowship of Isis, designed to worship 'Isis of the thousand names'. Huntington Castle remained its base, horrifying the local villagers, who initially did not take kindly to Olivia's rituals for a variety of reasons ('the kind of thing you sit through at weddings when couples insist on writing their own vows', said one witness). Wisely, Olivia left the castle door open and the villagers were eventually mollified when a series of celebrities – including Van Morrison, Hugh Grant and Mick Jagger – showed up to have a look. Brigitte Bardot's sister contributed two stuffed canvas dragons.

The Fellowship was modest in its demands from participants: dispensing with dogma, it suggested only that members believe in love and beauty. Nor did it insist that anyone should abandon their own religious practices. The result was an organization that flourished across a number of countries. Olivia died in 2013 but the Fellowship lives on.

## Ceremonial Magic

We have looked at ceremonial magic throughout the previous chapters, reaching what might be regarded as its finest hour in the final years of the nineteenth century and continuing into the twentieth. Yet ceremonial magic did not die out: offshoots of the Golden Dawn are still active, as are the Ordo Templi Orientis and the Society of the Inner Light. Curiously, for something that is so significant to the development of magical practice, ceremonial magic is probably one of the least known paths today and some of its practitioners would debate whether it even falls under the heading of paganism.

Ceremonial magic has always been a niche interest. Modern media has tended to focus on witchcraft or what it perceives to be black magic, so although elements of ceremonial practices occasionally make their way into film and television, these tend to be fragmented and often inaccurate. The legacy of the Golden Dawn pops up in some surprising places – if you check out Kate Bush's video for the song 'The Red Shoes', you'll find a version of the Lesser Banishing Ritual of the Pentagram, for instance! And aspects of ceremonial magic occur in fantasy literature (Katherine Kurtz, whom we mentioned earlier, is a good example of someone who writes accurate rituals). But generally, ceremonial magic is little known beyond its practitioners. However, a study of some of its leading lights will prove interesting.

One of these was William Gray (1913–1992), born in Middlesex and the son of an actress who was also a professional fortune-teller. Yet he worked quietly as a chiropodist in Cheltenham for much of his life. He wrote books on Hermetic

Kabbalism and ceremonial magic, and he trained a number of people, some of whom (such as Robert 'R. J.' Stewart) are still working and respected in the field today. With his father away at war, and his mother working in London for the War Office, the infant Bill was sent to live with an uncle and aunt who were members of the Theosophical Society, thus providing him with an early exposure to esoteric ideas. Gray, who was legendary for his mordant wit, described the Theosophists as 'elderly ladies of both sexes and genteel behaviour whose ideas of Nirvana centred around mysterious Oriental Masters who directed the destiny of all mankind from a secret spot in Tibet'.[41] He met Crowley's magical partner Victor Neuberg, although Gray's mother disapproved. He also went to see Dion Fortune, who was apparently hospitable but who refused to admit him to her order as he was under 21. He found a mentor in the form of a London-based Austrian esotericist named Emile Napoleon Hauenstein. He also became friendly with Robert Cochrane, whom we met earlier when considering Wicca. And he founded an order of his own, the Sangreal Sodality, which is still running under the guidance of Gray's student Jacobus Swart.

People who knew Gray described him as fiery, contentious, hugely knowledgeable but with a habit of falling out with people (a trait, it must be said, which he shared with a great many occultists) and possessing many of the prejudices of his day. Alan Richardson's book on him, *The Old Sod* (2003), is not titled as such for nothing. Gray is, however, regarded with considerable respect.

Real esotericism was not just dressing up in handsome robes and manipulating symbols for the sake of so doing. It was knowing how to apply the meaning of such symbols to Life itself, for the purpose of altering or directing its energy in accordance with intention. For example, a Magical Sword was not the physical symbol one handles in Temple practice, but its qualities as applied to the human being. Flexibility, sharpness, keenness, brightness, pointedness of action, and everything else to be thought of in connection with a well-balanced blade.[42]

As with Gray, Ronald Heaver is someone who is little known today. Yet Heaver influenced and indeed trained a generation of esoteric practitioners, including Gray himself, Peter and Eileen Caddy of the Findhorn Foundation, and Sir George Trevelyan, who founded the Wrekin Trust (a 'university of spirit').

As a sixteen-year-old, Heaver joined the Air Force during the First World War (he was underage) and was shot down, crashing over enemy lines. He was taken prisoner and despite sustaining injuries that would lead to bouts of paralysis throughout his life he managed to escape to Britain. He established a sanctuary near Glastonbury after experiencing a spiritual transformation while crossing Westminster Bridge in London. His sanctuary was simple and the means by which people engaged with it were equally straightforward: they were encouraged to sit in silence for a time and report on their experiences, which seem often to have been profound.

Glastonbury itself is one of the most popular destinations for modern pagans in the UK. It is the home of a number of sites dear to the pagan heart, including the Chalice Well, a garden built around a chalybeate (iron-bearing) spring on the slopes of the nearby Tor. Glastonbury is popular among pagans partly because it was the home of the Avalonians: a diverse bunch of writers, artists, sculptors, occultists and archaeologists who were a kind of West Country version of the Bloomsbury set and who included among their ranks Dion Fortune and her friend Alice Buckton, who was also a friend of Tennyson – he gave her his cloak, which she wore when in residence in Glastonbury – and who, in 1912, purchased the Chalice Well.

The Chalice Well is now run by a trust founded in 1959 by the redoubtable Major Wellesley Tudor Pole. (The lead singer of punk band Tenpole Tudor is his grandson.) Originally from Weston-super-Mare, Tudor Pole was a stalwart of the British Empire: an adventurous soldier with an enquiring mind. Meeting the head of the Bahá'í faith in Constantinople in the early 1900s, he became a keen adherent. He served in the Directorate of Military Intelligence in the Middle East throughout the First World War, and information received by him proved pivotal in altering plans to conduct the war in Palestine. After the war, in collaboration with Winston Churchill, he set up the Silent Minute alongside the Lamplighter Movement, which culminated in the establishment of Remembrance Day commemorations. The Silent Minute itself is a curiously potent idea: a 'null', if you like; the absence of action. After the war, one Gestapo officer described it as a weapon that the Germans could not counter: 'There is no power on earth, that can withstand the united cooperation on spiritual levels of men and women of goodwill everywhere.'[43]

Tudor Pole's association with Glastonbury began at a young age after he had a vision of himself as a monk at the abbey. His letters to novelist Rosamond Lehmann reveal an endearingly gung-ho, Sax Rohmer-style attitude towards adventures on the astral plane.

We may also include the (pen) name of Gareth Knight in our line-up: writer and magician Basil Wilby, born in 1930. He was trained in Dion Fortune's Society of the Inner Light and has written over forty books on Tarot, the Arthurian mythos, Kabbalism and ritual magic. The magical working group that he founded, the Avalon Group, is still going today: they meet at Hawkwood College in the Cotswolds. Another order emerging from Fortune's group, the Hermetic Order of the Servants of the Light, has been helmed by Dolores Ashcroft-Nowicki for many years, though she recently stepped down from the post of director. She has worked with Gareth Knight, occultist W. E. Butler and many other Hermetic practitioners throughout the twentieth and twenty-first centuries.

The purpose of ceremonial magic started to become more geared towards personal spiritual development from the late nineteenth century, and this remains one of its central precepts. It thus continues the Hermetic legacy and is arguably less concerned with 'practical' magic or spellwork. Its practices include:

C Pathworking: this is a form of creative visualization and is a discipline that focuses on a particular context. For instance, a practitioner may choose to work with the Kabbalistic Tree of Life, regarded as a staple component of ceremonial magic, and undertake regular active meditations using the imagination to 'journey' between different stages of the tree. You can use taped visualizations, or work out your own.

◖ Ritual: ceremonial magic tends to focus on rituals for various occasions and purposes, and can involve various traditions – for instance, the Celtic, Egyptian or Greek pantheons. It also uses some basic ritual formats such as the Lesser Banishing Ritual of the Pentagram.

◖ Development of an actual and/or an astral temple: either by building one on the material plane (William Gray had one in his basement, which he had constructed himself entirely out of plywood) or developing one in the imagination.

Modern ceremonial magic is formal, often highly structured and tends to take place indoors, although there is no prohibition against conducting rituals outside. It is seen as a bit more old school than Wicca or even modern Druidry. But it is worth noting here that a lot of people in various traditions do cross over and often work in different paths. A Druidic grove may decide to do a ceremonial magical ritual for a change, or a Wiccan group may decide to work Druidically for a bit. People who involve themselves in magical practice tend to be inquisitive and experimental; magic has been described as 'geeky', and there is definitely an element of truth in this.

For instance, Gray's magical practice, on which he wrote extensively, is based upon the Kabbalah and on elemental magic. He follows a standard ceremonial magic approach in focusing on a fourfold system that encompasses the four directions; the four archangels (Raphael, Michael, Gabriel, Uriel); the seasons; and the 'weapons' of the ceremonial magician (the sword, the staff, the cup and the pentacle). This format – with the possible exception of the archangels – is now commonplace across pagan ritual work. As well as ceremonial magicians, Wiccans use it, as do Druids and some Heathens.

One of the most famous ceremonial magical rituals is called the Abramelin. It is often regarded as a ritual that the serious ceremonial magician aspires to and people who have completed it gain a lot of respect from their peers. It is an intensive set of practices and takes place over at least several months.

The idea behind the Abramelin ritual is that it prepares the magician to contact his or her holy guardian angel. Once you have done this, it is supposed to give you mastery over the Goetic demons, although many current practitioners say that the main aim of the ritual is to put you in touch with divinity rather than enable you to have power over demonic forces. It comes from the *Book of Abramelin* (which seems to have first been published in 1608), which tells the story of an Egyptian mage, Abraham or Abramelin, who teaches magic to a German Jew, Abraham of Worms. The work was translated by Samuel Mathers and was adopted by the Golden Dawn, and later by Crowley, who incorporated it into Thelema.

It is a long ritual – the original text says that it takes eighteen months, but Mathers suggested that it should take six. It is a strict, disciplined piece of work: you are supposed to pray every day at sunrise and sunset after cleansing yourself, preferably abstain from alcohol and sex, and conduct yourself scrupulously. In an ideal scenario you would set yourself apart from the world (author William Bloom left his job and moved to the Atlas Mountains to undertake this ritual). In the last two months, you should spend most of your time reading sacred works and praying. You also need a set of tools, such as an almond branch wand, a lamp and a seven-sided plate of silver or beeswax. At the culmination of the ritual, you invoke your holy guardian angel. After this, you can, if you wish, summon demons.

There is a lot of debate among occultists as to how the ritual should best be performed. The practical dictates of the rite entail that successful completion of it is relatively rare. Crowley is said to have performed it at his house in the Highlands, Boleskine (this burned down a few years ago), but was interrupted by the local butcher; this story may well be apocryphal. He adapted the rite so that it does not take so long to complete. His Bornless ritual has the same purpose of summoning the holy guardian angel and gaining power over demonic forces.

## Vodou

Also known as 'voodoo' and 'vodoun' depending on which branch of the religion it is and where it is practised, this is not a major part of British paganism, but it has started to emerge as part of some people's practice in this country outside the BAME community. It is distinct from Hoodoo, which we can define as folk magic and which bears a resemblance to the cunning craft practised in earlier centuries.

People coming to Britain have brought their own magic with them: Santería, Candomblé, the cult of Santa Muerte and some highly publicized instances of African practice have joined Vodou as part of the magical tapestry of this country. Beyond their original ethnic practitioners, these paths continue to enjoy a minor vogue among British occultists, particularly among the younger generation, regardless of ethnicity. This is due partly to a greater flow of information, either from migrants themselves, from books published by the main esoteric publishing houses or online. It is also due partly to a liking for novelty, to which pagans are as prone as anyone else, and to a craving for what are seen as more 'authentic' practices. For example, Vodou services usually involve possession by spirits, whereas trance mediumship or spirit/deity possession are still in their relative infancy within revivalist paganism. Vodou has a long history of working with spirits and possession, whereas modern paganism does not. Some pagans are therefore looking to other spiritual traditions with an older track record.

Media coverage on Vodou in this country tends to be poorly informed at best: what is described as 'Voodoo' or 'African witchcraft' is often simply criminal activity, such as child abuse. In a nation where racism remains often institutionalized and unrecognized, the practices of anyone who is non-white are often mischaracterized, misunderstood or simply sensationalized. My personal experience of Vodou ceremonies are that they are structured experiences that can lead to significant spiritual development. We hosted a ceremony in Glastonbury some years ago with a houngan (a Vodou priest) who came over from the States; he was Puerto Rican in origin and thus the form of Vodou he practised was from this part of the world. The ceremony required some effort to set up: we constructed a large altar covered in candles, fruit, flowers and offerings such as rum, perfume and cigars. Vodou spirits like different offerings and it is considered good form to give them what they like. Once this was done, and everyone had assembled (dressed in white), the ceremony began. The houngan taught us some chants, which everyone began to sing, and the evening then progressed in three stages: initially the Ghede, or spirits of the dead, were invoked, then some of the Rada Loa (older, originally African spirits such as La Sirène, Papa Legba, Erzulie Freda) and then the Petro Loa (fiery, fierce spirits mainly from the New World). The ceremony lasted for about six hours (although we did have a cigarette break), involved a lot of trance possession and ended with the summoning of Baron Samedi, one of the Ghede, who are above all cheerful spirits. Baron Samedi often makes sexual comments and pinches women's bottoms – as he is dead, he no longer fears anything, including offending people. For Westerners who are largely unused to trance mediumship, the ceremony was a little unnerving, or at least unfamiliar, but it was an upbeat occasion, not at all sinister, and I got the impression that there is a strongly cathartic element to it.

Vodou and Hoodoo are generally considered by anthropologists to be a form of folk practice: when disenfranchised people, subject to substantial societal and political oppression, seek power, they may do so through magic. The Loa – the spirits of Vodou – resemble the gods of ancient Greece in that they embody recognizable human concepts. Someone may consult a houngan or his female equivalent, a mambo, to petition Erzulie Freda to get his girlfriend back, just as his classical equivalent might have petitioned the goddess Aphrodite.

## Shamanism

Shamanism is both a path in itself and part of other spiritual paths, such as Druidry. It is in some respects contentious because much of it is taken from Siberian and Native American and South American practices, among others, and, as with Vodou, in some quarters there is seen to be an issue with cultural appropriation – a lack of respect for the traditions from which these practices come. There is certainly an element of justification in this charge. The 'weekend shaman' is a phenomenon known to most pagans and esotericists, and is rightly scorned.

So what do shamans do? Although shamanism is an ancient set of practices found across the world, there are some commonalities. Shamans are often said to have been marked out by suffering a childhood illness that leaves them with heightened psychic powers and the capacity, through a variety of techniques but also innate ability, to move into other spiritual realms in order to help people (and sometimes to curse them). My direct experience of shamanism was in Siberia with a woman named Maria. Her ancestors had been shamans, including her grandmother, but the Soviet secret police had put paid to a lot of practitioners after the Revolution, having first carefully noted down what they did. Maria lived in a tiny village in the Altai region. Just down the road was a massive quartz cliff housing a cave that was supposed to have been the home of a yeti tribe. Humans and yeti lived peacefully together until the humans gave the yeti alcohol, whereupon they killed a child and were slaughtered by the villagers. There is now an archaeological dig in progress as the cave may have been the home of an early human species. You could go into a truly wild flight of fancy about the yetis being a remnant of these early people in this remote region, but I am not going to do that here. Suffice to say that the people of Maria's village had lived there for a very long time.

Maria had a serious illness as a child, and her grandmother, who had been secretive about her beliefs for obvious reasons, gave her a special bag with a hare appliquéd on it for her to keep ritual tools in. Maria worked in an *iyill*, the Siberian version of a yurt, and when the party I was travelling with turned up, she was busy: it was the first three days of the new moon and her little garden was filled with a queue of people. Some of them had travelled a long way to see her. They had a variety of problems – some were ill, some had family members who were ill, and a couple of them thought they might have been cursed. Maria explained that some shamans did work with black magic, and a local one (now deceased) had been particularly prone to cursing people. Nor had he stopped now that he was resident in the afterlife – she and her colleagues had to keep popping up to the astral plane in order to sort him out. Like Native American practitioners, she relied on tobacco to fuel, literally, the connection between herself and the spirit world (a relatively recent addition to Siberian practice). But her home was filled with Russian Orthodox icons. She is probably like the cunning person who, hundreds of years ago, worked with spirits but also with God, the Virgin, Christ and the saints. She also bore a resemblance to Haitian houngans and mambos, who also work with a variety of composite traditional elements.

In addition to her regular practice, Maria had taken on the major task of a soul-retrieval project. Some years before, the body of a woman, known colloquially as the 'Ice Princess', had been discovered in the permafrost of an upland plateau. Heavily tattooed, this ancient person had been buried with a wealth of grave goods and she was now being studied in an institute in Akademgorodok near Novosibirsk, some seven hours away from Maria's village. This was causing tensions throughout the Altai region, as the people of the mountainous Altai wanted her body brought back. So Maria had been entrusted with the task of retrieving the woman's soul – in nine parts. Unfortunately this could not be done all in one go so Maria had to make nine seven-hour-each-way trips to the city. All sorts went on – the car ran off the road, which she attributed to a black-magic attack – but eventually the Ice Princess's remains were returned to the Altai, and I do not know what happened after that. Soul retrieval – which can be done with living people who have experienced trauma as well as the dead – is an integral part of shamanic work throughout the world.

Maria was a fairly typical shaman although she was interested in other things: she had read up on Madame Blavatsky and Atlantis, for instance, and she was intrigued by Indian thought, eventually travelling to India in the late 2000s. She was in contact with shamans across the world, since some of her colleagues had Internet access and swapped information with Native American practitioners in particular. Like every other spiritual tradition, shamanism is a growing, living practice that draws on a variety of other practices, sometimes from unusual sources.

# Conclusion

In this book we have covered a substantial span of time, ranging from the comparatively little we know about prehistoric magical practices and religion, to the poorly documented Celtic peoples, the Saxons and Vikings, and then the magic that was practised throughout Christian Britain. We have looked at two main strands: magical practice itself, and paganism. We have seen these entwine, separate and entwine once more.

In a sense, we come full circle in the twenty-first century, when most of the magical work that is undertaken in the British Isles can no longer be said to be Christian and is often done in the name of pagan deities who have a variety of different origins. The tapestry of magical practice and pagan thought that we see today has its roots not so much in the ancient world, although the images of that world continue to inspire, but in more recent centuries – from later Druidry, Rosicrucianism, Theosophy, Freemasonry, the occult orders and lodges of the Victorian period, and folk magic. Their development has been influenced by literary fiction, art and craft, the work of academics, film and television. Hermetic practice and folk craft may have mutated and changed over the years, but they are still practised today.

What we see in the twenty-first century is a wide range of paths and beliefs: generally non-dogmatic and tolerant, but

– particularly with the advent of the Internet – prone to schism and dissent. But where are these movements headed?

At the moment, what we can say for certain with regard to paganism in the British Isles is that it is continuing to grow. Members of various groups report a concern about the way in which the demographic is ageing, since people coming into paganism tend to do so in their thirties rather than their teens. Popular media can inspire youthful interest in the various paths; sometimes people continue to pursue and deepen their interests, and sometimes they do not, as with many other areas of human life.

It is extremely difficult to predict what's going to be the next big thing: Vodou saw a curious resurgence in the 2000s, with (mainly white) groups springing up in South Wales and the North of England among young people. There is currently a move among the smaller magical lodges to cut back their online presences and operate more according to personal recommendation and word of mouth; some of them have been doing this for a while and a number of them are quite strict about criteria for membership. Wicca has a huge online presence and a number of big public gatherings – the various annual Witchfest events, for example – but it can be quite hard to find a reputable coven to join. Druidry is possibly one of the most accessible movements, with the Order of Bards, Ovates and Druids as well as some smaller Druidic groups having a highly visible web presence as well as running correspondence courses. Crowley's legacy of the Ordo Templi Orientis and the Illuminates of Thanateros, among others, continue to be powerhouses of esoteric work, as do the various offshoots of the Golden Dawn itself. But as well as these big groups, there are many people who prefer to work individually and under the radar – which makes it hard to estimate the actual number of pagans working in Britain today. The 2011 census indicated at least 80,000, but not everyone chooses to indicate their religion on a census form.

Finally, we return to the elephant in the room mentioned in the Introduction, which really deserves a book in itself. The reader will have noted that I have made no claims about the ontological or theological status of pagan beliefs: whether or not the gods are real; whether magic 'really' works. This is for several reasons – primarily that this is a historical overview, not a theological analysis. But I have also aimed to reflect the way that pagans and magical practitioners treat belief. Because the community is not text-based – there is no biblical or Koranic equivalent to which we can refer – pagans tend to take, overall, a mutually tolerant approach to other people's beliefs. They do not compare beliefs in the same way that more mainstream faiths do: I have said earlier that, for instance, one does not encounter followers of Freya taking issues with worshippers of Rhiannon. Pagans do have conversations about belief, but (as opposed to discussions about practice and the 'right' way of doing things, when fur can fly) they tend not to question other people's beliefs in spirit or deity. This can make for a curiously amicable approach between very different groups.

Attitudes towards belief itself, on an individual basis, are varied. They may be deistic: people who believe in the literal reality of gods, goddesses and spirits. They may be agnostic: people who neither believe nor disbelieve, but who like other aspects of ritual, or who regard deities in a more Jungian sense, as psychological archetypes, for example. Or they may be atheistic: some occultists may not believe in God, but in a kind of mechanistic approach to the universe, as though it is a giant computer.

Politics can be an engine of dissent, as we have seen in our discussion of Heathenism, but I have never heard a pagan accuse another pagan who worships a deity with perceived ancient roots as believing in something unreal. There are 'modern' gods: some of the 'folk saints' in Vodou such as Santa Muerte or St Expedite may be questioned, although it is still held as being perfectly acceptable to believe in them, and some of the deities in the contemporary Goddess movement such as the Glastonbury entity of Nolava may also be up for debate. You might hear pagans contending that, just because a god might be mentioned in a work of popular fiction, this does not mean that this god is not real (perhaps the entity of Pan or Herne the Hunter inspired people to write about them, for example). So tolerance extends to belief in something that may not be consensually agreed to be real – an interesting theological proposition, but one for another book, perhaps.

What I think we can be definite about is that interest in magic is not going away any time soon. As the proprietors of an occult shop in Glastonbury, my partner and I get enquiries every week – and sometimes every day – from people who want magical work undertaken for them. This work is the same sort of work that it has always been: how to find love, how to get a lover back, how to win a court case, how to heal from an illness, how to remove a curse. We may not undertake this work – it varies – but the enquiries keep coming. Our distant ancestors would, I think, recognize these needs, and the many different people migrating into the UK or visiting it as tourists certainly recognize them, too. We read Tarot and the runes for people, sell scrying mirrors that would not have been unfamiliar to John Dee, and wands and regalia that the original members of the Golden Dawn would have been familiar with. Times and technology change but these preoccupations remain constant: you can see people's spellcasting and rituals on Instagram and Facebook and YouTube, but those rituals themselves have their roots in a pre-technological age. Social media remains a medium, not a message. Quite random people (taxi drivers, travellers on trains, tourists in pubs) tell me about their spiritual experiences, their encounters with ghosts, their grandmother's ability to read palms. And in an increasingly technological society and a rational age, there seems to be a hunger for different experiences, for wonder and enchantment, for the mystical. Folk magic is alive and well and bubbling under the scientifically focused world. This is a hunger that the magical orders and lodges, that Wicca and witchcraft and Druidry, endeavour to satisfy. Perhaps in counterbalance to the mechanistic, materialistic outlook of late capitalism, they are now firmly not only out of the broom closet, but growing.

# APPENDIX I:

# A Short Guide to Magical Tools and Ritual

The ritual I outline below is a standard sort of format that will be recognized by pagans working within Wicca, Druidry, Heathenism, the ceremonial tradition and to some extent chaos magick. This format most probably derives from the Golden Dawn originally, although that magical order drew on earlier aspects of magic, such as working within a circle.

Most magical practitioners work with an altar. As with most other aspects of the craft, there is no single 'right' way to build an altar – and indeed, it is a wonderfully individual thing! Some of us have altars crowded with many statues of gods and goddesses. Some people prefer to have seasonal greenery – snowdrops, primroses, hawthorn or autumn leaves – on their altar. Some altars are very abstract. I have known ones that feature action figures and cartoon cats. It all depends on your own preferences.

Most people use a large box or a small table for their altar. We use a little ornamental table, for example, but my altar used to be the top of an old cupboard. You can get very elaborate, specially made altars, but these are not necessary. Ideally, the top of the altar should be about waist height, as this is easiest for working.

Don't see this altar as a finished product. Altars change over time, with the seasons, with the periods of your life, with your working requirements. A very basic altar, however, holds the following:

as many candles as you like and as are safe
a chalice or cup
an athame or knife
your wand, if you have one
an incense holder
a small dish of earth, or a stone or crystal,
or anything that symbolizes earth

Some people prefer to have a cloth on their altar (practically, this is in case your candle overflows), but although useful and pleasant, it is not essential. In the case of the ritual tools like the chalice, you might choose to have an expensive and ornate chalice for your altar, or you may just use a glass.

Make sure you have everything to hand, on a table or your altar. There is nothing more irritating than getting halfway through your ritual and then realizing you have forgotten the matches. Once you have done this, you will be ready to begin.

Please remember that this is only one way of doing a ritual. Many traditions have different ways, invoking different elements in different combinations. These are to be respected, but not necessarily unquestioningly followed. If I am in a ritual which is run by other people, that – for example – invokes fire in the east rather than air, then that may not be the way I would do it at home, but it is simply a matter of politeness to follow one's host's methods. I would expect equal respect if they came to me. Nor do you have to follow the colour codes rigorously. If you like all-white candles, then use them. Over time, you will find your own way of working with ritual, and do feel free to experiment: you will not be struck down by lightning if you miss a bit out. The gods, if they exist, are very forgiving.

And we all make mistakes – even very senior priests and priestesses. A friend of mine has been doing rituals for thirty years and heard himself, in the middle of a huge ceremony at Stonehenge, proclaiming the element of water in the south of the circle, the bit that is usually dedicated to fire … Everyone grinned at him and he may have felt like a small pile of smouldering ash, but he just grinned back, apologized and carried on.

The moral is: take what you are doing seriously, but don't take yourself too seriously. I don't think ritual is to be undertaken lightly, but it is perfectly all right to have a moment of laughter and confusion in the middle of the proceedings.

## Drawing the Circle

Place your candles in the four quarters of your working space, as follows, and light them:

EAST: white (or yellow, if you prefer)
SOUTH: red
WEST: blue
NORTH: green (or black)

Place a second white candle on your altar and light it.

Take your knife, athame or wand. Face east. Hold up the athame (I'll use this as an example), in your working hand (that is, if you are left-handed, use that hand). Hold your other hand down towards the ground and picture a thread of energy coming up from the earth, through your hand, across your body and down the arm that holds the athame, to be projected outwards through the tip of the blade. It does not matter what colour you imagine the energy to be – white, or blue, or gold, for instance. Then walk clockwise (sunwise) around your perimeter, drawing the circle in the air, usually at just above head height.

Some people express intentions as they do this – for example, if you're doing a ritual dedicated to working with the moon, you might want to say what the ritual is about: 'On this night, at this new moon, I call upon the lunar powers, the moon powers, the powers of light in darkness, on She who is the Lady of the Moon –' until you have reached the east again and your circle is complete. Usually, the person drawing the circle imagines that thread of energy emerging from the tip of the wand, or finger, and forming a circle: for example, as a thread of white light, or neon blue, or gold.

### Can you step out of the circle?

Yes. Sometimes something just happens outside the circle (crying child, howling dog) and you have to deal with it. Most of us 'draw' a doorway in the air and step through it, to show that we're aware that it is sacred space. Don't just bolt through it, though! Patricia Crowther suggests taking the circle down and re-drawing it. But don't obsess about breaking the circle: again, you won't be struck by lightning if it happens.

### How big does the circle have to be?

Big enough in which to work comfortably, but it depends on the size of your room. You can project energy as far as you need to – not miles to the far-off horizon, but as far as is needed to accommodate a big group of people if necessary. More traditional Wiccans hold that the circle must be 275 centimetres (9 ft) in diameter (nine is the number traditionally associated with the moon): if you want to do this, cut a cord 137.5 centimetres (4½ ft) in length, place it in the middle of your potential circle, and measure outwards. You can delineate the working circle in white chalk, or with a white rope.

### Can a circle be drawn outside, without an altar?

By all means. There is nothing to say you have to work inside or outside.

### Why do we draw it sunwise?

Again, it is that connection with the natural world, the way that the sun travels. There is an old view in traditional witchcraft that to walk anti-clockwise, or 'widdershins', is unlucky, and this view has somehow become ingrained in our inner selves – at least when drawing the circle. Unwinding it is another matter, as we will see.

What is important is the connection that you yourself make between earth and air and the wider world. You're delineating it with energy that comes from the earth, not from yourself, to make sacred space. Magic is all about making connections, and this very basic part of ritual is an aspect of that.

## Consecrating with Water

Once you have drawn your circle (using energies of earth and air), it is customary to consecrate it with water and with fire. I usually do water first, out of a feeling that if you consecrate with fire first, the water puts it out!

Take your chalice or cup full of water and go around the circle from east to east, sunwise. Flick a few drops as you go – if you find yourself in a group, it is customary to anoint each person's brow as you go around. You may wish to speak as you do so: 'I consecrate this circle with the element of water, the purifier, the cleanser, element of river and spring and sea, of the falling rain . . .' or whatever words come most naturally to mind. As you do so, don't just concentrate on the words, but on imagining water, in the form of rain, mist or even salt spray.

## Consecrating with Fire

And now do the same thing with incense, either a joss stick or incense in a censer. Again, you may choose to speak as you do so: 'I consecrate this circle with the element of fire, the energiser, element of noonday and high summer and the leaping flame in the hearth . . .' Do the same for fire as you did for water – imagine the light of the sun, or the heat of flame.

## Calling the Quarters

It is usual for most pagan ritual to 'call the quarters', locating the circle and placing you firmly within your ritual space. So I will begin with the general properties of the quarters and then move on to the specifics.

Because there are so many correspondences, and so many deities, I have included only a few here. Please also bear in mind that correspondences might vary and some of them are not very old, so they are not set in stone.

### East:

TIME: dawn

SEASON: spring

ELEMENT: air (fire in some systems, in which case just swap air and fire correspondences around)

RITUAL TOOL: athame (or wand, if using fire in this quarter)

ZODIAC SIGNS: Gemini, Libra, Aquarius

COLOUR: white/pale yellow

ANIMALS: the hawk, birds in general

GODDESSES/GODS: Bride, Mercury, Thoth

## South:

TIME: noon
SEASON: summer
ELEMENT: fire (air in some systems)
RITUAL TOOL: wand (or athame, if using fire in this quarter)
ZODIAC SIGNS: Aries, Leo, Sagittarius
COLOUR: gold/red
ANIMALS: the stag, the fox, the lion, the dragon
GODDESSES/GODS: Lugh, Bel, Hephaestus, Hestia

## West:

TIME: evening
SEASON: autumn
ELEMENT: water
RITUAL TOOL: chalice
ZODIAC SIGNS: Cancer, Scorpio, Pisces
COLOUR: green/blue/sea colours
ANIMALS: the cow, the salmon of wisdom from Celtic legend,
seals and water creatures
GODDESSES/GODS: Rhiannon, Isis, Danu, Llyr/Mannanan,
Osiris

## North:

TIME: midnight
SEASON: winter
ELEMENT: earth
RITUAL TOOL: pentacle, dish of salt, crystals
ZODIAC SIGNS: Taurus, Virgo, Capricorn
COLOUR: black/indigo blue/dark green
ANIMALS: the bear, the badger, the snake
GODDESSES/GODS: Arianrhod, Frey, Freya, Odin, Morrigan

SPIRITS OF PLACE: To me, this is one of the most important aspects of calling the quarters, and is very rarely done. This may mean that we depart from more standard systems of correspondences – for example, Gwyn (as a deity of the underworld) would traditionally be associated with the north, but since he is supposed to live beneath the Tor, and that is east of us, this is why we call him in the east.

I live just west of Glastonbury, and so when I call the quarters, this is how it goes:

EAST: I call upon the spirits of the East – spirits of spring, of dawn, of morning! I call upon the spirits of the air, spirits of the winds! I call upon the hawk, the peregrine soaring in the clear skies! I call upon the spirits of the Tor, that rises to the east of these Levels, of Gwyn the Hunter, of the goddess Bride, of Orion who strides from the sides of the Tor! Behold! The gateway to the east is open.

SOUTH: I call upon the spirits of the South – spirits of summer, of noonday, of the sun at its zenith! I call upon the spirits of fire, spirits of flame and simmering heat! I call upon the great stag running, of the fox in the woods! I call upon the spirits of the Polden Hills, the low hills, the Quantocks! Behold! The gateway to the south is open!

WEST: I call upon the spirits of the West – spirits of river and spring, spirits of evening and autumn! I call upon the spirits of the crashing seas, of twilight, of the salmon leaping in the pool of wisdom, of the spotted cow beside the darkening pool! I call upon the spirits of Severn Sea and Severn Shore, of Brean and Brent Knoll! Behold! The gateway to the west is open!

NORTH: I call upon the spirits of the North – spirits of winter, spirits of midnight, spirits of the iron cold! I call upon the spirits of earth, of standing stone! I call upon the great Bear in the starry heavens, of badger beneath the earth! I call upon the spirits of the Mendips, spirits of cave and gorge, spirits of copper and tin, spirits of the high bare hills! Behold! The gateway to the north is open!

What this does is to anchor your ritual space, your sacred space, in its environment, and honours the spirits around it. Note that I have used a certain kind of phrasing. I have said that there is no single right way to do ritual, but when you look at older forms of magic, they speak of 'summoning' the spirits of the quarters. Frankly, I feel this is a little rude. If you believe in them then you are not dealing with beings that are under your control. They may bite back, just like any other wild thing when it is treated with disrespect.

You do not have to use the 'behold!' invocation, either. It is used in Druidic ritual, but you could just state that, for example, the northern gate or door or portal is open.

As with the consecrations, the power of calling the quarters does not lie in the words you use (though in public ritual, it does help if they are opened and closed fairly dramatically – but public ritual contains a strong quality of public theatre, and not everyone takes to the 'am dram' character of some ritual work). Its power lies in the images you invoke – when I call the east, for instance, I see in my mind's eye a high mountain scene, glimpsed between two birch trees. A hunting peregrine soars up into the clear morning air and the atmosphere is cold in the early light. Snowdrops ring the foot of the birches and the morning star is still a lamp in the sky.

But that's my own vision. Other people may have a very different visualization – of a gate of clear quartz, for example. What you are doing, however you envisage it, is building up your own relationship with the quarter and the elements that are associated with it.

## The Body of your Ritual

Your circle is now cast and consecrated and you are ready to begin. This sample ritual is to the new moon, but since you're probably working alone, it is really up to you what to do. Here are some of the things that people generally do in this 'central' part of the ritual:

spellwork
visualization/guided meditation
prayer
dance
song
invocation
Tarot or other divination

For the new moon, for instance, you might wish to sit in front of your altar, close your eyes and meditate on the new moon. Focus on something that you want to begin at this time and visualize it. Send a prayer to the goddess or god for this new project, in your own words. Draw a symbol of the new moon and place it on the altar, until the moon's next significant phase.

It is often helpful to know what other pagans actually *do*, so here are some examples of rituals I have undertaken recently:

> **RITE TO VENUS:** this is a ritual I do annually with a group around Beltane and is based on one of the old festival dates dedicated to the goddess Venus. The centrepiece of the room is a bowl of roses and after calling the quarters, each participant is given a rose. Each of us is then invited, for example, to turn to our neighbour and say why we value them, or we might do a meditation on Venus.

> **SERPENT RITUAL:** my group has been working with the Druidic Animal Oracle recently, so this was a Druidic ritual to honour the serpent (the animal that was chosen at random during the previous session). Before the ritual, we all spoke, in-circle, about what snakes mean to us – some people disliked them, some had grown up with them, some of us are from places other than Britain and had to deal with cobras on a daily basis! So we called the quarters according to the snakes that might be found there – an adder for the northern quarter, a cobra for the south, for instance. Then, once the circle had been set up, we underwent a guided meditation, taking us through the snake's life.

> **RITUAL OF LIGHT:** this was undertaken at a workshop on Dartmoor. Rather than calling the quarters, a group of us simply stood in a circle and were given a nightlight. Then we were asked to hold hands, with the 'nightlight' hand still holding the light. One of the little candles was lit and the flame was passed around the circle without breaking the connection, so that we all stood in a circle of flickering flames. Then some words were spoken to the goddess and we each blew out our neighbour's light. A very simple ritual, but effective and beautifully done.

## Closing Down

Once you have done all that you wish to do within your ritual, you need to close it down. This is straightforward. Starting in the north (some people begin in the east, however), you begin the winding down by thanking the spirits of each of the quarters, for example:

> NORTH: I thank the spirits of the North – spirits of winter, spirits of midnight, spirits of the iron cold. I thank the spirits of earth, of standing stone. I thank the great Bear in the starry heavens, the badger beneath the earth. I thank the spirits of the Mendips, spirits of cave and gorge, spirits of copper and tin, spirits of the high bare hills. Behold! The gateway to the north is now closed!

... and so on for west, south and east. Once you have closed the quarters, you now close the circle, beginning in the east but moving anti-clockwise to 'unwind' your circle. Reverse the casting that you made at the start of the ritual, picturing energy passing through your athame, back down your arm and across your body, and into the earth.

That's it! Most traditions recommend having something to eat and drink afterwards, to ground you again, and this is always a good idea.

# Addressing Some Issues within Paganism

## Cultural Appropriation

I have used the personal example in my story about Maria in Chapter Seven to illustrate what a modern shaman from an indigenous background actually does. The collection of techniques involved in shamanism are popular in the West but as I have mentioned, they have attracted criticisms of cultural appropriation, which often gets misrepresented as undue political correctness. There are rather too many examples of white people claiming heritage from, say, a Native American tribe and charging hundreds of dollars for workshops. We do need to be really careful what we lay claim to.

A good example is the chakras: is the Western use of the chakra system (found throughout the New Age but popular in paganism as well) culturally appropriative given that chakras are considered in Indian thought to be a real thing, a real part of the body? In that case, working with the chakras is just like working with your liver or your lungs. This is a difficult topic, but some guidelines are emerging. Don't claim to be part of a culture if you're not, just because you like it and you feel entitled to it. Don't rip off other people's ideas or terminology. If you're going to use them, ask permission. If you're not able to do that, give credit where it is due. Much of paganism holds that deities and spirits are real. What if you're white and are convinced that a Vodou spirit is contacting you? It is possible that this actually is the case: Vodou holds that the spirits walk with all of us, not just people from a black African heritage. However, this does not entitle you to set yourself up as an expert, and you need to prioritize the experience of people who *are* from that background, because spirituality as a whole is often not separate from other issues, such as race and gender, and power imbalances. It is essential to be sensitive to other people's feelings, backgrounds and experiences.

If you are drawn to a path, I think it is important to check out exactly who and what you are reading or studying with or listening to, because of the issues above. This is particularly pertinent in the case of shamanic workshops in the West. I have come across many that are not only superficial but expensive – and not only in the West. It is, in my opinion, fine to charge money for what you do – we've all got to make a living. Maria, in my example, did expect to be paid, but she worked on a fair market rate and she sometimes didn't charge people at all. There are some hair-raising examples of indigenous shamans in Brazil charging a lot of money to conduct ayahuasca ceremonies, for example. Use your intelligence. We are all human and there are dubious people found in all walks of society and all societies. Just because someone is presented to you as a tribal elder from the Amazon and you feel guilty about the way his people have been colonially treated, that does not necessarily make him a good guy. He may or may not know what he's talking about.

## A Word of Warning about Cults

Paganism in general is not overly prone to cults, mainly because pagans tend to be resistant to being told what to do. But there are elements of cult-like behaviour among some groups. Paganism also attracts narcissists – as do many other religions and political systems. And like those other groups, the problem is not just with the narcissists themselves, but with the people who enable them, and those who see someone else's behaviour as an excuse to grab some power. When you look at a cult, you don't just look at the central figure of the guru – you look at the people who surround him or her as well.

In any group there is a danger of a cult of personality forming around the leader. Janet Farrar and Gavin Bone for Progressive Witchcraft and Philip Carr-Gomm for Druidry are excellent examples of leaders who work really hard to try to counteract this. As long-term and responsible practitioners, they are well aware of the pitfalls of being treated like gurus, and won't tolerate it. Some leaders, however, do fall into this trap. Don't hand over your power. Treat people like fellow professionals and don't be gullible. Ask around the pagan scene and find out who is genuinely respected and who is not. Look online and read the forums. Don't sign up to something just because it is fashionable. By all means shop around – there is a lot out there, it can be confusing, and you sometimes need to try different things before you find the right thing for you. However, once you have found it, try to stick with it for at least a year – the butterfly approach isn't helpful to anyone.

I always recommend that people read some basic books before they jump in. The Pagan Federation's magazine *Pagan Dawn* has listings of 'moots' – these are meetings of pagans, often from different paths, which are usually held in pubs once a month or so. Some of them offer a talk followed by general chit-chat.

## What Not to Do

❦ If anyone asks you for a large sum of money to join anything, be cautious. People will charge for workshops, but take a look at similar events and get a rough idea of the market rate. I'd regard £60–£150 as a reasonable amount for a day's workshop, but courses should not really run into four figures unless they're over a long period of time. For example, a year's worth of weekend courses, held every six weeks, could just about go over £1,000, but it should not be thousands of pounds. The New Age is less scrupulous in this respect than paganism, generally.

❦ Even if you are joining an organization that states that it has a sexual component (like the Rajneeshis, for instance), it should go without saying that no one should be pressurising you into sex. I have heard of cases of predatory high priests, and there are several cases of predatory high priestesses as well (claiming, for instance, that women should be allowed to sleep together without informing their male partners, and pressure being put on newcomers). Mixing sex with magical practice is fraught with hazard and best left well alone until you really know what you're doing. Newbies who think that sleeping with the high priest or priestess will somehow fast-track them into knowledge or authority, or both, are wrong.

❦ Don't join any spiritual group that insists that you cut off contact with family and friends. This has happened recently and insidiously with a group in the u.s.: they present as a 'family' who look after each other, and it is only some way down the line that people suddenly wake up and realize that they haven't seen anyone outside the group for some time.

❦ Don't do anything you are seriously uncomfortable with. And don't let people gaslight you – 'oh, it's only because you're not doing it enough/you're doing it wrong.' My late partner had this experience with a neuro-linguistic programming group in the 1970s. If techniques – like hyperventilation, for example, where you breathe rapidly until you are in an altered state – don't seem to be working for you, it is probably because they are *not* working, not because you are not doing them properly.

C By all means give respect to group leaders, as a matter of courtesy, but don't hand over all your power to them. This is as much your responsibility as a functional adult as it is theirs.

C Try and keep a balance. Magic is exciting but it often promises what it can't deliver. By all means use magic to improve yourself: do a wealth spell if you're poor. But be prepared to solve your problems via mundane means too, like getting a job.

C Don't attribute everything that happens to you after joining a group or starting a practice to be down to magic. Examples of this from the Internet have been: 'I had a row with my husband and a button popped off my shirt. What does it mean?' ('Don't buy cheap clothes' was one response). One of our contacts described something that they claimed was an 'energy experience' but which sounded to me like indigestion. Don't be a drama queen. Not everything that happens to you is esoteric.

C It is very unlikely that anyone will ever curse you properly. Going to Egypt on a package tour and visiting a pyramid does not mean that you are now suffering from the Mummy's Curse (I have come across this one several times).

C Don't get into magical wars with people: it is boring and unnecessary. As in all other arguments and personality clashes, state your case and walk away. This particularly applies to the Internet. I see rows every day in online paganism and most of them are completely pointless.

C Paganism can supply you with a social circle, but this should not be the main focus of it. I belong to one group, but rarely see or even communicate with fellow members between our meetings every six weeks or so. I count them as friends, too, but socializing isn't the main point of our meetings.

☾ Be careful about people's claims. If someone tells you that they are the inheritor of an ancient pagan tradition of witchcraft that has survived for hundreds of years in the British Isles, you need to take this claim with a pinch of salt. There may be people from other countries who come from genuinely older magical traditions (in the Slavic regions, for instance) but it is doubtful whether this is the case in the UK or among Americans of British or Irish heritage.

The above is mostly common sense, and it should apply to most aspects of life, not just your introduction to paganism. I have stayed in Druidry for over twenty years partly because of the calibre of the people I found within it, and I predict without needing a crystal ball that you will meet some exceptional individuals, and a fair number of abusive people as well. Just like everywhere else!

# References

## Introduction

1 William Gray, *Temple Magic* (St Paul, MN, 1988), p. 253.
2 Kari Sperring, in conversation with the author, February 2019.
3 Adrian Bott in Liz Williams, 'UK Pagans Respond to Questions on the Origins of Easter and Ostara', https://wildhunt.org, accessed 13 April 2017.

## ONE: Ancient Origins

1 Tacitus, *Annals*, trans. John Jackson (Loeb Classical Library) (Cambridge, MA, 1937), 14.30.
2 Julius Caesar, *Gallic War*, trans. W. A. McDevitte and W. S. Bohn, 1st edn (New York, 1869), 6.13.
3 Ibid., 6.14.
4 Ammianus Marcellinus, *Res Gestae* [AD 353–78], www.mountainman.com.au.
5 Pliny the Elder, *Natural History*, trans. John Bostock and H. T. Riley (London, 1855), 16.95.
6 Kathleen Mulchrone, trans., *The Book of Lecan* (Dublin, 1939).
7 Pliny, *Natural History*, Book 4.
8 Caesar, *Gallic War*, 6.16.
9 Strabo, *Geography*, trans. Benjamin Fortson (Aberystwyth, 1995), 4.1.13.
10 Lucan, *Pharsalia*, trans. J. D. Duff (Loeb Classical Library) (Cambridge, MA, 1928).
11 Tacitus, *Annals*, 14.31.
12 Ibid., 14.32.
13 Ibid., 35.1.
14 Pomponius Mela, *De chorographia* [AD 43], trans. Arthur Golding, www.sacred-texts.com.

15 'It Was a Very Confined Space and I Don't Think Anyone Would Have Got Out Alive', https://bbs.hrmtc.com, accessed 15 November 2017.

## TWO: Saxons and Vikings

1 Gildas, *On the Ruin and Conquest of Britain*, www.tertullian.org, 16 December 2017.
2 Kari Sperring, in conversation with the author, February 2019.
3 The Venerable Bede, *An Ecclesiastical History of the English People*, trans. A. M. Sellar (London, 1907), pp. 5–6.
4 *The Laws of King Athelstan* [AD 924–39], www.sourcebooks. fordham.edu.
5 Thomas H. Ohlgren, *Mediaevistik* (Bern, 1988), vol. I, pp. 145–73.
6 Tacitus, *Agricola and Germany*, trans. A. R. Birley (Oxford, 1999), Chapter 9, www.books.google.co.uk.
7 Bill Griffiths, *Aspects of Anglo-Saxon Magic* (Ely, 1996), p. 181.
8 *County Folk-lore*, vol. III: *Examples of Printed Folk-lore Concerning the Orkney and Shetland Islands*, collected by G. F. Black and ed. Northcote W. Thomas (London, 1903), p. 144.
9 Griffiths, *Anglo-Saxon Magic*, p. 14.
10 Saxo Grammaticus, *Gesta Danorum*, trans. Oliver Elton (New York, 1905), Book 6, Chapter 5.
11 Jonathan Arnold, *Theoderic and the Roman Imperial Restoration* (Cambridge, 2014), p. 139.
12 Adrian Bott, 'The Modern Myth of the Easter Bunny', *The Guardian*, 23 April 2011.
13 Bede, *An Ecclesiastical History of the English People*, p. 38.
14 Gregory I, *Letter to Abbot Mellitus, Epistola 76*, PL 77: 1215–16, ed. T. Hofstra, L.A.J.R. Houwen and A. A. MacDonald (Groningen, 1995), pp. 149–73.
15 J. Blair, *Anglo-Saxon Pagan Shrines and their Prototypes* (Oxford, 1995), pp. 1–28.
16 See '1,000-year-old Onion and Garlic Eye Remedy Kills MRSA', *BBC News*, www.bbc.co.uk, 30 March 2015.
17 Daniel McCoy, *Sources*, www.norse-mythology.org, accessed 16 January 2018.
18 Andy Orchard, *Dictionary of Norse Myth and Legend* (London, 1997), cited in 'Norse Temple of Uppsala Adam of Bremena', www.allaboutheaven.org, accessed 17 January 2018.

19  I. Yu. Krachkovsky, trans., *Ibn-Fadlan's Travel to Volga* (Leningrad, 1939), www.onlinehome.us.

20  Runatal, *Rationale*, www.notendur.hi.is, accessed 22 January 2018.

21  Neil Price, *The Viking Way: Religion and War in Late Iron Age Scandinavia* (Oxford, 2002), p. 64.

22  Julius Caesar, *Gallic War*, trans. W. A. McDevitte and W. S. Bohn, 1st edn (New York, 1869), 1.50.

23  J. Sephton, trans., *Eiríks saga rauða* (Liverpool, 1880), Chapter 4, www.sagadb.org.

24  H. Davidson, trans., *Gods and Myths of Northern Europe* [London, 1900], ebook.

25  Griffiths, *Anglo-Saxon Magic*, p. 100.

26  Francis Melville, *The Book of Faeries* (London, 2002).

## THREE: Magic of the Middle Ages and the Witches Who Weren't

1   *Canon Episcopi* [*c.* 900], www.personal.utulsa.edu.

2   P. G. Maxwell-Stuart, 'The Emergence of the Christian Witch', *History Today*, v/11 (November 2000), www.historytoday.com.

3   D. N. Dumville, 'Sub-Roman Britain: History and Legend', *History*, LXII/205 (1977), pp. 187–8.

4   John Stowe, *Annales of England* [1592], www.openlibrary.org/works.

5   Francis J. Child, *The English and Scottish Popular Ballads, A Gest of Robyn Hode* [*c.* 1450] (Northfield, 2006), vol. IV.

6   Francis J. Child, *The English and Scottish Popular Ballads*, vol. III, p. 122.

7   Richard Heygate and Philip Carr-Gomm, *The Book of English Magic* (London, 2009), p. 176.

8   Rachel A. C. Hasted, *The Pendle Witch Trial, 1612* (Lancaster, 1993).

9   Matthew Hopkins, *The Discovery of Witches – In Answer to Several Queries, Lately Delivered to the Judges of Assize for the County of Norfolk* [London, 1647], www.quod.lib.umich.edu.

10  Owen Davies, *Popular Magic: Cunning-folk in English History* (London, 2007), p. 69.

11  Alan MacFarlane, *Witchcraft in Tudor and Stuart England* (London, 1970), p. 130.

12  James Sharpe, *Instruments of Darkness: Witchcraft in England, 1550–1750* (London, 1997), p. 67.

13  Keith Thomas, *Religion and the Decline of Magic* (Harmondsworth, 1971), p. 209.
14  Ibid.
15  John Aubrey, *Miscellanies* [London, 1696], ebook (New York, 2008), p. 157.
16  John Aubrey, *Remains of Gentilisme and Judaisme* [1686], ebook (Oxford, 2008), p. 41.
17  Thomas, *Religion and the Decline of Magic*, p. 215.
18  William Drage, *Daimonomageia: A Small Treatise of Sicknesses and Diseases From Witchcraft* (London, 1665), p. 5.
19  C. L'Estrange Ewen, *Witchcraft and Demonianism* (London, 1970), p. 406.
20  Thomas Ady, 'An Essex Cunning Man Exposed', in *The Witchcraft Papers: Contemporary Records of the Witchcraft Hysteria in Essex, 1560–1700*, ed. Peter Haining (London, 1974), p. 191.

## FOUR: High Magic and the Seventeenth Century

1   James Elimalet Smith, *Legends and Miracles and Other Curious and Marvellous Stories of Human Nature* (London, 1837), p. 6.
2   Tobias Churton, *The Golden Builders: Alchemists, Rosicrucians, and the First Freemasons* (New York, 2002), p. 5.
3   'What Is Hermeticism?', www.hermeticfellowship.org, 20 March 2014.
4   Gabriele Ferrario, 'Al-Kimiya: Notes on Arabic Alchemy', www.sciencehistory.org, 15 October 2007.
5   Charlotte Fell Smith, *John Dee: 1527–1608* (London, 1909).
6   William Lilly, *History of His Life and Times* [1681], *The Retrospective Review*, ebook (Bavaria, 2011).
7   Owen Davies, 'Top Ten Grimoires', www.guardian.co.uk, 8 April 2009.
8   *The Magic and Demonology of Babylonia and Assyria*, www.wisdomlib.org, 4 April 2018.
9   Psalms (New York, 1880), vol. II, p. 107.
10  Reginald Scot, *Discoverie of Witchcraft* (1584), Book XV, p. 215.
11  Johann Weyer, *On the Illusions of the Demons and on Spells and Poisons* [1563], ed. George Mora (Binghamton, NY, 1991).
12  Carl Edwin Lindgren, *The Way of the Rose Cross: A Historical Perception, 1614–1620*, archived on 8 November 2012, *Journal of Religion and Psychical Research*, XVIII/3 (1995), pp. 141–8.

13 *Dr Wallis's Account of Some Passages of his Own Life* [1696], as contained in Part XII of Peter Langtoft's *Chronicle* [1725], www-history.mcs.st-and.ac.uk.

## FIVE: The Georgians

1 *British Mercury; or, Annals of History, Politics, Manners, Literature, Arts Etc. of the British Empire*, VI/27–39 (1788).
2 Ibid.
3 William Mason, *Caractacus: A Dramatic Poem* (London, 1759).
4 John Wood, *A Description of Bath* (Bath, 1765).
5 Geoffrey Ashe, *The Hell-fire Clubs: A History of Anti-morality* (Stroud, 2000), p. 49.
6 John Wilkes, *The North Briton*, XLVI: *Numbers Complete*, vol. IV, p. 271.
7 Ashe, *The Hell-fire Clubs*, p. 142.
8 Henry Evans, *The Master Mason* [June 1927], www.themasonictrowel.com.
9 Ibid.
10 Ibid.
11 A. E. Waite, *The Secret Tradition in Freemasonry* [1911], vol. II, ebook (London, 2008).
12 Christopher Hodapp, Freemasons for Dummies blog, 23 April 2007.
13 Alexander Gilchrist, *Life of William Blake: Pictor Ignotus* (London, 1863; enlarged, 1880), vol. I, p. 149.
14 Francis Barrett, *The Magus*, Book 2: *A Complete System of Occult Philosophy*, p. 140, www.celticearthspirit.co.uk.
15 Ibid.
16 Ibid.
17 BBC *History Magazine*, www.historyextra.com, accessed 2 September 2019.

## SIX: The Victorians

1 Stephen Hebron, 'The Romantics and Classical Greece', www.bl.co.uk, accessed 8 August 2019.
2 B. R. Haydon, letter to Mary Russell Mitford (12 February 1824), in Stanley Jones, 'B. R. Haydon on Some Contemporaries: A New Letter', *Review of English Studies*, new series, XXI/102 (May 1975), p. 189.

3  Review of Keats's *Endymion* in *Blackwood's Edinburgh Magazine* (August 1818).
4  Suzanne Barnett, *Romantic Paganism: The Politics of Ecstasy in the Shelley Circle* (New York, 2018), p. 167.
5  Charles Godfrey Leland, *Aradia* [London, 1899], Chapter 1, www.enwikisource.org.
6  Ibid.
7  Ibid.
8  Raven Grimassi, 'Aradia: An Introduction to the Holy Strega', www.moonshadow13.weebly.com, accessed 17 July 2018.
9  Aidan Kelly, 'The Gospel of Diana', www.patheos.com, accessed 17 July 2018.
10 Sabina Magliocco, 'Who Was Aradia? The History and Development of a Legend', *The Pomegranate: The Journal of Pagan Studies*, 18 (2002), www.journals.equinoxpub.com.
11 R. Lowe Thompson, *The History of the Devil* (London, 1929), p. 133.
12 The Wellcome Collection, 'Edward Lovett', www.wellcomecollection.org, June 2018.
13 Edward Lovett, 'Superstitions and Survivals among Shepherds', *Folklore*, xx/1 (30 March 1909), pp. 64–70.
14 A. R. Wright and E. Lovett, 'Specimens of Modern Mascots and Ancient Amulets of the British Isles', *Folklore*, xix/3 (30 September 1908), pp. 288–303.
15 Ibid., pp. 300–301.
16 'More about Theosophy and the Society', www.theosophicalsociety.org.uk, accessed 19 July 2018.
17 'Edith Nesbit', www.blavatskynews.blogspot.com, 2011.
18 Éliphas Lévi, *Transcendental Magic: Its Doctrine and Ritual* (New York, 1968), p. 1.
19 Robert Hadji, 'Nesbit E[dith]', in *The Penguin Encyclopedia of Horror and the Supernatural*, ed. Jack Sullivan (London, 1986), pp. 299–300.
20 R. A. Gilbert, *A. E. Waite: Magician of Many Parts* (Wellingborough, 1987), p. 361.
21 Jean-Pascal Ruggiu, 'Rosicrucian Alchemy and the Hermetic Order of the Golden Dawn', www.meleph.free.fr/alchemy.htm, accessed 20 June 2018.
22 Dennis Denisoff, 'The Hermetic Order of the Golden Dawn, 1888–1901', www.branchcollective.org, accessed 1 May 2018.

23 Leslie Evans, 'The Memorable Life of Edith Nesbit',
www.boryanabooks.com, accessed 12 June 2018.

24 Edward Pease, *The History of the Fabian Society* (New York, 2009),
p. 33.

25 Aleister Crowley, *The Confessions of Aleister Crowley*
(New York, 1979), Chapter 87.

26 Amy Clukey, 'Enchanting Modernism: Mary Butts, Decadence,
and the Ethics of Occultism', *Modern Fiction Studies*, LX/1
(March 2014), pp. 87–8.

27 Ifor Williams, ed., *The Poems of Taliesin*, trans. J. E. Caerwyn,
Mediaeval and Modern Welsh Series, 3 (Dublin, 1987).

## SEVEN: Modern Magic

1 H. Rider Haggard, *The Days of My Life*, ed. C. Longman, ebook
(Adelaide, 2003).

2 Ronald Hutton, *Triumph of the Moon: A History of Modern Pagan
Witchcraft* (New York, 1999), p. 152.

3 Kenneth Grahame, *The Wind in the Willows* [1908], Chapter 7,
www.online-literature.com.

4 Saki [H. H. Munro], 'The Music on the Hill' [1930], in *The Short
Stories of Saki* (New York, 1958), p. 179.

5 Ibid., p. 180.

6 E. M. Forster, 'The Story of a Panic' [1928], in *The Collected Tales
of E. M. Forster* (New York, 1959), pp. 28–9.

7 Richard Stromer, 'An Odd Sort of God for the British: Exploring
the Appearance of Pan in Late Victorian and Edwardian
Literature', http://soulmyths.com/oddgod.pdf, p. 8, accessed
20 March 2018.

8 Helen H. Law, *Bibliography of Greek Myth in English Poetry*
(New York, 1932).

9 Aleister Crowley, *The Magical Record of the Beast 666*, ed. John
Symonds and Kenneth Grant (London, 1972), pp. 235–6.

10 Hutton, *Triumph of the Moon*, p. 177.

11 S.E.G. Hopkin, 'Cheering Satanism', *The Spectator*
(November 2009), www.spectator.co.uk.

12 Phil Baker, *The Devil is a Gentleman: The Life and Times of Dennis
Wheatley* (Cambridge, 2009), p. 298.

13 Ibid.

14 Ibid., p. 309.

15  Ibid., p. 609.
16  Dion Fortune, 'Sexual Ethics in Occultism', *Inner Light Magazine* (1940), reproduced in Dion Fortune and Gareth Knight, *The Circuit of Force* (Loughborough, 1998), p. 160.
17  Hutton, *Triumph of the Moon*, p. 195.
18  Ralph Merrifield, 'G. B. Gardner and the 20th Century "Witches"', *Folklore Society News*, 17 (June 1993), p. 10.
19  June Johns, *King of the Witches* (New York, 1969).
20  Pamela Couchman, in conversation with the author, February 2018.
21  Linda Woodhead, in conversation with the author, February 2018.
22  Cecil Williamson, 'History', www.museumofwitchcraftandmagic. co.uk, accessed 9 July 2018.
23  Adam Stout, 'The Fifth Mount Haemus Lecture', www.druidry.org, accessed 9 July 2018.
24  Adele Cosgrove-Gray and Ross Nichols, 'Reminiscences', www.druidry.org, accessed 12 July 2018.
25  Philip Carr-Gomm and Ross Nichols, 'Reminiscences', www.druidry.org, accessed 12 July 2018.
26  Thomas Carlyle, *On Heroes, Hero-worship and the Heroic in History* (London, 1841).
27  Heathen Women United, 'Who We Are', www.heathenwomenunited.org, accessed 13 July 2018.
28  'Patricia Monaghan: Robert Anton Wilson', *Booklist*, xcv/18 (15 May 1999), p. 1680.
29  Ashley Palmer, Reverend in the Church of Satan, interviewed in *The Independent*, www.independent.co.uk, 2 June 2017.
30  Mary Beard, interviewed in *The Guardian*, www.theguardian.com, 3 September 2010.
31  Dion Fortune, *The Sea Priestess* [1935] (San Francisco, CA, 2003).
32  Jane Harrison, *Prolegomena to the Study of Greek Religion* (Cambridge, 1922), p. 285.
33  Hilda Ellis Davidson, *Roles of the Northern Goddess* (Abingdon, 2002), p. 11.
34  Richard Nilsen and Lori Woolpert, 'Rediscovering the Goddess: An Interview With Marija Gimbutas', *Whole Earth Review* (Spring 1989).
35  Jaques Leslie, 'The Goddess Theory', *Los Angeles Times*, 11 June 1989, pp. 22–6.

36 Sally Binford, *The Politics of Women's Spirituality*, ed. Charlene Spretnak (New York, 1982).

37 Zsuzsanna E. Budapest, interviewed by Kamila Velkoborska, *Zlín: Proceedings in Humanities*, II (2011), p. 249.

38 Starhawk [Miriam Simos], *The Spiral Dance: A Rebirth of the Ancient Religion of the Great Goddess* (San Francisco, CA, 1999), p. 103.

39 Interview by Stephen Price, featured in Robertson's obituary, *The Telegraph*, 22 November 2013.

40 Ibid.

41 Alan Richardson and Marcus Claridge, *The Old Sod* (Cheltenham, 2011), pp. 22–3.

42 Ibid., pp. 58–9.

43 Wellesley Tudor Pole [1960], www.chalicewell.org.uk.

# Select Bibliography

Ashe, Geoffrey, *The Hell-fire Clubs: A History of Anti-morality*
(Stroud, 2000)
Baker, Phil, *The Devil is a Gentleman: The Life and Times of Dennis
Wheatley* (Cambridge, 2009)
Churton, Tobias, *The Golden Builders: Alchemists, Rosicrucians,
and the First Freemasons* (New York, 2002)
Davies, Owen, *Grimoires: a History of Magical Books* (Oxford, 2010)
—, *Popular Magic: Cunning-folk in English History* (London, 2007)
Farrar, Janet, and Gavin Bone, *The Inner Mysteries: Progressive
Witchcraft and Connection with the Divine* (Portland, OR, 2014)
—, *Progressive Witchcraft: Spirituality, Mysteries, and Training in
Modern Wicca* (Newburyport, MA, 2004)
Fortune, Dion, *The Magical Battle of Britain* (Cheltenham, 2012)
—, *The Sea Priestess* (Newburyport, MA, 2003)
Gilbert, R. A., *A. E. Waite: Magician of Many Parts*
(Wellingborough, 1987)
Gray, William, *Temple Magic* (St Paul, MN, 1988)
Griffiths, Bill, *Aspects of Anglo-Saxon Magic* (Ely, 1996)
Heygate, Richard, and Philip Carr-Gomm, *The Book of English Magic*
(London, 2009)
Hutton, Ronald, *Blood and Mistletoe: The History of the Druids
in Britain* (New Haven, CT, and London, 2009)
—, *The Rise and Fall of Merry England: The Ritual Year 1400–1700*
(Oxford, 1994)
—, *The Stations of the Sun: A History of the Ritual Year in Britain*
(Oxford, 1996)
—, *Triumph of the Moon: A History of Modern Pagan Witchcraft*
(New York, 1999)
—, *The Witch: A History of Fear, from Ancient Times to the Present*
(New Haven, CT, and London, 2018)

Knight, Gareth, *A History of White Magic/Magic and the Western Mind* (Cheltenham, 1978)

Leland, Charles Godfrey, *Aradia* (London, 1899)

Thomas, Keith, *Religion and the Decline of Magic* (Harmondsworth, 1971)

# Acknowledgements

I would like to thank Trevor Jones, with whom I have run a witchcraft shop for the past fifteen years, and whose capacity for historical analysis and common sense have made this book possible.

I would also like to thank the (contemporary) Druids of OBOD for some exceptional conversations over the years: always thought-provoking.

I should like to thank Ronald Hutton, without whom much of my understanding of paganism simply would not have been possible. And I should like to thank the town of Glastonbury – always interesting, often infuriating, but definitely the crucible of contemporary paganism in Britain.

# Index